Praise for AN APOCALYPSE OF LOVE

"Cyril O'Regan has explored in immense detail and with an abundance of new insights Voegelin's question of the gnostic dimension in modernity, and Balthasar's question of Christian theology's relationship to its problematic margins of gnosticism, apocalyptic, neoplatonism, pantheism and esotericism. The bulk of his scholarly contribution can sometimes hide its equally substantive theological significance for the future. The great merit of the fine essays in the current volume is that they bring this significance more fully into view."
—John Milbank, Emeritus Professor, University of Nottingham

"This is a superior collection of essays, amounting to a kind of Platonic form of the *Festschrift*. It is in the genre of the Festchrift to range from the scholarly to the personal. This volume runs from awe-inspiring scholarly pieces, like Marion's chapter about *Kenosis* and Astell's essay on O'Regan's poetry, to invaluable personal reminiscences (Cunningham), chapters of spirituality (Nussberger and Cavadini), and chapters about the frequent targets of O'Regan's pen, such as Hegel (Walsh). This volume of essays walks and talks like a *Festchrift*, but many of the contributors go so far beyond the regular brief for such volumes that they establish a kind of dazzling, superior norm for the genre."
—Francesca Murphy, University of Notre Dame

"*Apocalypse of Love* is a fitting title for this collection of essays that pay homage to the breadth and depth of Cyril O'Regan's vast work. The essays here are superb, offering glimpses into his intellectual development during his days at University College Dublin, reflections on St. Joseph, after whom he was named, and rich insights into his work on aesthetics, Thomas, Kant, Hegel, Russian Orthodox thinkers, Balthasar, and much more. Put together by students, colleagues, and friendly critics, these essays are, like O'Regan's work, well worth reading. They take us ever deeper into one of the most astute guides of philosophy, theology, and literature in the modern era. We are in their and his debt for such a beautiful journey."
—D. Stephen Long, Cary M. Maguire University Professor of Ethics, Southern Methodist University

"Cyril O'Regan's work represents one of the jewels of contemporary philosophy and theology. The range and depth of his thinking are extraordinary. The insights are at times stunning; you leave a lecture with your mind on fire; or you read a passage and step away to get your bearings. He has a way of changing the whole intellectual landscape in a brilliant turn of phrase or in the twinkling of his eye. His rhetorical skill can be overwhelming; he did not kiss the Blarney Stone back in Ireland; he

swallowed it. It is a joy to welcome the celebration of his achievements to date. It is an added bonus to have a superb introduction and overview of his work."
—*William J. Abraham, Perkins School of Theology, Southern Methodist University, Dallas Texas*

"This exceptionally probing and appreciative collection of essays offers a multi-faceted assessment of Cyril O'Regan's contributions to contemporary theology. Throughout the volume a portrait emerges of O'Regan's academic theology as "superbly attuned" to Hegel, Newman, Heidegger, and Balthasar, and more broadly to the *ethoi* of both modernity and post-modernity. The collection also draws out implicit features of O'Regan's own theology and brings them into the open, raising the reception of his considerable corpus to a new level of clarity, sophistication, and promise. The book additionally presents an enriching engagement with O'Regan's poetry, augmenting the reader's understanding of his inter-disciplinary approach to contemporary theology. Last, the volume offers reflections on O'Regan as a teacher, mentor, and friend, and in these pages the reader beholds an image of Cyril O'Regan as "delighting in the truth" (Augustine), practicing a theology of "ecstatic surrender," and as exceedingly generous in his engagement with the thought of both his intellectual allies and opponents."
—*Mark McInroy, Assistant Professor of Systematic Theology, University of Saint Thomas, Saint Paul, MN*

"*An Apocalypse of Love* offers readers a golden chain of commentaries whose unity is found in the relationship of each idea to the others rather than in a single thesis. The book contains thoughtful contributions that at once summarize and interpret Cyril O'Regan's wide-ranging work, doing so in such a way that we are left desiring to re-read O'Regan and yet also to move past him to the winding pathways he has spent his career urging us to explore. From poetry to Hegel to the deep mysteries of the cross, *Apocalypse* asks us to consider the glories and devastations of a life given over to genuine wonder at God's work and the modern world."
—*Anne Carpenter, Assistant Professor of Catholic Theology, Saint Mary's College of California*

"Martin and Sciglitano have assembled a fitting tribute to the achievements of an exceptional theologian. The essays in this volume—by an outstanding group of scholars—cover themes as profound and wide-ranging as O'Regan's own contributions. More impressively, they pay homage to O'Regan's work by drawing it into dialogue with constructive proposals at the intersections of theology, philosophy, and literature. Readers will find here an indispensable resource for engaging a truly indispensable conversation partner."
—*Patrick Gardner, Assistant Professor of Catholic Studies, Christopher Newport University*

AN APOCALYPSE OF LOVE

AN APOCALYPSE OF LOVE

ESSAYS IN HONOR OF CYRIL O'REGAN

Edited by
Jennifer Newsome Martin
and Anthony C. Sciglitano, Jr.

A HERDER & HERDER BOOK
THE CROSSROAD PUBLISHING COMPANY
NEW YORK

The Crossroad Publishing Company
www.CrossroadPublishing.com

© 2018 by Anthony C. Sciglitano, Jr. & Jennifer Newsome Martin

Crossroad, Herder & Herder, and the crossed C logo/colophon are registered trademarks of The Crossroad Publishing Company.

All rights reserved. No part of this book may be copied, scanned, reproduced in any way, or stored in a retrieval system, or transmitted, in any form or by any means, electronic, mechanical, photocopying, recording, or otherwise, without the written permission of The Crossroad Publishing Company. For permission please write to rights@crossroadpublishing.com

In continuation of our 200-year tradition of independent publishing, The Crossroad Publishing Company proudly offers a variety of books with strong, original voices and diverse perspectives. The viewpoints expressed in our books are not necessarily those of The Crossroad Publishing Company, any of its imprints or of its employees, executives, owners. Although the author and publisher have made every effort to ensure that the information in this book was correct at press time, the author and publisher do not assume and hereby disclaim any liability to any party for any loss, dam- age, or disruption caused by errors or omissions, whether such errors or omissions result from negligence, accident, or any other cause. No claims are made or responsibility assumed for any health or other benefits.

Cover and text design by Sophie Appel

Library of Congress Cataloging-in-Publication Data available from the Library of Congress.

ISBN 978-0-8245-9918-8 (cloth)
ISBN 978-0-8245-9828-0 (tradepaper)

Books published by The Crossroad Publishing Company may be purchased at special quantity discount rates for classes and institutional use. For information, please e-mail sales@CrossroadPublishing.com.

To Cyril O'Regan,
lo più che padre

*"Therefore, I pray you, gentle father dear,
to teach me what love is: you have reduced
to love both each good and its opposite."
He said: "Direct your intellect's sharp eyes
toward me, and let the error of the blind
who'd serve as guides be evident to you.
The soul, which is created to love,
responds to everything that pleases, just
as soon as beauty wakens it to act.
Your apprehension draws an image from
a real object and expands upon
that object until soul has turned toward it;
and if, so turned, the soul tends steadfastly,
then that propensity is love—it's nature
that joins the soul in you, anew, through beauty."*

—Dante, *Purgatorio* XVIII, lines 13–27

CONTENTS

Acknowledgments   xi

Foreword: A Personal Reflection   xiii
Lawrence S. Cunningham

Introduction   1
Jennifer Newsome Martin

CHAPTER 1. The Mystery of St. Joseph in the Memory of the Church: A Father Rich in Mercy   13
John C. Cavadini

CHAPTER 2. Kenosis, Starting from the Trinity   32
Jean-Luc Marion | Translated by Tarek R. Dika

CHAPTER 3. Balthasar's Theology of Christ's *Impasse* and "Dark Night"   49
Danielle Nussberger

CHAPTER 4. Theology in the Middle Voice: Thomas Aquinas and Immanuel Kant on Natural Ends   64
Corey L. Barnes

CHAPTER 5. Haunted by Heteronomy: Cyril O'Regan, Hegelian Misremembering, and the Counterfeit Doubles of God   80
William Desmond

CHAPTER 6. On Hegel: Sorcerers and Apprentices   95
David Walsh

CHAPTER 7. Christian Theology after Heidegger   120
Andrew Prevot

CHAPTER 8. Delighting in the Truth: St. Augustine and
Theological Pedagogy Today   136
Todd Walatka

CHAPTER 9. Philosophical and Theological Historiography
in *The Red Wheel*   149
Brendan Purcell

CHAPTER 10. O'Regan as Origen in Alexandria   164
Ann W. Astell

CHAPTER 11. "As love, the giver is perfect": Love at the Limit
in the Thought of Cyril O'Regan   183
Jay Martin

CHAPTER 12. The Unity of Cyril O'Regan's Work: Narrative
Grammar and the Space for a Post-Modern Theology   203
Anthony C. Sciglitano, Jr.

Poetic Epilogue   229
Cyril O'Regan
"On the Nile"   229
"Waiting for the Barbarians I"   231
"Requiem for Marguerite (d. 1310)"   233

Contributor Biographies   239

ACKNOWLEDGMENTS

Grateful acknowledgments are owed to the many contributors who eagerly took to this task and helped to honor Cyril, his work, and his friendship in such a substantive and rich manner. In particular, Geraldine Meehan provided uncommonly sympathetic and pragmatic insight for this volume, knowing better than we where to look for contributors and pointing the way in a perfectly clandestine manner. We are also thankful to the early readers of the full manuscript who agreed generously to provide endorsements for our volume, including William Abraham, Anne Carpenter, Patrick Gardner, D. Stephen Long, Mark McInroy, John Milbank, and Francesca Murphy.

Gwendolyn Herder graciously took on this project at Crossroad Publishing Company, where Chris Myers has been an excellent guide and steward of our progress. His is a gentle and helpful hand. We want to thank also the superb team at the press of editors, designers, and those in marketing as well.

In keeping with its new Open Access policy, the Metropolitan Museum of Art supplied free of charge the beautiful cover image, the oil painting "The Supper at Emmaus" by Diego Rodríguez de Silva y Velázquez (1622–23), which depicts the moment of recognition at which the disciples knew Jesus for who he truly is (Luke 24:13–35). The Met appears to believe that art ought to be shared rather than hoarded; we are immensely appreciative for their generosity.

We are exceptionally grateful for the generous support of the University of Notre Dame's Institute for Scholarship in the Liberal Arts (ISLA), the McGrath Institute for Church Life, the Department of Theology, and Professor Lawrence Cunningham in particular, whose financial contributions have made the publication of this volume possible.

JNM: I am indebted to my co-editor Tony Sciglitano, whose fantastic sense of humor, aesthetic sensibilities, and especially good taste in whiskey has made light the burdensome and pleasant the tedious. I am also grateful to my enormously supportive colleagues in the Program of Liberal Studies at the University of Notre Dame, particularly for the consistent and compassionate friendship of Andrew Radde-Gallwitz. And though the entire project is in a sense an expression of gratitude for the formative influence of Cyril O'Regan both personally and academically, I offer an explicit thematization of it here. Finally, to my husband and always first reader Jay Martin, I owe the greatest debt for the performance of his own decades-long "apocalypse" of love. Polish poet Czesław Miłosz famously said that "one can believe in God out of gratitude for all the gifts"; such a proposal is manifestly easy to accept in the face of the giftedness all around me.

ACS: It has been a privilege to work on this volume with Jennifer Newsome Martin. Her steady and efficient editorial hand, her keen eye for detail and insistence on excellence have elevated this volume. It helps that she is a pleasure to work with (or, with which to work). I am also grateful for the bourbon that catalyzed this collaboration. I want to thank my family who have always been supportive of my academic life and without whom it would have been impossible. In particular, I want to thank my cousin, Brian Sorrentino, who many years ago gave me my first Hegel book, Miller's translation of the *Phenomenology of Spirit*, and thus made possible the impossible. And, of course, my gratitude goes to my wife, Julie, whose love suggests the impossible of another plane every day.

FOREWORD

A Personal Reflection

Lawrence S. Cunningham

For well over a decade, Cyril and I had adjoining offices in Malloy Hall on the campus of the University of Notre Dame, and rare was the day when he was not at my door or I at his. I would jokingly refer to our quotidian visits as my chance for spiritual direction. One of my few sorrows since my retirement is not having the pleasure ("pleasure" is the *mot juste*) of his daily company. Professionally, we served as colleagues in the department and labored together on any number of academic committees, and it was always a signal honor to be asked by him to be a reader of dissertations for many of his numerous Ph.D. students. I would always tell those students that they needed to appreciate how blessed they were to have a professor who would spend so much time with them and help make them better writers, but—and this is most important—teach them to resist any temptation to indulge in cant, padding, or sloppy thought. On such pages this most pacific of men would yield the red pen with militancy. However, unlike some self-regarding academics, he never performed this correction with a view to humiliating a student.

While I have given up my Malloy office, Cyril and I still see each other on a regular basis. Our favorite rendezvous is a Friday lunch at a local Indian restaurant where we spend an hour or so engaged in academic gossip (of which he is *facile princeps*), catching up on current work, commenting on sports (in which he takes a keen interest), and taking the pulse of the department in particular and the university in general. Most of lunch is punctuated by not-too-raucous laughter when Cyril can let loose with that sly wit and baroque language for which he is justly famous. I have seen many faculty members imitated by their graduate students, but Cyril is hard "to do," since most students do not have the vocabulary to pull it off, and they most certainly do not have the command of that wicked patois of his native Ireland.

Cyril and his wife Geraldine Meehan are unabashedly companionable, and that company decidedly includes their well-loved son Niall (my wife is Niall's Confirmation sponsor) and the family dog, Matilda, to whom I have added the name "Prancer" for her vigorous gait when (usually) Cyril takes her on walks. Walking Matilda is not much of a chore for Cyril, since I have observed over the years that—like many a person who came late to driving—he is a determined walker who seems to prefer that mode of conveyance on his daily trips to and from campus. I have it from reliable sources that when he taught at Saint John's University in Collegeville, Minnesota, he regularly walked from his home in St. Joseph across the highway to the campus of Saint John's, even in those notoriously cold Minnesota winters.

Here is something about Cyril that rather astonishes me: he never seems to be in a hurry. For someone who is a prodigious scholar, a fully engaged teacher, a generous giver of time for all sorts of academic committees, and a committed family person, he appears to go through life seemingly never harried. I am equally astonished that he does not wear a watch or keep an appointment book; if he possesses a cell phone, it is one of the better-kept secrets in the Western world. Still and all, he is always on time for meetings, classes, and writing deadlines and makes those deadlines while never seeming to be in a rush. How he manages this placid way of proceeding I mark down to his intelligence.

When he writes—and he does so prodigiously—he writes fully. I have often teased him by saying that my essays are about as long as the book reviews he writes. When he speaks informally at campus "talks," he does so from fully written texts that are as much a joy to read as they are to hear. What many do not know is that Cyril is also a regular writer of poetry. He has on occasion shown me completed poems that are wonderfully crafted but austere in a fashion that his prose is not. Why he has not published more of his poetry is a mystery to me; if he has published it, it is his secret. Does he have a *nom de plume*?

Of course, it is Cyril's scholarly writing that has made his reputation. His first major publication, *The Heterodox Hegel* (1994), was a revision of a dissertation written under the direction of Louis Dupré at Yale with the subtitle "Trinitarian Ontotheology and Gnostic Narrative." The subtitle hints at the subsequent direction of his research with the publication of the two books *Gnostic Return to Modernity* (2001) and *Gnostic Apocalypse: Jacob Boehme's Haunted Narrative* (2002), while he has in production two more books mining the Gnostic theme under the tentative titles *German Idealism and Its Gnostic Limit* and *Deranging Narrative: Romanticism and Its Gnostic Limit*. In a similar vein, his Père Marquette lecture has been published under the title *Theology and the Spaces of Apocalyptic* (2009).

The above-cited works create a perfect background for his interest in and expert commentary on the magisterial theological corpus of the late Hans Urs von Balthasar. He has written much and directed some wonderful dissertations on the thought of the famed Swiss theologian. He took a vacation from his writing on Gnosticism to investigate the intellectual matrix out of which Balthasar's theology arose, which resulted in a two-volume work under the generic title *Anatomy of Misremembering*. The first volume, on Balthasar's response to philosophical modernity, with special emphasis on Hegel, is already published (2014), and the second volume, on metaphysics and the prospects of theology, with a focus on Heidegger, is in press as of this writing.

To take on a serious study of Balthasar is to wrestle with the life work of a man whom the late Henri de Lubac called the most learned man in Europe.[1] To understand Balthasar fully is to commit oneself to a generous understanding of the Christian past, ranging from the Fathers East and West as well as the grand medieval tradition and that of the early modern. Hence, it comes as no surprise that Cyril has written rich essays on Balthasar in relation to Newman, Eckhart, and Augustine, to mention just a few. That sweeping knowledge of the past has allowed Cyril to construct Notre Dame courses that take into account these traditional figures, and to make forays into the world of contemporary theology, philosophy, and literature. With all due deference to the late Isaiah Berlin, Cyril is one of those thinkers

---

1 Henri de Lubac, "A Witness of Christ in the Church: Hans Urs von Balthasar," *Hans Urs von Balthasar: His Life and Work*, ed. David L. Schindler (San Francisco: Ignatius Press, 1991), 272.

who exemplifies both the hedgehog and the fox.[2] He escapes those tired categories of "liberal" and "conservative," and it would be otiose to try to pigeonhole him as such. His intellectual interests are too capacious and too wide for such lazy labels. He is "catholic" to the bone in the etymological meaning of the word.

Elsewhere in this volume old friends, former students, and present colleagues will memorialize Cyril's scholarship with a set of celebratory essays to honor his sixty-fifth birthday. Such an occasion, despite the fact that the social security checks may commence, only marks mature middle age, so it is with hope that we look forward to decades of further work coming from his learned pen. There are academics who retire at sixty-five, but they tend to be those who, in reality, retired long ago and are, if truth be told, only retiring their yellowed lecture notes. Those who have a genuine inquiring intelligent mind, like that of our honoree, will say what Thomas Merton said at the end of his classic *The Seven Storey Mountain*: "*Finis libri sed non quaerendi*"—the book ends here but not the search.

I have known Cyril since he came to Notre Dame and count him among my best friends. Of him I can only repeat what that old wisdom writer, Jesus, Son of Sirach, said: "Faithful friends are a sturdy shelter/whoever finds one finds a treasure. Faithful friends are lifesaving medicine" (*Sirach* 6:14, 16).

---

2 Isaiah Berlin, *The Hedgehog and the Fox: An Essay on Tolstoy's View of History*, ed. Henry Hardy (Princeton, NJ: Princeton University Press, 2013).

INTRODUCTION

Jennifer Newsome Martin

An Apocalypse of Love: Essays in Honor of Cyril O'Regan is a celebratory collection of critical essays by contemporary theologians and philosophers in honor of Cyril Joseph O'Regan (b. 1952), Huisking Professor of Theology at the University of Notre Dame and author of the magisterial two-volume *The Anatomy of Misremembering: Von Balthasar's Response to Philosophical Modernity, Volume I: Hegel* (The Crossroad Publishing Company, 2014) and *Volume II: Heidegger* (The Crossroad Publishing Company, forthcoming). Given its genre as an homage, this volume comprises a tribute to and a celebration of the ongoing legacy of a notable modern theologian. Far beyond this function, however, it is also a constructive investigation of the state of contemporary theological scholarship in response to O'Regan's interventions, which help to set the terms for what it might mean to do pioneering work in systematic theology, especially that which is philosophically and literarily inflected.

Certainly, the voluminous contributions of Cyril O'Regan to contemporary theology cannot be subsumed under one simple category or heading. His academic range of expertise is frankly astonishing—John Henry Newman is treated alongside Valentinus, Jacob Böhme, moderns and post-moderns, Irish literature, experimental poetry, Gnosticism, Hans Urs von Balthasar, William Blake, Hegel, Heidegger, Schelling, Meister Eckhart, and Hölderlin, not to mention patristic and medieval authors. We requested from our contributors substantive, intellectually hefty essays that would not only honor Cyril's immense contributions to date, but also publicize and make more accessible the fullest possible range of his work. That includes not only the philosophically and theologically thick kinds of contributions such as *The Heterodox Hegel*, the *Gnostic Return in Modernity* series, and the two volumes of *The Anatomy of Misremembering*, but also—no less carefully prepared and intelligently wrought—the kinds of things he has written for the popularly pitched "Saturdays with the Saints" series before Notre Dame home football games, in the sheaves of his largely unpublished poetry, lecture notes for his graduate and undergraduate courses, and in the marginalia of the thousands upon thousands of draft pages of the (prodigious) number of theses and dissertations he has directed or co-directed over the years. His contributions to the field of contemporary theology are thus not only academic, but also pastoral, pedagogical, and personal. What is doubly extraordinary about O'Regan's original contribution to the theological project alongside its massive scope is that even in its diverse applications, both the range of work and the man himself present as a composition, with a recognizable tonality, timbre, and rhythm that resonates not only through his whole body of theological and philosophical scholarship, but also in the character of his personal, professional, and spiritual life.

These essays, which are generally irenic but not uncritical, certainly do not strive to be exhaustive in scope, but they are comprehensive at least in their efforts to address elements of the full range of O'Regan's interdisciplinary corpus. When taken collectively, the essays presented herein demonstrate and even perform the lithe and dynamic movement between genres that mark his theological, philosophical, and literary contributions. The reader may approach this text, then, as a kind of *silva rerum*, a "forest of things" that simultaneously allows for multiple and distinct perspectives, but one that is also correlated thematically; like Kristina Sabaliauskaitė's novel that bears the same name, the "family" of our contributors is likewise multi-generational. That is, this book creates a democratic space both for established and emerging theologians and philosophers to catalogue, assess, exemplify, extend, or supplement O'Regan's wide-ranging contributions in and on their own terms and according to each of the respective contributor's area of expertise, whether they be in the early, mid, or later stages of their academic careers. Essays include appreciatively critical analyses of Cyril's work on and engagement with Hegel, hermeneutics, historical theology, rhetorical and pedagogical styles, spiritual theology, Heidegger, love, mysticism, kenosis, Eric Voegelin, psychoanalysis, post-modernity, poetry—both published and unpublished—and a handful of more personal reflections. With respect to the last, we are especially pleased to have a personal appreciation offered by Lawrence S. Cunningham, Cyril's long-time office mate, colleague, and friend, as the foreword to the entire volume.

In "The Mystery of St. Joseph in the Memory of the Church: A Father Rich in Mercy," John Cavadini considers the central though utterly anonymous position of St. Joseph in the Church's living memory. His essay locates the phenomenon of friendship in this space of mystery—whether it be friendship with another person, the saints, with Christ, or in the Church—offering a richly theological meditation that mines the tradition (chiefly the *Protevangelium of James* and homilies from Origen) not only on the identity of Joseph as such, but on the ordinary mysteries of fatherhood, sonship, and marriage. Central to his discussion are kenotic themes of erasure and renunciation: of the hidden signifier of Joseph's paternity, Cavadini writes that "when we look back on the fatherhood to try to clarify or objectify or specify it, we see, in a way, nothing. We see an effacement rather than a claim; a hiddenness rather than assertion; silence and not speech...."

This thematic of kenosis as a theological datum is continued in Jean-Luc Marion's chapter "Kenosis, Starting from the Trinity," which supplies a somewhat oblique dialogue with Hegel on the pain of God by way of a biblically saturated and contemplative meditation on kenosis. Marion's interest is to protect the mystery not only of the various Scriptural accounts of variations on the theme of *kenos/kenon* but even more fundamentally the Trinitarian reality to which the Scriptures bear witness. Marion's meticulous exegesis of the biblical texts on emptiness more broadly suggests a certain hermeneutical delicacy with respect to the use of *ekenosen* in Philippians 2:7, insofar as it cannot justly be informed by reference to other New Testament texts. Continuing still the themes of darkness, kenoticism, and mystery, Danielle Nussberger's contribution, "Balthasar's Theology of Christ's *Impasse* and 'Dark Night'" makes an intervention in the sometimes contentious debates regarding Hans Urs von Balthasar's theology of Holy Saturday and the passive descent into hell by recalling the importance of spirituality to doctrinal speculation, an element that has sometimes been altogether forgotten or perhaps misremembered. In effect an act of memory itself, Nussberger's essay traces Balthasar's spiritual and intellectual debts to the poetry of St. John of the Cross's "dark night of the soul," particularly as it has been interpreted by Constance Fitzgerald as impasse. This notion of impasse signifies polyvalently, with implications both for Christology and the experience of the theologian herself, who moves through apophatic impasse toward a greater dynamism, depth, and creativity of thought.

In keeping with Cyril's own philosophical bent, many of the essays mark nodes of contact between the disciplines of theology and philosophy. In his "Theology in the Middle Voice: Thomas Aquinas and Immanuel Kant on Natural Ends," Corey Barnes draws together what he reads as cognate themes and problematics surrounding Thomistic final causality and Kantian natural teleology. His methodology for drawing these figures together is double, namely by way first of constelled historical eras—here specifically medieval scholasticism and Enlightenment—in the style of Walter Benjamin's *On the Concept of History*, and second, through appeal to Cyril O'Regan's project of middle-voice genealogy in *Gnostic Return*, borrowed at root from antique Roman rhetoric. The first methodological move liberates Aquinas and Kant from a potentially myopic focus on historical context that would restrict the thought of either to the bygone past, while the second secures a position between strictly disinterested genealogy and (post-Nietzschean) high genealogy, which operates under the assumption that all discourse is fundamentally interested and thus inseparable from power plays. Without claiming a relation of dependence between Thomas and Kant, Barnes productively draws these thinkers into a mutually illuminating dialogue on causality.

As one might well expect, Hegel features prominently among these more philosophically oriented contributions. Included in this category are the thematically similar but materially distinct essays from William Desmond and David Walsh. Desmond's "Haunted by Heteronomy: Cyril O'Regan, Hegelian Misremembering, and the Counterfeit Doubles of God" offers a favorable appraisal of O'Regan's rich contributions to scholarship on Hegel's philosophy of religion, particularly in *Anatomy of Misremembering* and *Heterodox Hegel*, alongside some shorter (review) articles, prioritizing issues surrounding his own notion of the counterfeit double and the operation of misremembering, insisting throughout that the preservation of divine transcendence is non-negotiable. The thematic of the counterfeit God—Hegel's "God," whose irreducible otherness is radically relativized to "self-completing immanence"—especially comes to the fore, particularly the paradoxical intimacy of the false representation with the original and the phenomenon of the "perfected double," the conceptual perfection of which may turn out to disclose rather than to disguise its own spuriousness.

David Walsh's "On Hegel: Sorcerers and Apprentices" presents a sustained study not directly of O'Regan's reception of Hegel but rather of Eric

Voegelin's, which amounts to a cleverly slantwise critical engagement with O'Regan by other means. Voegelin operates in this essay as a double stand-in. First he substitutes for Walsh himself, insofar as Voegelin's trajectory with respect to his reading of Hegel is one of dramatic denunciation that warms gradually to the recognition of affiliations and even filiations with Hegelian and Schellingian strands of German Idealism. Second, Voegelin might be thought to substitute for O'Regan's mode of critique of Hegel. Walsh argues fundamentally for a hermeneutic of charity and generosity rather than suspicion vis-à-vis Hegel, in his reassessment of Hegel in a light more positive than not. He reconfigures stock interpretations of Hegel by allowing for a sustained valuation of history as having ongoing importance rather than eventual consumption into obsolescence, the possibility for a genuine transcendence in Hegel's philosophy of religion, and the sense that Hegel's "system" was neither ossified nor hyperbolized, but actually a dynamic organic whole that grew through the annual lecture additions that "came to overwhelm the margins of the 'system' which, it turns out was only a syllabus for a viva voce performance."

Andrew Prevot's essay, while acknowledging the centrality of Hegel as an interlocutor with modern Christian theology, prioritizes Heidegger's place in what he terms the philosophical "counter-canon" of seductive but ultimately duplicitous figures with which Christianity must contend. He first considers the methodological role of philosophical contestation in Christian theology in general, which must move beyond polemic into substantial engagement (Hans Urs von Balthasar is a prominent interlocutor here), and in Cyril's performance of Christian theology in particular. Second, he turns his attention to specific texts in Cyril's œuvre that deal explicitly with Heidegger, including review essays, book chapters, and the heretofore unpublished manuscript drafts of the second volume of *Anatomy of Misremembering* on Balthasar's contestations with Heidegger. Finally, Prevot accounts for O'Regan's engagement with contemporary Christian thought that bears some degree of Heideggerian influence, namely that of Jean-Luc Marion and William Desmond.

While Cyril is perhaps most well-known for his challenging theological works, his students, both graduate and undergraduate, know him also as a patient, deft, and deeply generous teacher. Todd Walatka's chapter, "Delighting in the Truth: St. Augustine and Theological Pedagogy Today," provides an appreciation of Cyril's theological pedagogy by means of an analysis of book four of St. Augustine's classic *De Doctrina Christiana*. Walatka suggests that Cyril's mode of teaching evinces a perceptiveness with respect to diagnosing error alongside an equal spirit of generosity that would render his "opponents" in their best possible light, a sensitive attentiveness to the needs of a given audience such that even the most erudite or cerebral points get communicated effectively (i.e., not just a performance of erudition for its own sake), and the way in which the life of the teacher himself or herself allows the luminosity of Truth to illuminate it and even spill out over the borders of the self to illuminate the lives of others.

Continuing with the more pedagogical theme, Brendan Purcell considers the kind of wide-angled multi-disciplinary formation Cyril might well have had as a student at University College Dublin in the 1970s that arguably formed his intellectual trajectory along three particular lines: first, the privilege of interdisciplinarity; second, the performance of acts of memory that would stand against the breach of cultural amnesias; and third, the incorporation of Russian religious thought into his work, particularly the kenotic theology of Sergei Bulgakov. He traces these themes through an outline of Aleksandr Solzhenitsyn's novel *The Red Wheel*.[1] Purcell sees Cyril alongside both Solzhenitsyn and Voegelin as offering an urgently needed alternative to yet another moribund system of thought.

Sr. Ann Astell's "O'Regan as Origen in Alexandria" offers an analysis of some of Cyril's poetry, particularly a selection from his unpublished cycle *Origen in Alexandria*. Punctuating poetic analysis with details of Cyril's early family life, Astell provides a sophisticated argument—including the observation of the suggestive anagrammatic potential at play in their names—that Origen and O'Regan operate as something like doubles for one another, since both theologians across time and geographic space bear sometimes contesting obligations to orthodoxy and to experimentation. In particular, Astell's treatment of the poems brings out themes of origin, place, identity, paternity, spirit, and the nature of art and especially language itself, insofar as it bears multiple registers of signification, with biblical images and text interspersed both with mythical figures and ancient rhetoricians. These

---

1 An earlier version of this article appeared as Brendan Purcell, "Philosophical and Theological Historiography in Aleksandr Solzhenitsyn's *The Red Wheel*," *Claritas: Journal of Dialogue and Culture* 3, no. 1, article 7 (2014). We are grateful to Purdue University for permission to reprint this slightly amended version.

variously assumed "impersonations" of such myriad voices are employed by the speaker of the poems as a means to deeper self-knowledge, "an opening to love, compassionate confession, and praise."

The final two essays, from Jay Martin and Anthony Sciglitano, Jr., consider in quite different ways the corpus of Cyril as a whole, prioritizing, respectively, the implicit place of love within his œuvre as precondition for diagnoses and argument, and a unified commitment across his writings to the rehabilitation of the post-modern in Catholic theology. Martin's "'As love, the giver is perfect': Love at the Limit in the Thought of Cyril O'Regan" takes its title from a line in *Gnostic Apocalypse: Jacob Boehme's Haunted Narrative*. He offers a reading of Cyril on the theme of love through a lens of Lacanian psychoanalysis in general and Lacan's commentary on Plato's *Symposium* in particular. Despite there being no explicit theology of love in Cyril's work, Martin suggests provocatively that love is the "hidden hiddenness" that operates below the surface even as a (if not *the*) fundamental means by which O'Regan diagnoses and adjudicates the theological viability of competing or counterfeit discourses. In sum, O'Regan's hermeneutic is demonstrably agapeic, a claim that Martin plots largely along Johannine and Irenaean lines but also complicates by his correlation of *agape* with *eros*. By situating Cyril's diagnostic project within the psychoanalytic register of desire, Martin's essay suggests ultimately that the agapeic is itself radically transformed in Cyril's thought precisely insofar as ordinary desire is conformed to the highest gospel imperative of love of God and love of neighbor.

Finally, Anthony Sciglitano argues that the sum of Cyril's work thus far suggests that post-modern Catholic theology is not only possible but also desirable, and, moreover, that Catholic ecclesial existence is a genuinely viable option in post-modernity. His essay draws out the multiple modes of argument that Cyril employs across his writings, which include lending explicit or implicit support to theological formulations that allow for plural vision as well as repudiating thinkers who "(a) render theological pluralism impossible, (b) render theology impossible, or (c) eliminate or derange Christian doctrine and forms of life under pressure from modern intellectual assumptions and regulations that frequently act as stipulations rather than arguments." The essay demonstrates clearly that Hegel's revisionist and ontotheological interpretation of Christianity is non-identical with traditional Christianity; the latter is thus more resistant to the post-modern critique, which would mistake one isomorphically for the other. This claim is reinforced by a thorough account of O'Regan's invocation of Christian Narrative Grammar against Hegelian metanarrative, which allows not only plural formulations and frank admissions of epistemological finitude in the face of the ever-greater mystery of God, but also accommodates coherence between particular points of doctrine, Christian spiritual practices and forms of life, and a vigorous doxology.

In addition to the fine essays included here, we are also extremely fortunate to be able to publish in this volume a selection of Cyril's original poetry. It amounts to quite a small percentage of the massive poetic work he has produced over the course of his writing life, poetry that occupies a primordial space prior to the philosophical and theological studies for which he is better known.[2] On the whole, O'Regan's poetry is insistently somatic, the images unapologetically raw and solid but rendered in language stunningly lyrical, delicate, and rich with understated allusions not only to biblical and classical literature but also to other modern poetry, literature, and philosophy. Included in the epilogue to *An Apocalypse of Love* are three original and strangely prescient poems, two from his collection *Origen in Alexandria* ("On the Nile" and "Waiting for the Barbarians I," both discussed at some length in Astell's essay) and one long narrative poem on the violent execution of Marguerite de Porete, "Requiem for Marguerite (d. 1310)," taken from the collection *Poems: Sacred and Profane*.

In "On the Nile," the speaker of the poem admits his own contingency and the potential of total self-erasure, even as the words of the poem themselves become lexically fixed in the very act of writing: "If the world is a sketch/In the possible, it may/Be I am never here, was not/There, fated only to remember/Another's notes and words/In the fog of the never happened" (lines 28–33). "Waiting for the Barbarians I" is a nod to the poetry of Alexandrian native and poet Constantine Cavafy (1863–1933), which likewise tends to overlay mythical elements on images drawn more immediately

---

2 For an analysis of *The Companion of Theseus*, another lengthy cycle of O'Regan's (unpublished) poems, see Jennifer Newsome Martin, "Poetry and the Exculpation of Flesh," in *The Irenaean Spirit and the Exorcising of Philosophical Modernity: Cyril O'Regan and Christian Discourse after Modernity*, ed. Phillip Gonzales. Eugene, OR: Cascade Books (Wipf & Stock Publishers, forthcoming).

INTRODUCTION   9

from the surrounding milieu of the Alexandrian desert.[3] While Cavafy's orators, consuls, praetors, emperor, and senators seem to have received and internalized the revelation like Godot's that the barbarians have not come and may not ever come, the denizens of O'Regan's silent city in his first "Barbarians" installment wait still, choking on bones. Those in his "Waiting for the Barbarians II," however, "say/The unsayable. They are already here/They are our souls turned inside out" (lines 12–14). "Marguerite" implicitly connects the *corpus* of its namesake's *The Mirror of Simple Souls*, itself a mystical meditation on divine love, with the *corporeal* nature of her burnt and broken body, her corpse, which post-figures that of the suffering Christ, unveiling love and beauty even or especially in its disfigurement:

> But inexplicable this finalizing of flesh
> to paper curling at the edges, first brash
> yellow, then sullen brown, dull black
> to end in no color at all, ready
> to fly to the blue beyond the steady
> chattering of windless morning,
>
> this folding in which bones see
> and the tempest of ash sniffs
> the apocalypse of beauty. (lines 7–15)

Here and throughout, O'Regan's poetry self-consciously queries the fragilities and vulnerabilities of bodies and language together, in a medium within which, in Cyril's own words, "logocentrism is broken in the name of a broken truth which is our only hope."[4]

Words are odd things indeed, as T.S. Eliot famously reminds us in *The Four Quartets*,[5] straining, cracking, breaking, slipping, sliding, perishing, decaying, and otherwise unrepentantly restive with respect to fixed or exhaustive meaning, particularly when met with the (im-)possibility of trans-

---

3 See, in particular, Constantine P. Cavafy, "Waiting for the Barbarians," in *C.P. Cavafy: Collected Poems*, trans. Edmund Keeley and Philip Sherrard (Princeton, NJ: Princeton University Press, 1975).

4 Personal correspondence, July 13, 2016.

5 T.S. Eliot, "Burnt Norton," *The Four Quartets*.

lation. When this collection was first conceived, for example, we initially considered taking its title from the Irish word *"agus,"* which means "and," and titling the book *Agus & Agus*. The original title, though probably impenetrable to the casual reader and certainly absolutely dreadful for market considerations, did have the benefit not only of providing a definitive nod toward O'Regan's Irish identity, but also of being maximally evocative on several other fronts. First, it is self-consciously grammatical as a series of three copulas, indicating his constitutively Yale school interest in depth and narrative grammar, deformative grammars of Gnosticism, grammars of the theological tradition, and so on. Second, the copular by definition connects and joins, as O'Regan's work straddles disciplines and opens up avenues which may have been previously narrowed or even closed, whether in the registers of theology and philosophy, religion and literature, fidelity to tradition and speculation, *fides* and *ratio*, poetry and prose, reading and being read, academic theology and sanctity. Third, the peculiar formulation of "and & and" gestures not only to the facility and inventiveness with which Cyril employs the English language, but also his willingness to unsettle rigid logocentric patterns that presume to speak beyond their competence. Fourth, it is suggestive of the confirmed fact that Cyril's work is deeply viable and generative, somehow simultaneously productive and yet also self-erasing, as it reproduces in those he influences (especially current and former students) something recognizable of his range, tone, and vision, but never allows or permits mere repetition. His mark indeed is indelible but does not blot out. Fifth, and finally, O'Regan is a distinctly fecund theologian insofar as his general *modus operandi* is unrelentingly expressive, where something more can always be said—though the mystery deepens in direct proportion to the speech—in his efforts to articulate the ever-greater reality of God as infinite mystery.

For the sake of simplicity, however, we opted ultimately for the slightly more accessible but no less apt title, *An Apocalypse of Love*. After all, the collective impression of these essays, when taken together, is that what is revealed or unveiled indeed is precisely *love* as the unifying if non-categorical force both of O'Regan's life and work as an academic, scholar, thinker, public intellectual, mentor, teacher, advisor, Catholic, and friend. The act of knowledge is at root an act of love. As Hans Urs von Balthasar suggests in *Theo-Logic I: Truth of the World*, objects and persons become known when they receive the gaze of the one who looks upon them with loving kindness:

> This special gaze, which is possible only in the loving attention of the subject, is equally objective and idealizing. That these two qualities can be compatible is the grand hope of the object. It hopes to attain in the space of another the ideality that it can never realize in itself. It knows or guesses what it could be, what splendid possibilities are present in it. But in order to develop these possibilities, it needs someone who believes in them—no, who sees them already existing in a hidden state, where, however, they are visible only to one who firmly holds that they can be realized, to one, in other words, who believes and loves. Many wait only for someone to love them in order to become who they always could have been from the beginning. It may also be that the lover, with his mysterious, creative gaze, is the first to discover in the beloved possibilities completely unknown to their possessor, to whom they would have appeared incredible. The beloved is like an espalier that cannot bear fruit until it is able to climb up on the sticks and wires that support it.... Unless the knower presented the ideal, the object known would never have dreamed of aspiring to it, or else it would have grown faint because the attempt would have seemed too fantastic. It takes the faith and confidence of the knower animated by love to give the thing known faith and confidence in the truth of the ideal held before it. At love's bidding, the object ventures to be what it could have been but would never have dared to be by itself alone.[6]

The interpretive lens that has emerged in the assembly of this volume as a whole is the place and exercise of love in Cyril's life and thought. He performs love's bidding. Yet the character of that love remains elusive: sometimes it is the call of the Love who names itself as the God of Jesus Christ and at others it is the undisclosed Love that hovers over the waters. Although his theological style and achievements are indeed as inimitable as they are profound, still they are but his penultimate gift. What transcends theological genius is the intensity of a theological life given over to Love's bidding, the life of teacher, poet, and friend that has so convincingly made

---

6 Hans Urs von Balthasar, *Theo-Logic: Theological Logical Theory, Volume I: Truth of the World*, trans. Adrian J. Walker (San Francisco: Ignatius Press, 2000), 114–15.

all who know him a neighbor. Cyril proves that, yes, love alone is credible, but that it is also manifestly possible.

CHAPTER ONE

The Mystery of St. Joseph in the Memory of the Church

A Father Rich in Mercy*

John C. Cavadini

A COLLEAGUE (NOT FROM the Theology Department!) once asked me who was my favorite saint.[1] When I responded "St. Joseph," he seemed utterly taken aback and exclaimed, "But we don't know anything about him! How can he be anyone's favorite saint?" There was a lot implied in my colleague's astonished response, and fair enough, since, considered from the point of view of bare facts about St. Joseph's life, we do not have much to go on (granting, for the moment, that there can be such a thing as "bare facts" about anyone's life). But how many such "facts" does one really need in order to find a person, even on the horizontal plane of this life on earth, so attractive that one wants to befriend him or her? One need not have a

---

1 * This paper is affectionately dedicated to Cyril Joseph O'Regan, who, in addition to being named after St. Joseph, is a parishioner of St. Joseph's Church in South Bend, Indiana.

This essay was originally presented in an earlier form as part of the "Saturdays with the Saints" lecture series hosted by the McGrath Institute for Church Life at the University of Notre Dame on September 10, 2016. I would like to thank Greg Cruess for his editorial assistance in preparing this paper for publication. Greg's marvelous work is especially evident in the notes.

lengthy c.v. at hand to be able to strike up a friendship with someone and to feel one's life inestimably enriched thereby. The dimensions of personal attractiveness are not easily reduced to "bare facts" about one's life. Perhaps, too, a mutual friend or a trusted advisor has introduced you, providing a few essential indications of character as the basis for a possible friendship. In such a scenario, the trustworthiness of the friend or advisor introducing you is part of the appeal of the prospective friend. Even more, the perspective of the mutual friend or trusted advisor is already a factor in the potential friendship and may continue as an important part of the friendship as it develops.

In the case of St. Joseph, the trustworthy friend in the analogy is the Church, and the introduction provided is the set of memories of St. Joseph preserved in Scripture. These memories belong to the Church as a kind of personal subject. The Church is, in a way, a collective person—that is, the People of God, whom Pope Benedict XVI calls a "collective subject," in fact "the living subject of Scripture."[2] He elaborates that "the Scripture emerged from within the heart of a living subject—the pilgrim People of God—and lives within this same subject."[3] The individual authors of the biblical books "form part of" this collective subject, who is, he continues, "the deeper 'author' of the Scriptures" on the human level.[4] Later on, Benedict explains how this works, making particular reference to the Fourth Gospel and the dynamics of remembering:

> On one hand, the author of the Fourth Gospel gives a very personal accent to his own remembrance ... on the other hand, it is never a merely private remembering, but a remembering in and with the "we" of the Church: "that which ... *we* have heard, which we have seen with our eyes, which we have looked upon and touched with our hands." With John, the subject who remembers is always the "we"—he remembers in and with the community of the disciples, in and with the Church. However much the author stands out as

---

2 Benedict XVI, *Jesus of Nazareth: From the Baptism in the Jordan to the Transfiguration*, trans. Adrian J. Walker (San Francisco: Ignatius Press, 2007), xxi.

3 Ibid., xx.

4 Ibid., xxi.

an individual witness, the remembering subject that speaks here is always the "we" of the community of disciples, the "we" of the Church.[5]

He goes on to emphasize that "because the personal recollection that provides the foundation of the Gospel is purified and deepened by being inserted into the memory of the Church, it does indeed transcend the banal recollection of facts."[6] It is, of course, important to remember that the memory of the Church, insofar as the memories contained are scriptural, is inspired. Benedict puts it this way: "This people does not exist alone; rather it knows that it is led, and spoken to, by God himself, who—through human beings and their humanity—is at the deepest level the one speaking."[7]

Scriptural memories are, as it were, definitive memories in the overall remembering of the Church that comprises apostolic tradition. The main content of this memory is, of course, the mystery of Christ, the Word made flesh, as *Dei Verbum,* the Second Vatican Council's Dogmatic Constitution on Divine Revelation, sums it up:

> It pleased God, in his goodness and wisdom, to reveal himself and to make known the mystery of his will (see Eph 1:9), which was that people can draw near to the Father, through Christ, the Word made flesh, in the Holy Spirit, and thus become sharers in the divine nature (see Eph 2:18, 2 Pet 1:4).... The most intimate truth thus revealed about God and human salvation shines forth for us in Christ, who is himself both the mediator and the sum total of revelation.[8]

Jesus "completed and perfected revelation," and "everything to do with his presence and his manifestation of himself was involved in achieving this: his

---

5 Ibid., 231 (italics in original).

6 Ibid.

7 Ibid., xxi.

8 Second Vatican Council, "*Dei Verbum*: Dogmatic Constitution on Divine Revelation" (hereafter *DV*), in *Vatican Council II: The Basic Sixteen Documents*, ed. Austin Flannery (Northport, NY: Costello Publishing Company, 1996), 2.

words and works, signs and miracles, but above all his death and glorious resurrection from the dead, and finally his sending of the Spirit of truth."[9] Everything in Christ's life, in other words, participates in the mystery of his person that sums up revelation. As the *Catechism of the Catholic Church* puts it, "Christ's whole life is mystery.... From the swaddling clothes of his birth to the vinegar of his Passion and the shroud of his Resurrection, everything in Jesus' life was a sign of his mystery."[10]

It goes without saying that St. Joseph is very much implicated in such a statement. To acquire a friendship with St. Joseph means, therefore, if it is authentic, a deeper acquaintance with the mystery of the Lord, and the more intimate the friendship, the deeper the appreciation of the mystery of the Incarnation. The reverse is also true. The more one has accepted the invitation of revelation to become friends with the Lord Jesus and through him the Father, the greater possibility there is for an intimate and living friendship with St. Joseph in Christ. For the whole of St. Joseph's life and identity is saturated with the mystery of Christ, and the mystery of St. Joseph in the memory of the Church is constituted wholly by its reference to the all-encompassing mystery of Christ that it reflects.

Why don't we take the recommendation of our trusted advisor the Church and strike up a friendship with St. Joseph? Though it is spare enough in detail, what is authoritatively remembered under the guidance of the Holy Spirit is overwhelmingly sufficient as the basis for an intimate and satisfying friendship. We can begin with the two infancy narratives of St. Matthew and St. Luke. They are notoriously different from each other to the point of potential, if not actual, conflict.[11] I regard the difference between

---

9 *DV*, 4.

10 *Catechism of the Catholic Church*, 2nd ed. (Washington, DC: Libreria Editrice Vaticana, 2000), §§514–15.

11 John Meier, for instance, traces the differences that the infancy narratives contain with regard to the movement of the Holy Family within Judea and Galilee and the chronology of their journeys. While he therefore concludes that "both narratives seem to be largely products of early Christian reflection on the salvific meaning of Jesus Christ in the light of OT prophecies," he nonetheless concedes that with regard to the historical value of the narratives, "a totally negative judgement may be too sweeping" (211–12). Indeed, he goes on to point out that certain major points of agreement between the two independent narratives (such as Jesus's birth in the reign of Herod and the names and identities of Mary and Joseph) are thus *more* likely to

the two narratives, as uncomfortable as it can feel for those who would like an easy reconciliation between them, as providential, for it shows that these two narratives are independent traditions, and yet—astonishingly—they agree on the most essential points. Included among these are some of the most unlikely points, namely, that Mary and Joseph were husband and wife, but that before they began to live together as husband and wife, during their betrothal, an angel announced (in one narrative to Joseph, in the other, to Mary) the conception of Jesus, which, in addition, was said to have taken place through the Holy Spirit, without intercourse between Mary and Joseph or indeed between Mary and any other man.[12] It is interesting, at least, that the Gospel of Mark does not identify Jesus as the Son of anyone but God, except when it says, simply, that he is "the carpenter, the son of Mary."[13] These points of agreement are anything but "bare facts," though they are indeed claims on historical truth. Such matters as the virginal conception of Jesus or the appearance of angels in dreams or otherwise cannot even in principle be historically verified, and yet the independence of the two inspired traditions does verify that these memories are as ancient as any there are about Jesus and are not simply the fabrications of the evangelists. They are as likely (or as unlikely, I suppose you could say) as the truth of the Word made flesh, as the truth of the Incarnation itself, for they are the essential elements of the location of the Incarnation in place and time. The Incarnation is thus distinguished from myth, for it is located in place and

---

be historical according to a rigorous historical-critical appraisal. My own interpretation of the infancy narratives identifies a few further essential characteristics that, despite being impossible to verify even to a contemporary observer of the Gospel events, nonetheless have positive historical value as preserved in the memory of the Church and received in faith. See John Meier, *A Marginal Jew: Rethinking the Historical Jesus* (New York: Doubleday, 1991).

12 See Joseph A. Fitzmyer, *St. Joseph in Matthew's Gospel* (Philadelphia: Saint Joseph's University Press, 1997), 9. There one finds the full list of the twelve points of coincidence between Matthew's infancy narrative and that of Luke.

13 Fitzmyer's explanation for this usage in Mark's Gospel, that Joseph had died, is unconvincing (cf. ibid., 5). Also, even if Joseph had indeed died, the fact that the Gospel of John can and does call Jesus "son of Joseph" (John 1:45, 6:42) and uses the word "father" for Joseph (6:42), in itself is perfectly consistent with the usage of the Gospel of Luke. In any event, the irony of the likelihood of the crowd "knowing" anything reliable or true about Jesus's origin is always a factor in John's Gospel.

time, and yet it is not reduced to mere history (if there is any such thing), for it was initiated outside of history and its significance transcends history. Between "myth" and "history" we find "mystery."[14] And for all the special significance of our developing friendship with St. Joseph, all friendships are located in an analogous domain of mystery, for the interior essence of someone's truly historically located love is never simply reducible to its location in history, nor does that make an account of it a "myth."

The Gospels do not tell us much about what Joseph thought about all of this. They do not give us an account of what today we might call Joseph's psychology, but the Gospel of Matthew does evoke an image of a man with a rich interior life, intent on doing God's will, always on the lookout for indications of his will, and ready to obey. Matthew recounts that Joseph was disturbed by the discovery that Mary was pregnant, and considered divorcing her, though we are not told whether this was because he thought she must have been unfaithful, or that he was already aware that some mystery larger than human devising had entered Mary's life, in which he was not sure of his further place.[15] Matthew tells us that as a "righteous" or

---

14 I have developed this theme at greater length in John C. Cavadini, "A Brief Reflection on the Intellectual Tasks of the New Evangelization," *Josephinum Journal of Theology* 19, no. 1 (2012): 111–12. There, I argue that, for Origen's sophisticated *apologia* in the *Contra Celsum*, the Gospels present Jesus as a true historical agent, not reducible to myth, but neither reducible to history precisely because "in this history a divine purpose is being accomplished that cannot be derived from or reduced purely to a human purpose from within history." In a later article, I develop this idea further to show how Origen, in rejecting what he sees as Valentinian mythmaking in the interpretation of Scripture, preserves the literal sense of the Song in his *Commentary on the Song of Songs*. See John C. Cavadini, "The Church as the Sacrament of Creation: A Reading of Origen's *Commentary on the Song of Songs*," *Communio* 42, no. 1 (2015): 114–15. God's abiding love, apparent also in the Gospel's testimony to St. Joseph, thus preserves this sacred history as a true mystery received in the faithful memory of the Church.

15 The Gospel can be read either way, as the tradition shows, even as early as the *Protevangelium of James* (13–14). See *The Protevangelium of James*, in *New Testament Apocrypha, Volume I: Gospels and Related Writings*, ed. Wilhelm Schneemelcher, trans. R. McL. Wilson (Philadelphia: Westminster Press, 1963), 370–88. Nevertheless, a careful reading of the Matthean infancy narrative suggests that Joseph's decision to divorce Mary discreetly does not require the conclusion that he therefore suspected her of infidelity. Joseph is simply described as "being a just

"just" man he decided to divorce her, following the Law, the best indication of God's will that he knew, yet "quietly," yielding the benefit of the doubt in so doing to Mary or to God or both, as the *Protevangelium of James* seems to suggest. In obeying the Law "quietly," Joseph is obeying both its letter and its spirit, divorcing Mary not as a public vindication of his own person, but as a refusal to claim that he knows God's intentions fully and as an openness to what they might be. In this, the evangelist is saying, does his righteousness—or, we could translate, sanctity—essentially consist.

We can see that this is true to Matthew's intentions, for when the angel reassures Joseph in a dream that he should take Mary into his home, he does so without any hesitation. The Gospel of Luke, for its part, does not register even a protest, worry, or anxiety on behalf of Joseph, and we might begin to think that he is an afterthought, merely a narrative or dramatic prop, were it not that the Gospel indicates his lively involvement in his family's life as husband and father up to and past Jesus's twelfth year. This sustained involvement is described in more detail than that of any other father in the Gospel of Luke—the father of Jairus being perhaps a suggestive second (cf. Luke 8:40–56) and not counting the fathers who are characters in parables. Luke privileges the reflective "pondering" of Mary, instead of Joseph's, and provides explicit memories of the thoughts and sayings that proceed from her pondering and return us to it.

But Luke is careful to point out that the angel's annunciation is to Mary, a virgin who was *betrothed,* and betrothed explicitly to Joseph. Thus, while Joseph is not consulted, neither is he just an also-ran who happens along at some random point in time. It is not Mary alone, but Mary precisely as betrothed who is addressed, and so her marriage to Joseph is part of the divine plan for the Incarnation and not incidental. In this matter, the Gospels of Matthew and Luke agree, though they bring out the point each in their own way. Neither Gospel is so indiscreet as to try to reproduce the conversations between Mary and Joseph about their marriage and their vocation, though they must have discerned it together, in some manner unique to themselves. The Gospels' reticence on this point, in a way, verifies that this domain is

---

man" [δίκαιος ὤν], an appellation intrinsically connected with the righteous figures of the Old Testament who also received the promises of God in faith. For a good explication of this non-suspicious interpretation, see Larry M. Toschi, *Joseph in the New Testament* (Santa Cruz, CA: Guardian of the Redeemer Books, 1991), 27–33.

truly spousal, truly intimate, and not for public view. Jesus enters this world embraced in an intimacy which, if not physical, is nevertheless truly spousal. It is important that we know that both Mary and Joseph are not simply passive instruments of God's will, and each evangelist implies this for one of them and verifies it for the other. God's will is accomplished in their free acceptance of it and in the bond of marital intimacy that is sealed in shared obedience to God's will.

In the case of Joseph, the two Gospel accounts converge in portraying him as having no "terms" for his involvement as husband and father, except for the terms that God offers, and they seem paltry enough. He is promised no "seed," as Abraham was, nor, more poignantly—since he is in the line of David—as David was. And though Mary is his betrothed, in neither account is Joseph even consulted about her pregnancy. Yet once he is sure it is God's will, he takes his place as her intended husband. He understands she does not thereby become his property; nor, for that matter, does he regard himself as his own private property. He becomes a husband and a father in dialogue with God's Law in its fullest dimension. He is depicted as someone whose exercise of husbandhood and fatherhood, and therefore of manhood (since these offices are exclusively those of a man) yield him no claims that he cares to exact on his own behalf. He rather exercises these offices of his manhood as instances of complete openness to God's will, without fanfare or display. And yet he is no less a man, and in fact one could argue that he is the Bible's most explicit revelation of what it means to be a man, for St. Joseph's identity is completely coincident with his roles as husband and father, without remainder.

We are not informed by the Gospels as to whether Joseph's "terms" had included an expectation of sexual intercourse with Mary at some point, or indeed what Mary thought about it, though we are given some clues. Mary's protest in Luke that she "does not" or "had not" known man implies something more than simply that she had not yet had sex, because, as the Old Testament shows and as the Lucan example of her kinswoman Elizabeth continues to show, God is perfectly capable of working a miraculous or otherwise wondrous conception *through* marital intercourse. The commonsense answer to Mary's question would be that through future sex with her husband Joseph, God would raise up the Savior. Her question seems to verify the angel's description of her as "full of grace," because she seems to be fully open to a possibility within God's domain that would go beyond what she has or could have glimpsed, another possibility, perhaps undiscerned as yet. This, oddly enough, tallies with the corresponding openness we have seen in St. Joseph, implied in Luke, and specified in Matthew. Matthew, furthermore, goes to the trouble of making it explicit that Joseph did not engage in sex with Mary before or during Mary's pregnancy, even though by that time it would probably not have been forbidden.[16] The Gospels do not mention anything explicit beyond this statement, but they do make it clear that the sex life of Mary and Joseph was something intimately relative to the mystery of the overarching designs of God in the birth of Jesus, and that Mary and Joseph both came to understand that this would involve a unique degree of renunciation or bypassing of married sex.[17] The Gospels allow them to continue their discernment unobserved by the reader, as part and parcel of pondering the dimensions of the awesome mystery of which their marriage is a part and thus of the uniqueness of their marriage.

The Gospels ask of us, the Church, the same attitude of openness toward the uniqueness of this marriage. The clues provided justify the ancient discernment of the Church that these spouses never had sex, and that this renunciation was part of the trueness of their true but unique marriage, rather than militating against it. *The Protevangelium of James* (usually dated to around 150 A.D.) testifies to the antiquity of belief in the perpetual virginity of Mary, and, contrary to the insults often heaped upon the text, not only proclaims

---

16 Although determining the precise details of betrothal and marriage practices at the time of Jesus is quite difficult, it seems likely that some amount of leniency with regard to sexual relations after betrothal but before marriage was practiced in the first century. In the Mishnah (*Kethuboth* 1:5) and Babylonian Talmud (*Kethuboth* 9b–10a, 12a), for instance, there is much discussion of the claims that a man can bring against his betrothed on the grounds of virginity precisely because such a leniency was common (see esp. 12a). As Raymond Brown notes, however, these same rabbinic traditions also refer to a difference between what was common practice in Judea and the comparatively stricter regulations in Galilee that tolerated no such leniency. See Raymond Brown, *The Birth of the Messiah: A Commentary on the Infancy Narratives in the Gospels of Matthew and Luke* (New York: Doubleday, 1993), 123–24.

17 It should be noted that the renunciation of marital relations between Mary and Joseph existed uniquely in reference to their immediate situation—the reception of the mystery of the Incarnation. It did not have direct implications for other married couples, not even Elizabeth and Zechariah, who also received the promise of a child, but one born from the natural course of marital relations. See also my "The Sex Life of Mary and Joseph," *Nova et Vetera* 13, no. 2 (2015): 365–77.

the doctrine, but cautions against an overly hasty assumption about what it might mean. The birth of Jesus takes place in the midst of an obscuring heavenly light, so that its exact character cannot be ascertained.[18] Salome puts her hand to the flesh of Mary to see if her hymen is intact, a gesture reminiscent of that of Doubting Thomas in the Gospel of John (John 20:24–29) and so indicating that the doctrine is in some sense tied to the mystery of the new creation in Christ.[19] She does discover that Mary's hymen is intact, and yet as a result her hand withers, though it is immediately healed. She is not judged overly harshly, but just harshly enough to allow the reader to see that though it is true, the reader should be warned against assuming he or she has or could fully grasp the mystery of the childbearing of the Virgin, a physical truth yet, like the resurrection itself, is not fully reducible or even fully specifiable in its physical dimensions. Karl Rahner's warning to his readers some 1,800 years later—that "there are physical events which, however naturally they may appear to be the direct consequences of the constitution of man, yet must be recognized by the more penetrating and comprehensive eye of faith"—is fully congruent with this text.[20]

Famously, the *Protevangelium of James* also depicts St. Joseph as an elderly widower, fully conscious of how ridiculous it will look for him to seem to be in the position of Mary's husband.[21] It will look as though he was so lustful that he, though he already had a long life and family, could not resist the attraction of a new, young wife. This is the writer's solution to the seeming counterevidence to the perpetual virginity of Mary—namely, the mention of "brothers" of Jesus in the Gospels. In this text, Joseph, afraid of disobeying God, receives Mary and puts up with looking foolish, and this solution has persisted in the Eastern Church and iconography. Without commenting on his age, Origen accepts as settled doctrine the perpetual virginity of Mary and consequently that Joseph's sons by an earlier marriage are the "brothers" of Jesus.[22] In modern times, this theory has (with modifi-

---

18   *Prot. Jas.* 19:2.

19   Ibid., 19–20; cf. John 20:25.

20   Karl Rahner, *Mary, Mother of the Lord: Theological Meditations*, trans. W.J. O'Hara (New York: Herder, 1963), 64.

21   *Prot. Jas.* 9:2.

22   Origen, *Homilies on Luke, Fragments on Luke*, trans. Joseph T. Lienhard

cations) been accepted by writers as diverse as Elizabeth Johnson and Gerald J. Kleba,[23] who depict Joseph as a widower with children but a young one, in his late twenties or thirties, thus bypassing the later objection of St. Jerome, who insisted that Joseph could not credibly pass as Mary's husband if elderly and suggested he was a virgin. This suggestion, accepted by St. Augustine, came to be the dominant position in the West.[24] It is especially beautifully treated in Pope St. John Paul II's evocation of the mystery of St. Joseph in the apostolic exhortation *Redemptoris Custos*, for there he explains how Joseph's own voluntary renunciation of marital relations makes him no less a true human father to the Lord Jesus:

> In this mystery of the Incarnation, one finds a true fatherhood: the human form of the family of the Son of God, a true human family, formed by the divine mystery. In this family, Joseph is the father: his fatherhood is not one that derives from begetting offspring; but neither is it an "apparent" or merely "substitute" fatherhood. Rather it is one that fully shares in authentic human fatherhood and the mission of a father in the family. This is a consequence of the hypostatic union: humanity taken up into the unity of the Divine Person of the Word-Son, Jesus Christ.... Within this context, Joseph's human fatherhood was also "taken up" in the mystery of Christ's Incarnation.[25]

(Washington, DC: The Catholic University of America Press, 1996), 7.4. Cf. Origen, *Commentary on Matthew*, 10.17.

23 For a feminist theological point of view that tends to favor this theory, see Elizabeth A. Johnson, *Truly Our Sister: A Theology of Mary in the Communion of Saints* (New York: Continuum, 2003), 195–99. In contrast to this approach, see the more popular narrative reconstruction of the life of St. Joseph in Gerald J. Kleba, *Joseph Remembered: The Father of Jesus* (Irving, TX: Summit Publishing Group, 2000), 20, 151–52.

24 For a concise review of this development, see Joseph T. Lienhard, *St. Joseph in Early Christianity: Devotion and Theology* (Philadelphia: Saint Joseph's University Press, 1999), 17–18.

25 John Paul II, *Redemptoris Custos: On the Person and Mission of Saint Joseph in the Life of Christ and of the Church* (Washington, DC: Office for Publishing and Promotion Services, United States Catholic Conference, 1989), 21.

Contemporary iconography that depicts St. Joseph as a young man thus has Jerome to thank for it. For Jerome's case to work, however, the word for "brothers" in Greek [*adelphoi*] must be taken to be flexible enough to refer to more distant relations, or to reflect a Semitic idiom that was that flexible. This was Jerome's position. Contemporary scholarship exhibits a sharp division on the matter,[26] and it is doubtful that it can ever be conclusive one way or the other. The benefit of the doubt actually works in favor of the tradition here.[27]

We have seen how the *Protevangelium of James* receives the mystery of St. Joseph in the memory of the Church. Now I'd like to turn to the next-earliest contributor, Origen. While it is true that the major flowering of devotional and theological literature about St. Joseph does not really take place until the fourteenth century, and that it was the public gratitude of St. Teresa of Avila to him that caused it to grow even more richly, the ancient Church is not without depth of reflection on St. Joseph. In my view, with regard to patristic commentary on St. Joseph, Origen's is certainly the deepest. In his *Homilies on Luke*, commenting on Luke 1:26–27, Origen states:

> Again I turn the matter over in my mind and ask why, when God had decided that the Savior should be born of a virgin, he chose not

---

[26] John Meier, after surveying the relevant scriptural evidence, concludes that "from a purely philological and historical point of view, the most probable opinion is that the brothers and sisters of Jesus were his siblings" (332). Richard Bauckham, on the other hand, while recognizing that the interpretation of Meier and others is possible given the evidence, argues that such a conclusion is not therefore necessary or even inevitable. He points out that "the references to the brothers of Jesus, including their association with his mother, in the Gospels and other early Christian literature are perfectly consistent with the view that they were his step-brothers [i.e., children of Joseph from a previous marriage]. Positive evidence that they were the sons of Mary, as well as of Joseph, is lacking." See Richard Bauckham, *Jude and the Relatives of Jesus in the Early Church* (Edinburgh: T&T Clark, 1990), 24.

[27] Meier certainly goes too far if he intends to restrict the significance of *adelphoi* to true half-brothers, which in the traditional view would not include sons of Joseph by another wife. (They would be step-brothers.) However, if Luke can call Joseph Jesus's "father," knowing he is not, he can also use the word "brother" in a similarly loose way; nor do any of the evangelists have to speak in a way that would not have been normal usage for those not "in" on the secret of the true conception of Jesus. They would have seen "brothers" and called them by that name.

a girl who was not betrothed, but precisely one who was already betrothed.[28]

Origen tells us that he found the key to understanding this in a letter of Ignatius of Antioch, writing:

> I found an elegant statement in the letter of a martyr—I mean Ignatius, the second bishop of Antioch after Peter. During a persecution, he fought against wild animals at Rome. He stated, "Mary's virginity escaped the notice of the ruler of this age."[29]

In his letter to the Ephesians, Ignatius had commented that there were three secrets wrought in God's silence and kept hidden from the prince of this world, namely the virginity of Mary, her childbearing, and the death of the Lord.[30] Ignatius is taking up a Pauline theme, namely, the essential "hiddenness" of the mystery of the Incarnation, as part of a logic or "wisdom" that is not of this world. Origen brings out this Pauline logic:

> The Apostle maintains that the opposing powers were ignorant of [the Lord's] Passion. He writes, "We speak wisdom among the perfect, but not the wisdom of this age or the wisdom of the rulers of this age. They are being destroyed. We speak God's wisdom, hidden in a mystery [*in mysterio absconditam*]. None of the rulers of this age knows it. If they had known it, they would never have crucified the Lord of glory.[31]

The logic of the Incarnation is not a logic of this world, of manifest credential, rhetorical leverage, intimidating erudition, or powerful status. Origen

---

28   *Hom. Luc.*, 6.3.

29   Ibid., 6.4.

30   See Ignatius of Antioch, *The Epistle to the Ephesians*, in *Early Christian Writings: The Apostolic Fathers*, trans. Maxwell Staniforth (New York: Penguin, 1987), 19.1.

31   *Hom. Luc.*, 6.5; quoting 1 Corinthians 2:6–8.

reminds his hearers that in the temptation scenes in the Gospels, the Savior never revealed to the devil that he was the Son of God, refusing to yield to the temptation precisely of pulling rank, of reducing himself to the logic or wisdom of this world, as it were, as though his status *qua* status would conquer the devil. He refuses to play the devil's game but is operating according to another wisdom of which, according to Christ's will, as Origen points out, the devil was kept ignorant. The devil, relying on the logic of this world, was waiting for someone to find bragging irresistible, to pull rank, to rely on status *as* status, for that itself would be his victory, their coming out into the "light" or logic of the wisdom of this age, by which he could then "see" them. The devil, Origen notes, is "fickle and depraved," his malice so great that he cannot "see" someone unless that person accepts the terms of his malice.[32] This means, too, that the mystery of Christ, even when revealed fully, remains a mystery, its wisdom irreducibly *hidden in mystery*, resisting and rejecting the logic of this world and its prince.

At any rate, Origen locates St. Joseph and his marriage to Mary squarely within the logic of hiddenness intrinsic to the mystery of the Incarnation. There is a discreet beauty here in the Providence of God. In a way, there is nothing so hidden, both in the sense of unobservable and in the sense of unremarkable or ordinary, as the conception of a child in the intimacy of a married couple—even, initially, to the couple themselves. It is just here, in the bosom of this intimacy, that the mystery of the Incarnation was "hidden," in the conjugal intimacy shared by a "righteous" man and a woman "full of grace." Origen comments, first quoting Ignatius:

> "Mary's virginity escaped the notice of the ruler of this age." It escaped his notice because of Joseph, and because of their wedding.... If she had not been betrothed or not had ... a husband, her virginity could never have been concealed from the "ruler of this age." Immediately, a silent thought would have occurred to the devil: "How can this woman, who has not slept with a man, be pregnant? This conception must be divine. It must be something more sublime than human nature."[33]

The devil is on the lookout for status claims, for achievements or wonders

---

32 Ibid., 6.6.

33 Ibid., 6.4; *humana natura ... sublimius*.

bragged about, and yet all he sees is the intimacy of a married couple, to him boringly human, low status, and ordinary. But this is not just a show. The devil is not fooled by show; in fact, he is known for pomp and for lies. The virginity is truly "hidden" in this intimacy, because it is not a limit or a block but the very substance of Mary and Joseph's deeply shared conjugal intimacy. It is not an ascetical purity that Mary has worked at and Joseph doesn't dare stain, an achievement that stands as something more sublime than human nature and aloof from real contact. The devil would notice that right away. To dwell as Origen does, for the length of this whole homily, on why the angel came to a girl who was betrothed, is to insist that the Word made flesh was conceived in a true marital intimacy of husband and wife and most safely hidden there by God.[34]

Ignatius comments that this "secret" of God, as he puts it, emerges from the great silence of God, and although he does not quote this part of the sentence, Origen sees to it that St. Joseph is the carrier, as it were, of this silence, which continues to cling to the mystery as hidden. St. Joseph has no terms and offers to no one an account of his life. He accepts a fatherhood that is not a fatherhood, becomes a father in renouncing a natural paternity, allows the designation "father" to be used of him without advertising that his is a very special case. His silence marks the intimacy of his total self-gift and, one could say, self-immolation into a paternity he cannot brag about and an identity of which he can give no account except to and in the heart of Mary his wife. But this, in traditional piety—and not without biblical reason, if Ignatius and Origen are reading correctly—makes him not the *image* but the *shadow* of the Eternal Father whose identity is dark and unknowable because it consists in the complete effacement of identity that is the begetting of the Son, like a supra-cosmic black hole of which St. Joseph is the visible version. But what is darkness and self-effacement and blankness on the one side of self-immolation is generation and paternal love and affection on the other side, toward Jesus.

Origen does not neglect the fatherly side of St. Joseph. We can turn

---

[34] Origen emphasizes that Joseph's role in the economy of the Incarnation is not simply a passive one when he describes the birth of Jesus in the crèche: "The shepherds found Joseph, who arranged matters for the Lord's birth," literally, who was the "dispensator" of the Lord's birth, the agent of God's providential dispensation, "and they found Mary, who bore Jesus in childbirth, and the Savior himself, 'lying in a manger.'" *Hom. Luc.*, 13.7; commenting upon Luke 2:16.

to that point briefly, for his remarks can help us understand the sources of devotion to St. Joseph and ultimately the title of this essay, where we will conclude. In *Hom. Luc.* 17, Origen comments on Luke 2:33, "And his father and mother were astonished by the things that were being said about him." Origen points out that Luke had already made it crystal clear that "Jesus was the son of a virgin, and was not conceived by human seed. But Luke has also attested that Joseph was his father."[35] Origen then asks, "What reason [*causa*] was there that Luke should call him a father when he was not a father?" He goes on to comment that the simple explanation is that "the Holy Spirit honored Joseph with the name of 'father' because he had reared Jesus."[36] And Origen does not deny that explanation,[37] but continues: "[O]ne who looks for a more profound [*altius*] explanation can say that the Lord's genealogy extends from David to Joseph. Lest the naming of Joseph, who was not the Savior's father, should appear to be pointless, he is called the Lord's 'father,' to give him his place in the genealogy."[38]

In other words, if Mary gives the Lord her flesh, Joseph, for his part, provides the Lord with his identity, his place in the line of human history, someone who is not *just* "flesh" but has a family identity. The significance of this inclusion, apart from verifying his status as Son of David, is more apparent if we recall an earlier passage from *Hom. Luc.* 11, commenting on the census at Bethlehem:

> Someone might say, "Evangelist, how does this narrative help me? How does it help me to know that the first census of the entire world was made under Caesar Augustus; and that among all these people the name of 'Joseph, with Mary who was espoused to him and pregnant,' was included; and that, before the census was finished, Jesus was born?"[39]

---

35 *Hom. Luc.*, 17.1.

36 Ibid. Cf. Origen, *Homilies on Leviticus*, 12.4.1.

37 Cf. also *Hom. Luc.*, 19.3, where Origen reiterates this explanation.

38 *Hom. Luc.*, 17.1.

39 Ibid., 11.6; quoting Lk 2:4–5.

Origen is pointing out that this seems to be nothing more than a bare historical fact. It seems to contain nothing spiritual. Origen answers his own question almost as if he had read the *Catechism*'s statement that "Christ's whole life is mystery" (§514–518), at least as his life is recorded in Scripture. He continues:

> To one who looks more carefully, a mystery [*sacramentum*] seems to be conveyed. It is significant that Christ should have been recorded in the census of the whole world. He was registered with everyone, and sanctified everyone. He was joined with the world for the census, and offers the world communion with himself. After this census, he could enroll those from the whole world "in the book of the living" with himself.[40]

It is Jesus's identity as the son of Joseph that permits him to be enrolled in a particular line of human descent, not in a way that reduces Christ to that line of descent but in a way that catches all of our lines of descent up into a descent derived from him, the most authentic genealogy of all, the *book of the living*. By refusing to conquer Satan by revealing his identity as Only-Begotten of the eternal Father, but by emptying that identity into hiddenness, into his identity as Joseph's son, into his place in the genealogy of Joseph, the Savior catches all of our genealogies up into the Book of Life.

In a surprising way, then, the paternity of Joseph, through Mary as her husband, and in Christ, is thus extended to us. Through his fatherhood, we are all enrolled in the Book of Life. St. Joseph is thus more than a friend. We can call him "Dad," just as Jesus did, if we want to,[41] as the deepest way of evoking the mystery of St. Joseph in the memory of the Church. And yet when we look back on that fatherhood to try to clarify or objectify or specify it, we see, in a way, nothing. We see an effacement rather than a claim; a hiddenness rather than assertion; silence and not speech; something easily overlooked; someone of "no particular interest."[42] The generous obedience

---

40 Ibid.; quoting Rev 20:15 and Phil 4:3.

41 As St. Luke reminds us, Jesus himself "was obedient to them" (2:51).

42 In connection with a discussion of St. Bernadette's devotion to St. Joseph, Andrew Doze comments that "what touches upon Joseph is generally carefully hidden

of St. Joseph to the vision of God is astonishing. No one asked him how he felt about his wife's being consulted, when he was not, on an intimate matter affecting their whole married life, or about raising someone else's kid and giving up his own natural paternity. But his sacrifice in generous obedience to the will of God became a home in this world for Jesus, his legal son, and for Mary, his wife, both treasures of divine initiative. They were hidden, as it were, in and by his paternal love, as though by Harry Potter's cloak of invisibility, completely concealed from the Prince of this World, to whom love is always and wholly invisible. This act submerges Joseph in the "deep silence of God" itself, as Ignatius calls it.[43] St. Paul says in Colossians 3:3, "For you have died, and your life is hid with Christ in God." There is something intrinsically "hidden" about the Christian life, and we see the form of this hiddenness revealed, in advance, in St. Joseph. His life, by its very structure, cannot provide an accounting of itself without undoing itself.

A mosaic of St. Joseph, commissioned by Pope St. John XXIII, and placed over the side altar in St. Peter's Basilica, where the Blessed Sacrament is reserved, uniquely depicts the warmth and beauty of this saint. In the mosaic, Joseph is on his back porch, hanging out at home. He is holding the child Jesus in his right arm. Jesus is not a month-old infant; rather, he looks to be about two years old. This depiction gives Joseph's figure a look of immense strength, because he manages to hold such a big, active kid on one arm with no trouble. In his left hand he holds his identifying iconic sign, the staff blooming with the lilies of purity. He holds it a little stiffly, as though a neighbor had chanced upon him and asked him to pose for a picture with his son, insisting that Joseph hold the staff too. He is in the middle of taking care of his two-year-old, and someone has asked him to pose. But he tolerantly obliges, picks up the baby, and looks at the camera. His face is calm but hardly grave; instead, even though posing for an annoying family picture, his face seems to take it in stride and seems to radiate happiness. It is a face familiar to any dad.

Here is the hiddenness of St. Joseph, who accepts the utterly common lot of a dad holding his kid, without fanfare, though he is holding the Word

---

and is of no particular interest" (60). Andrew Doze, *St. Joseph: Shadow of the Father*, trans. from the French by Florestine Audett, RJM (New York: Alba House, 1992).

43 Cf. note 30 above.

Incarnate and could claim glory and fame. Jesus, for his part, pays no attention to the imaginary photographer, but rather seems wholly delighted with his dad, for what on St. Joseph's side is the continuous immolation of self-gift, is on Jesus's side the brilliant radiance, comfort, and charity of paternal love, that cloak of invisibility that gives even the Word of God a genuine childhood. This same love keeps him hidden from the Prince of Darkness until it is time for him to confront him alone, armed only with the love he had learned, in part, from his earthly dad. If, as St. Augustine taught, true sacrifice is always a work of mercy, then St. Joseph's whole fatherhood is "rich in mercy" and is, in fact, one great work of mercy that extends all the way to us. Devotion to St. Joseph, therefore, means that as the genuine mystery of his paternity is revealed to us little by little, we grow up to accept the form of the Christian life as—in Baptism—a hidden one, a death to the noise of the world and a life in the silence of God, which is nothing other than his eternal paternal love.[44]

---

44   On the word "Father" as applied to God, see the very helpful explanation at CCC §2779–85, esp. §2779. St. Joseph may well be an avenue to the "purification of hearts" to which this section refers.

CHAPTER TWO

Kenosis, Starting from the Trinity[1]

JEAN-LUC MARION | *Translated by Tarek R. Dika*

AN ERUDITE AND SERIOUS specialist on Hegel, German Idealism, modern gnosis, and contemporary theology, Cyril O'Regan has frequently offered diagnoses of his contemporaries that are as exact as they are often surprising. I have myself benefited from O'Regan's diagnoses, since he has kindly read my work, posing a question to which I had never—at least not consciously—given much attention: that is, why I have not discussed Hegel as directly as I have Kant, Nietzsche, Husserl, and Heidegger, whose texts I have always examined. In an essay on my work, he asked himself (or me) whether I would eventually have to "cross, double-cross, cross over and through" Hegel.[2] Here I would like to sketch a discussion with Hegel by focusing on the question of kenosis, following O'Regan's own indications on this question.[3] In so doing, I will only inscribe myself in the margins of

---

1 A shorter version of this contribution was published in *Communio: Revue Catholique Internationale* 49, no. 6 (2015).

2 Cyril O'Regan, "Jean-Luc Marion: Crossing Hegel," in *Counter-Experiences: Reading Jean-Luc Marion*, ed. Kevin Hart (Notre Dame, IN: University of Notre Dame Press, 2007), 132.

3 Ibid., 105ff. On kenosis in the work of Cyril O'Regan, see *The Heterodox Hegel* (Albany: State University of New York Press, 1994), 205ff. and 216ff.; "Von Balthasar's Valorization and Critique of Heidegger's Genealogy of Modernity," in *Christian Spirituality and the Culture of Modernity: The Thought of Louis Dupré*, ed. P.J. Casarella & G.P. Schner (Grand Rapids, MI: Eerdmans, 1998); *Gnostic Re-*

the learned inquiries he has carried out on the re-interpretations that Hegel (but also Luther, Boehme, and many others) has given of this theme, which is absolutely *crucial*, so to speak, and which decides everything.

But before all other considerations, it needs to be recognized that we speak too casually about "kenosis," and we decide with far too much levity, as though we really know what, in this rare Greek word, is at stake. This is not the case.

I.

First, the scriptures make neither frequent nor univocal use of this word. The most common use of the root indicates an emptiness, the absence of something expected or due. Thus, the bad winemakers send the master's attendant back "empty-handed" (Mark 12:3), and God, according to the *Magnificat*, "sent the rich away empty" (Luke 1:53). Thus, this emptiness is equivalent to the deception provoked by what arrives "in vain, empty, *kenos*" (in opposition to Scripture, James 4:5). Thus, the "vainglory" (Galatians 5:26; Philippians 2:3) and "empty phrases" (1 Timothy 6:20; 2 Timothy 2:16), by which the "vain man" deceives himself (James 2:20), allows himself to be "taken by empty and vain arguments" (Ephesians 5:6; cf. Colossians 2:8).[4] Consequently, it is necessary to avoid emptiness and vanity; in effect, Paul stresses that "our coming to you was not in vain" (1 Thessalonians 2:1), that he knew not to "run in vain" (Galatians 2:2; cf. Philippians 2:16), that "in the Lord your labor is not in vain" (1 Corinthians 15:58; cf. Thessalonians 3:5). It is necessary above all "not [to] accept the grace of God in vain" (2 Corinthians 6:1). On the contrary, do everything "so that the cross of Christ might not be empty and vain [*ou kenôthê*] (1 Corinthians 1:17): not to think that the law saves, for then "faith becomes empty" (Romans 4:14); convince oneself well that "if Christ has not

---

turn in Modernity (Albany: State University of New York Press, 2001), 69ff.; and *Gnostic Apocalypse: Jacob Boehme's Haunted Narrative* (Albany: State University of New York Press, 2002), 78ff., 117ff., and 153ff. Thank you to N. Philipps for collecting this information for me.

4 The vanity justified by Paul being one exception: "this reason to boast, nobody will render it empty [*ou kenôsei*]" (1 Corinthians 9:15; cf. 2 Corinthians 9:3). One can relate this to the citation of the "vain projects" (in Acts 4:25) fomented by the people (according to Psalm 2:1).

been raised, then our proclamation has been in vain and empty and your faith has been empty and vain" (1 Corinthians 15:14). In a word, believing comes down to affirming that "grace toward me has not been vain, empty" (1 Corinthians 15:10). These uses, which are limited, all indicate a lack, a bankruptcy—in short, a radical failure [*un défaut, une failllite, bref un* échec *radical*]. One rediscovers here the classical use of the term, which connotes not only the state of vacuity, but, medically, the process of evacuation— literally, the purging of "excrement."[5] In this context, its use in "he was emptied of himself [*ekenôsen*]" (Philippians 2:7), which is here described as an extraordinary, redemptive operation to be imitated par excellence, contradicts all the other uses (Pauline, apostolic, or from the synoptics), which are negative. Hence a delicate hermeneutic situation arises: the use of the verb *kenon*, here in its inflected form, cannot be interpreted by reference to other, similarly positive uses. This occurrence is an *hapax legomenon*.[6]

Thus, we have no other guide by which to conceive this "exinination" (to stick to a neutral and indeterminate term) of Christ than the thing itself—the consideration of the mystery of the Cross alone, of the death and the resurrection of Jesus, the Christ, the eternal Son of God and truly man. But how to follow this question without immediately losing one's way, allowing oneself precisely to be "taken by [the] empty and vain arguments" of our conceptions? It is necessary, here more than anywhere, to display the greatest prudence, the greatest respect, for we are approaching sacred ground, which neither our feet nor our thought can approach with complete rigor, and which one risks profaning, not only with responses, but already in the way one poses questions. For it concerns the most unfathomable mystery, the most unapproachable, the most reserved—not only the "mystery of lawlessness [*mustêrion tês anomias*]" (2 Thessalonians 2:7), but the "great mystery of our religion [*mustêrion tês eusebeias*]" (1 Timothy 3:16): how the salvation of all can come from the suffering and death of one, how and why the one who nobody "can convict of sin" (John 8:46), the only one that remains "without sin" (Hebrews 4:15), this one who even God "for our sake he made him to be sin" (2 Corinthians 5:21)? Here, a hushed tone becomes the only agreeable attitude, the least kindness, the indispensable reserve that every theologian must borrow, as too

---

5   Plato, *Philebus* 35b, *Republic* 585a.

6   *Hapax legomenon* = what is only used once. This reinforces the hypothesis that Philippians 2:6–11 is indeed the citation of an anterior hymn.

every believer and even non-believer, provided that he pays attention to what he says and whereof he speaks.

The question becomes all the more necessary once one knows the (relatively modern—in fact, sixteenth-century) origin of the debate that has since become the problem of kenosis, even of "kenoticism." That is, starting from the Lutheran conception of the hypostatic union (of the "communication of idioms"), certain theologians influenced by the Calvinist doctrine known as *"ad extra"* have come to ask questions about the relationship, in the Passion, between the divine attributes and the human attributes of Christ. Must we not admit a diminution of the former in the moment of crisis of the latter? Is it necessary to understand it as a limitation and renunciation of their usage until the resurrection (M. Chemnitz, school of Giessen), or rather as a suspension and an occulation (J. Beretz, school of Tübingen)? In fact, this quarrel limits itself explicitly to deploying a rather common difficulty: the Passion of Christ unfolds in a suffering and a death so profoundly human that we cannot conceive how the divinity of the Son can still deploy Himself there; and therefore, without limiting the humanity of Jesus (by Docetism), it would be agreeable to restrict *here* the exercise of His divinity. This debate would have had a secondary role had it not led to an apparently inevitable dilemma: in the person of Jesus, divine nature and human nature deploy themselves in inverse proportion, and if the human nature recovers the entire scene of the humiliation (above all in the Passion), the divine in Him obscures itself all the more.[7] Why must one admit this contradiction between two natures in Christ, especially during the Passion? Because the humiliation that torture, suffering, and being put to death inflicts, contradicts, for a time at least, the glory, power, and conscience of His divinity. In the end, this seemingly banal distinction leads to one of Hegel's conclusions, which is not much of a conclusion (and we are, on this matter, often Hegelians without knowing it).

The contradiction between the attributes of Christ only imposes itself on naively pious reflection because it seems evident that the humiliation of human death does not agree with the glory of God. Or, more exactly, because the humiliation (suffering and death) seems *unbearable* to the glory, which can neither accommodate itself to it nor endure it. In fact, divine love

---

7 On the state of this historical question, see H.U. von Balthasar, *Mysterium Salutis Dogmatique de l'histoire du salut*, Vol. 12, *Le mystère pascal* (Paris: Cerf, 1972), 34–46.

(the love that God has and gives to man, but above all the love that defines the Trinity) *does not bear* the Passion and recoils before it, less from fear than from the fact that it cannot explain it, render it thinkable, or justify it. To do justice to the divinity of the Passion, to overcome the contradiction between the attributes in the person of Jesus Christ, more and better than love (*agapé*, charity) is needed, which here lacks speculative radicalness: "Thus the life of God and divine cognition may well be spoken of as a play of Love with itself; but this idea lacks the seriousness, the suffering, the patience, and the labor of the negative."[8] The negative, that is, the negative moment that consciousness (of self) introduces in the proposition in order to release all speculative power and lead abstract theoretical assertion all the way to the effectiveness of objective reason, substitutes itself for the subjective and sentimental impotence of love. This thesis proves to be essentially blasphemous from the very beginning. First, because it subordinates *agapé*—"the greatest" (1 Corinthians 13:13) of all the theological virtues, which alone goes "to the end [*eis telos*]" (John 13:1)—to the point that one "denies" it "before others" (Matthew 10:33ff.). This thesis radically lacks everything in not knowing "the only one who is good" (Matthew 19:17ff.) that all Revelation reveals at its foundation. Consequently, it has not only found its refutation in its theoretical consequences (indeed in its historical consequences, which I will not insist upon here), but it was in advance challenged by St. Paul, who defined *agapé* by assigning it precisely the four terms that Hegel desired to transfer to the negative: "*Agapé* bears all things, believes all things, hopes all things, endures all things [*panta upomenei*]" (1 Corinthians 13:7). In other words, it experiences and exerts the serious (*pisteuein*), suffering (*impomenein*), labor (*stegein*), and patience (*elpein*) more than everything in the world and beyond the world. It is a matter of edification, but of an "edification of Christ by Himself in *agapé*" (Ephesians 4:16), without any danger of sinking into vapidity, because nothing endures more than *agapé*, at least the *agapé* Christ accomplishes in his Passion. Certainly, it is possible not to believe it, because it is possible not to see it, as often happens also among philosophers, indeed more than they may think. The entire difficulty arises from what, *for us*, that is, according to our experi-

---

8 G.W.F. Hegel, *Phenomenology of Spirit*, trans. A.V. Miller (Oxford: Oxford University Press, 1977), 10. This one text should have held back the blind momentum of all those who rush to claim that they are at once both Hegelian and Christian.

ence and our beliefs about *agapé*, is self-evident about suffering and human death, such that the moment of the negative seems much more "serious" than what *we* understand under the banner—equivocal and devalued—of "love." But it is precisely a matter of knowing whether we think correctly, in *what we understand* by "love," what God understands by *agapé*. In other words, is it necessary to introduce the negative into the Trinity in order to reach the speculative "seriousness" of God or, inversely, to understand what philosophy takes to be "serious" by starting from *agapé*, such as it is put to work by the Trinity in Christ on the cross?

Rahner's principle—as celebrated as it is disputed, but in any case determinant—according to which "the 'economic' Trinity *is* the immanent Trinity and vice versa,"[9] finds here a privileged application. If *agapé* deploys itself in the Passion beyond what we can understand and experience of love and must be interpreted according to the very wont of God, it is necessary to understand it starting from the Trinity. But what access can we claim to have to the Trinity *in se* (the immanent Trinity)? None, at least not by ourselves. None besides what Christ, He who calls Himself the eternal Son of the Father, can reveal to us. But where and how does he reveal to us anything about the Trinity, if not precisely in the economy, in the extreme performance of *agapé*—extreme because accomplished in its foundation from its opposite, suffering and death?

II.

Having indicated this reversal of perspective, it remains to put it to work in reading Philippians 2:6–11. The first verse, "Christ Jesus, who, even though he was in the form of God, did not regard equality with God [*to einai isa theô*] as something to be grasped [*harpagmon*]," mobilizes many terms from the philosophical lexicon (*hyparkein, morphé, einai*), broadly understood, as does the following verse (*morphé, omoiôma, skhêma*). Despite recent

---

9 "Bemerkungen zum dogmatischen Traktat 'De Trinitate,'" *Schriften zur Theologie*, Vol. 4, (Einsiedeln: Benzinger Verlag, 1960), 115. See "Dieu trinité, fondement transcendant de l'histoire du salut," *Mysterium Salutis: Dogmatique de l'histoire du salut*, Vol. 6, *La Trinité et la création* (Paris: Cerf, 1971), 29. The discussion of this formula in G. Lafont, *Peut-on connaître dieu en Jésus-Christ?* (Paris: Editions du Cerf, 1969), 190ff.; H.U. von Balthasar, *Theodramatik* II/2 (Einsiedeln: Benzinger Verlag, 1978), 466ff.; and Y.-M. Congar is discussed in X. Morales, *Dieu en personnes* (Paris: Cerf, 2015), 71ff.

discussions about their translation (*form* or *condition*, *exist* or *subsist*, *resemblance* or *aspect*, *to be equal* or *equality*, etc.), the stakes are limited because the eventual differences only make sense when the legitimacy of metaphysical distinctions is admitted, which is perfectly modern and therefore unsuitable (more important perhaps would be the usage—extremely rare in the New Testament—of the infinitive *einai*). There remains one significant but enigmatic term—*harpagmon*—because it is introduced in the scriptures only this once and remains very rare in Hellenic Greek. Relying on two substantives (*harpax*, the thief, and *harpagé*, the prey, the loot) and the verb (*harpazein*, to seize, rob), one can come closer to a plausible translation. It can be a matter of positively being pulled out of the flames (Jude 23), of a rapture that transports Paul to the sky (2 Corinthians 12:2), the faithful caught up together with those in the clouds (1 Thessalonians 4:17), the infant menaced by the dragon at its birth (Revelation 12:4), or the snatching away of Phillip from the sight of the eunuch (Acts 8:39). It could also be a matter of seizing Jesus to make him king (John 6:15) or of seizing Paul to put him in a fortress (Acts 21:10). But in the majority of cases, it is a matter of despoliation (Hebrews 10:34), rapacious wolves (Matthew 7:15; cf. Luke 10:12), the greed of merchants (1 Corinthians 5:10; 6:10; Luke 18:11), the thief (Matthew 12:29), he who seizes the seed (Matthew 13:19), the "rapaciousness which cannot be controlled [*harpagé kai akrasia*]" (Matthew 23:25) of the Pharisees, of their "obscene rapacity [*harpagé kai ponêria*]" (Luke 11:39). Whatever is ultimately in view in the formula "the violent seize the kingdom," it is clear that, in any case, "they seize it by force [*harpazousin*]" (Matthew 11:12). *Harpagmon*, then, designates what one seizes with violence, possesses with force, and preserves in possession so long as one has the force to do so. It is not only a matter of "usurpation," which can be done without force; nor yet of "pursuit," because here the possession has indeed already been acquired; nor finally of "jealously holding onto," which omits the first gesture—violent appropriation.[10]

Nevertheless, this result only reinforces the difficulty. For to appropri-

---

10 Respectively: Lemaitre de Sacy, Vigouroux, and the TOB (Traduction œcuménique de la Bible); *La Bible*, new translation (Bayard); and *La Bible de Jérusalem*. See the article s.v. by W. Bauer and F.W. Danker, *A Greek-English Lexicon of the New Testament and Other Early Christian Literature* (Chicago: University of Chicago Press, 1957, 2000), 133ff.

ate the rank of God—is this not precisely what Christ was accused of? If they sought to murder him, it was "for blasphemy, because you, being a man, make yourself God" (John 10:33). Indeed, for a crime formulated in almost the same (rare) terms as in the hymn, "That is why the Jews sought all the more to kill Him, because He not only broke the Sabbath, but also said that God was His Father, making Himself equal with God [*ison heauton poiôn tô theô*]" (John 5:18). Moreover, one could be surprised that the science of exegesis nearly always passes over this nevertheless evident proximity in silence. It is as though (despite the supposed incompatibility of the dates) the hymn of the Epistle to the Philippians literally responded to and refuted the accusation raised against Jesus. And yet, is it not a matter here of what Christ never ceased to claim—to be on equal footing with the Father, to be God: "We have a law, and according to that law he ought to die because he has claimed to be the Son of God" (John 19:7)? Everywhere and always, it is a matter of this attestation: "All things have been handed over to me by my Father" (Matthew 11:27 = Luke 10:22). And: "For he said: 'I am God's son'" (Matthew 27:43). Or: "Jesus said to her, 'I am he, the one who is speaking to you'" (John 4:26). And again: "The Father and I are one" (John 10:30), for "I am in the Father and the Father is in me" (John 14:10). The accusation is indeed valid, and the crime established. And yet the condemnation reveals itself to be unjust.

The question does not consist in knowing whether Christ and the Son of God are "one" with the Father, but rather in knowing how: he is certainly on an equal footing with God, but everything depends on the manner in which this equality is accomplished. The accusers of the Temple, the scribes, and the Pharisees only understand this *manner* according to their understanding of possession—as a *seizing*, an eventually violent appropriation, a claim. In short, as an appropriation in the mode of jealousy toward God (which, for its part, supposes a God who is himself jealous) in the mode of a diabolical temptation: "God knows that when you eat of it your eyes will be opened, and you will be like God, knowing good and evil" (Genesis 3:5). Furthermore, when they loudly proclaim that they are "the descendants of Abraham," Christ reproaches them not only for conceiving it as a "search for glory," but also, and in fact, as a possession of diabolical origin: "you are from your father the devil, and you choose to do your father's desires [*epithumias*]" (John 8:33, 50, 44). Christ's adversaries see his claim to divine filiation as they understand their own descent from Abraham—a seizing. Never as a gift, which would appear *all the more* as one lets oneself be dispossessed by it [*qui apparaîtrait d'autant plus qu'on s'en laisse déposséder*].

This failure to understand can be found among the disciples even more clearly. They think like the other Jews, as all men do: if Jesus is the Christ, the Holy One of God, and if they are His disciples and apostles, the question of what they possess immediately arises, and so the question of what they can see only as an appropriation to claim for themselves, a privilege to possess. Hence the nagging question, perhaps from a possessive mother wanting to promote the career of her sons (Matthew 20:20–21), but repeated many times in "reasoned argument [*dialogismos*]," even "dispute [*philoneikia*]" (Luke 9:46 and 22:24) between the interested parties: "At that time the disciples came to Jesus and asked, 'Who is the greatest in the kingdom of heaven?'" (Matthew 18:1–5). Or again: "And when he was in the house he asked them, 'What were you arguing about on the way?' But they were silent, for on the way they had argued with one another who was the greatest" (Mark 9:33–34). The disciples conceive themselves as the "kings of the Gentiles," who "exercise authority over them" and "are called 'benefactors'" (Luke 22:25). They too want power, and the power to possess.

The point of disagreement is here. For the adversaries of Jesus, it is a matter of possessing his rank (for themselves, descendants of Abraham), together with the associated privileges. For the disciples, it is a matter of possessing positions of power in the kingdom to come, together with the associated privileges. For both, it cannot be otherwise in Christ's case, whom they imagine to *possess* the filiation that makes him equal to the Father, with the associated privileges. As they see it, he considers this filiation to be a possession, if not to enjoy, at least to conserve and defend—as they undoubtedly would if they could. To settle this conflict of interpretations—which reaches its acme precisely in the discussion with the disciples about their rank in the kingdom of heaven—Christ poses the contrary principle: "Whoever becomes humble like this child is the greatest in the kingdom of heaven" (Matthew 18:4), employing on this occasion the precise verb "humble" (*tapeinôsei*), which applies to him in the hymn ("he humbled himself [*etapeinôsen eauton*]," Philippians 2:8). Not only "Whoever wants to be first must be last of all" (Mark 9:35), but this inversion of values requires radical humility, whose fulfillment will begin with the washing of feet, among other acts: "Do you know what I have done to you? You call me Teacher and Lord—and you are right, for that is what I am. So if I, your Lord and Teacher, have washed your feet, you also ought to wash one another's feet. For I have set you an example, that you also should do as I have done to you" (John 13:12–15). Thus, primacy in the kingdom of God resides not in possession, but rather in dispossession; not in conservation, but rather in abandon, to such an extent that the (metaphysical) principle of the self-conservation of every being (*conatus in suo esse perserverendi*), which effectively puts the principle of non-contradiction to work (nothing can differ from itself), is here opposed by that which one might name the principle of self-contradiction: "If any want to become my followers, let them deny themselves and take up their cross and follow me. For those who want to save their life will lose it, and those who lose their life for my sake will find it." (Matthew 16:24–25).[11] To save and find oneself eventually saved, it is necessary precisely *not* to try to save *oneself* at all costs, as opposed to the spontaneous opinions of those who defy Christ on the cross to save himself, which is precisely what Christ on the cross above all must not attempt, for he must show that every resurrection comes from the Father alone, who has created *ex nihilo*. The savior is not he who saves *himself*, but rather he in whom others are saved, and who even finds himself saved by an Other: here, the Father. And Jesus, he who saves, does not save others unless, in saving them, he *does not carry out his own will*, but rather that of the Father to whom he has given himself over. In other words, because in saving others, he does not save himself first or in addition to the others, but bears witness to the kingdom to come and to the signs that accompany it. One can go so far as to "hate ... life itself [*misiei ... tên psuchên eautou*]" (Luke 14:26, 17:33; or John 12:25): "*ho misôn tên psuchên autou entô kosmô eis zôên aiônion phulaxei autên*, on the condition that one does not conflate self-denial with the resentment of self-hatred. Rather, self-denial is conceived as opposed to self-love to the point of having contempt for God. Conversely, one is to love God to the point of having contempt for oneself—to the point of leaving to God the care of oneself. Before God, I am more responsible for my brother than I am for myself. In effect, I can do much to save my brother, but nothing to save myself—nothing if not wait to be saved by God, and not by myself.

To renounce saving *oneself* becomes the one, unique condition for re-

---

11   See also Matthew 10:38; Mark 8:34–38; and Luke 9:24. Note that here it is a matter of the same *imitatio Christi* as in Philippians 2:5, and that "deny themselves [*aparnêsasthô heauton*]" corresponds to "emptied himself [*eauton ekenosên*]" (ibid. 2:7) or to "humbled Himself [*etapeinôsen eauton*]" (ibid. 2:8).

ceiving salvation. The conquest by the self for its proper salvation, as indeed every seizure by auto-appropriation—and this is its original defect and failure—conceals the fact that the essence of salvation consists in the gift, in the fact *that* it arrives, *if* at least it happens to me, from elsewhere than myself. And this gift can only arrive if it can let itself be received by its recipient, therefore only if the eventual recipient has renounced the fatal delusion to produce it by himself. Salvation can only come from elsewhere, happen to me only as a gift, and therefore supposes that I have abandoned the possibility and the care of its arrival to *it* and its happening to *me*. I can only receive to the extent that I abandon the mastery of that which I receive, and the extent of the salvation I receive to the gift itself. Thus, the gift can only be received in proportion to the abandon that he who receives it grants—who receives it precisely as what he does not possess, does not produce, and which does not come from him, but happens to *him* from elsewhere. No gift arrives without happening in possibility; possibility opens expectation, permits the reception and therefore also deception, and so supposes that I have consented to it, expose myself to it, do not close it off by seizing it in my hands, by my pretention to possession (*harpagmon*). The gift gives and does not ask anything—if only one abandons oneself to it. The abandon to the possibility of the gift fixes the only measure of the reception of the gift. To the extent that Christ "empties himself," "humbles himself"—that is, abandons himself to possibility to the point of exposing himself three times, first to humanity ("taking the form of a slave, being born in human likeness"), then to obedience ("he became obedient to the point of death"), and finally to the cross ("death on a cross")—his immense abandon opened up the space of an immense gift: "God also highly exalted him and gave him the name that is above every name" (Philippians 2:9). What is possessed is lost with the one who seizes it. For he who does not end in a gift, in a gift received, loses himself with his possessor. Only he who finds himself given regains himself saved, saved by he who gives it to him who receives it in the measure to which he abandons himself to it. In the death of Christ is revealed, all the way to the abyss which the fossil thickness of sin crosses at the foundation of the world, the principle that everything is lost but that which finds itself given, that nothing survives, if it is not on the way to a gift, that only the gift saves abandon, because only the gift makes of abandon the paradoxical condition of the gift. Christ on the cross proves, forever, that only he who guards his soul loses it, and that he who abandons it saves it.

III.

It henceforth becomes evident that "kenosis" can only be understood—supposing that we must ever understand it, for it alone makes us understand the "great mystery of our religion" (1 Timothy 3:16)—in a strictly Trinitarian horizon. The debate over the distinction of attributes ("moral" or "metaphysical"), which reduces the entire issue to an approximate psychology of self-consciousness which is in every way too human, has no pertinence and intends only to evade the seriousness of the question. The real difficulty, which for us is almost insurmountable, would consist in making out how, in the most accomplished lair of sin, across the sufferings that Thomas Aquinas described as "exceeding all those which humans can suffer in this life" (because his body was flesh more sensible than ours, because his purity of spirit renders the offenses even more profound, because finally his will was there committed without reserve for the salvation of all),[12] Christ was able to endure everything without himself revolting against God (but placing his spirit back in the Father, Luke 23:46) or accusing any man, whoever he might be (but forgiving, Luke 23:24). What did he thereby "accomplish" (John 19:30) and accomplish "to the end" (John 13:1)? He accomplished, in finitude, the foundation of sin and therefore the very act of *agapé* in extreme suffering, absolute abandon to the Father to receive the absolute gift, according to the Spirit, which accomplishes itself from all eternity in the (immanent) Trinity. What he says of his mission in the economy—that he does not consider the glory that puts him on equal footing with the Father as a possession to conserve, but receives it as a gift received without end in an abandon taken up without end: "I seek to do not my own will but the will of him who sent me" (John 5:30); "Yet I do not seek my own glory; there is one who seeks it and he is the judge. [...] If I glorify myself, my glory is nothing. It is my Father who glorifies me" (John 8:50, 54)—reveals exactly what he accomplishes eternally in the Trinity itself, without sin, without finitude, without passion. The glory that, in the economy, finds Christ according to the hymn (since "every tongue should confess that Jesus Christ is

---

12 St. Thomas Aquinas: "... *uterque autem dolor [sensiblisi & tristitia] in Christo fuit maximus iner dolores praesentis vitae*" (*Summa theologiae*, III, q. 46, a. 6, c.).

Lord, to the Glory of God the Father" [Philippians 2:11]), coincides exactly with what the Trinity in itself (immanent) accomplishes: "So now, Father, glorify me in your own presence with the glory that I had in your presence before the world existed" (John 17:5). Jesus Christ performs in his Passion exactly the same performance of *agapé* as in the Trinity, because the Son that he is from all eternity never "leaves" the Trinity, nor alienates or externalizes himself from it, according to the absurd and blasphemous doctrine (to go where?) of the philosophers (does the Son undo his filiation?). The inverse holds: Jesus Christ reintegrates the world—despite its finitude and its sin—in the Trinitarian play, he "gather[s] together all things" (Ephesians 1:10) in himself "so that God may be all in all" (1 Corinthians 15:28). The Trinitarian paradox—the Son possesses nothing that he has not received, and *for this reason* he is at the principle absolutely—Jesus Christ announces it and accomplishes it in the economy, from the foundation of finitude and our sin: "Then you will realize that I am he, and that I do nothing on my own, but I speak these things as the Father instructed me" (John 8:28). "Kenosis" does not introduce the negative, alienation, even the "death of God" in (or rather outside of) the Trinity. It renders manifest, to men stuck in the obscurity of sin and who deteriorate in the hatred of self and of all for all, the eternal play of the gift and abandon, where the three of the Trinity jubilantly triumph. The *chef d'œuvre* accomplished by Christ resides neither in the heroism of his virtues nor in the enormity of his suffering (for in itself neither the exemplarity of a model, nor the pain of atonement saves anyone); it resides in the fact that, like a brilliant musician, he performs the most perfect melody and orchestration on an instrument that has only one string (free will), a single string completely out of tune (by the perversity of evil); with this instrument—our nature which always plays falsely—he plays perfectly well according to his own nature. On the strength of this performance, he promises us that we, too, can succeed in playing well (or almost), provided that we let ourselves be inspired by the same Spirit as the one who unites him eternally to his Father. The final cry of the dying Christ marks agony no doubt, but also the triumph of he who knows himself to have won the race, who has gone to the end of himself and—above all—up to his Father, crossing the desert of our perversity. For there is a joy of Christ, which he gives us, provided that we learn how to abandon ourselves to it: "That they may have my joy made complete in themselves" (John 17:13). "I have said these things to you so that my joy may be in you, and that your joy may be complete"

(John 15:11). The resurrection of Christ begins with this cry of joy, cried out at the instant of his death. And in this life, we only divine the resurrection to the extent that we touch the breath, however distant, of this joy.

In fact, for us, the contemplation of the living God comes down to knowing how to see: to see the kenosis starting from the Trinity and not the Trinity starting from the kenosis. Indeed, in and across the deformation that the obscure and almost totally obfuscated prism of sin imposes—the perfect performance of the gift, eternal and glorious, up to the abandonment of the Son to the Father, according to an inconceivably just logic of communion by the Spirit. In other words, even on the cross, not only the dying of the Isenheim Altarpiece, then the cadaver, but indissociably, the resurrection that explodes with glory, also painted on the *verso*. It would be necessary—this would-be faith in the resurrection—to see the three in superposition, in a single view. To see the cross as the unique performance of the Trinity, the *representation* of which is for us permitted until the end of time.

There is no lack of texts that reveal flashes of the Trinity *in se* (immanent, as it is called) piercing through the confused shadows where the economy plays out. Thus, Christ sometimes directly addresses the Father as the Son: "I thank You [*exomologoumai soi*] Father, Lord of heaven and earth, because you have hidden these things from the wise and the intelligent and have revealed them to infants" (Matthew 11:25)—a sequence in which, as Luke 10:21 further specifies, Jesus "rejoiced [êgalliasato] in the Spirit." Whenever the miracle of the unconcealment of Trinitarian life is produced before the eyes of a human being (for this is the sole decisive miracle, which all the others try to release), Christ quivers with joy, in affirming that light has been brought, that his mission has been completed, and that the glory of God imposes itself within sin. The same occurs when Jesus, in the faith that surrounds him, sees that the miracle of resurrecting Lazarus becomes useful (and, therefore, possible), and he demands that his Father do so in order to manifest on earth the eternal play of the Trinity: "And Jesus looked upward and said, 'Father, I thank you for having heard me. I knew that you always hear me, but I have said this for the sake of the crowd standing here, so that they may believe that you sent me'" (John 11:41–42). It is a matter of making one perceive, through a miracle, the Trinitarian mission that renders this miracle possible and, therefore, effective. This is par excellence what happens when the "hour" comes and which is at the heart of the dispute in the temple about his mission. Jesus provokes the response of the Father: "It is for this reason that I have come to this hour. Father, glorify your name" (John 12:27–28). Above all, during the "sacerdotal prayer," the last before the instigation of the Passion, Christ announces the *admirabile commercium* of the glory abandoned as a *harpagmon* and rendered as a gift: "Father, the hour has come; glorify your Son so that the Son may glorify you" (John 17:1ff.). Thus, the Father makes himself understood directly to men by responding to the Son, or rather in responding *from* the Son. First, during the baptism: "And a voice from heaven said, 'This is my Son, the Beloved, with whom I am well pleased'" (Matthew 3:17; Mark 1:11; and Luke 3:22, which even makes a direct address to Jesus: "You are my Son."). The transfiguration does not consist so much in a vision as in a "voice coming from the cloud, saying: 'This is my Son, the Beloved; with him I am well pleased; listen to him!'" (Matthew 17:5; Mark 9:7; and Luke 9:35). Clearly, the calls the Son raises up to the Father find their confirmation immediately. To the demand "Father, glorify your name" responds "a voice ... I have glorified it and I will glorify it again" (John 12:28). The voice was heard, if not understood, because the crowd asked whether it was a clap of thunder or an angel; and Christ's ("The voice has come for your sake, not for mine," as in John 11:42, for the resurrection of Lazarus) was made in order to attest to the manifestation of what we call the immanent Trinity in the economic Trinity. We could even interpret the arrest of Jesus—or rather Christ's consent to an arrest that could perfectly well not have taken place—as a confirmation of his Trinitarian status as Son "in the form of God" (Philippians 2:6): "When Jesus said to them, 'I am he [*egô eimi*], they stepped back and fell to the ground" (John 18:6). As for the Spirit, he intervenes without speech, as the operator and director of the Trinitarian play, "like a dove" (Matthew 3:16; Mark 1:10; and Luke 3:24).

It is in this context of a *torn* opening of the Trinity (as the veil of the Temple is torn) that it is necessary to conceive the final words of Christ. Death evidently designates the abandon of every *harpagmon*—"My God, my God, why have you forsaken me?" (Matthew 27:46 and Mark 15:34). But, according to the eternal play of the immanent Trinity, the forsaking *permits* no less clearly the dispensation without return of the gift. *Because* the Son finally says: "Father, into your hands I commend my spirit" (Luke 23:46), in effect "Everything is finished [*telestai*]" *in the eyes of the Father* and the Spirit finds itself liberated *even in this world*: "Then he bowed his head and gave up his spirit" (John 19:30).

KENOSIS, STARTING FROM THE TRINITY

Some saw this, if not from the beginning, then at least occasionally, but—once seen—forever. Bearing witness to the fact without understanding it well, the disciples in the boat under the storm declared: "Truly you are the Son of God!" (Matthew 14:33). Or as the centurion and the guards "saw the earthquake and what took place, they were terrified and said, 'Truly this man was God's Son!'" (Matthew 27:54; Mark 15:39; Luke 23:47: "When the centurion saw what had taken place, he praised God and said, 'Certainly this man was innocent'" (Luke 23:47). Or approaching the entire Trinitarian manifestation within the economy as Peter to Caesarea: "You are the Messiah, the Son of the living God!" (Matthew 16:16; Mark 8:29–30; and Luke 9:20). And since Peter spoke in the name of all the remaining disciples, it is necessary to expand the recognition: "Lord, to whom can we go? You have the words of eternal life. We have come to believe and know that you are the Holy One of God" (John 6:68–69). Thus, to approach "kenosis" only signifies perceiving "how the most high [*to hupsêlon*], in coming down here, became the most low, let himself be seen in the most low without descending from the most high."[13] In other words, to learn how to see that in the immensity of his suffering and the absoluteness of his death (for he dies, if one may say so, more than any other man and "has not assumed birth but in view of death"),[14] the dereliction of Christ remains a forsaking, which returns and acknowledges before the Father the gift that this Father makes to him as to his Son in the unique Spirit. Even in the infernal desert of sin, which controls its empire with maximum force (physical, moral, and spiritual)—that is, in the experience of torture until death, of being forsaken, of the injustice of men, and *of course* of solidarity with the damned—Christ has performed the Trinitarian communion in his eternal perception. Happy will we be if, one day, we are able to say that it is "what we have seen with

---

13 Gregory of Nyssa, in *Discours catéchétique*, XXIV, p. 254, col. 65, ed. E. Mühlenberg, trans. R. Winling, Sources chrétiennes, no. 453 (Paris: Cerf, 2000).

14 Gregory of Nyssa, in *Discours catéchétique*, XXXII, p. 45, col. 80, ed. E. Mühlenberg, trans. R. Winling, Sources chrétiennes, no. 453 (Paris: Cerf, 2000). It is also in this sense that one must understand the less clear formulation of Hilary of Poitiers: "He empties himself of the form of God, i.e., of his equality to God; without, however, considering his equality to God as a *rapinia*, even though he remains in the form of God and equal to him, being God, marked by the seal of God [*quamvis in forma Dei et aequalis Deo per Deum Deus signatus extaret*]" in *De Trinitate* VIII, 45, p. 452, éd. G.M. Durand et al., Sources chrétiennes, no. 448 (Paris: Cerf, 2000).

our eyes, what we have contemplated" (1 John 1:1).

At the very least, one should never speak of a "divine kenosis" on the cross. The Trinitarian glory shows itself even in kenosis, but kenosis is not identical to it. Kenosis has to be contemplated starting from and with an eye toward the Trinity. Kenosis *exposes* the Trinity, but does not *explain* it. On the contrary, it is a matter of a revelation, through the obscurity of sin, of the Trinitarian play, where *l'agapé*—by its seriousness, its work, its patience, and its pain—passes beyond all that our poor understanding and our deep resentment imagines as the seriousness of the concept. There is infinitely more seriousness in the Trinitarian joy than can ever be found in the futility—certainly atrocious, but finite—of our sin. The Trinity operates even in kenosis, because the distance in it includes and surpasses even those—still finite—of evil, sin, and death. "For power (*dunamis*) is made perfect in weakness" (2 Corinthians 12:9) precisely because "Everything is in the power of God" (Mark 10:27 and Luke 18:27).

CHAPTER THREE

Balthasar's Theology of Christ's *Impasse* and "Dark Night"

DANIELLE NUSSBERGER

Introduction

A RECURRING AREA OF contention among Balthasar scholars is his theology of Holy Saturday. While some defend Balthasar's development of the tradition, others assert that there is utter discontinuity or even rupture between his theology of the descent into Hell and the traditional expression of the doctrine.[1] When they forget spirituality's vital role in the theological tradition, both parties fail to appreciate how Balthasar's innovations are attuned to the Spirit's movements in the lives and thought worlds of the saints.[2] The following is an act of remembering insofar as it suggests how

---

1 For a defense of Balthasar, see Edward T. Oakes, "The Internal Logic of Holy Saturday in the Theology of Hans Urs von Balthasar," *International Journal of Systematic Theology* 9 (2007): 184–99. For a critique of Balthasar in response to Oakes, see Alyssa Lyra Pitstick, "Development of Doctrine, or Denial? Balthasar's Holy Saturday and Newman's *Essay*," *International Journal of Systematic Theology* 11 (2009): 129–45. For an earlier example of this debate, see Alyssa Lyra Pitstick and Edward T. Oakes, "Balthasar, Hell, and Heresy: An Exchange," *First Things* 168 (2006): 25–32. See also Alyssa Lyra Pitstick's *Light in Darkness: Hans Urs von Balthasar and the Catholic Doctrine of Christ's Decent into Hell* (Grand Rapids, MI: Eerdmans, 2007).

2 Balthasar writes, "Above all, there are the graces of participation in the passion given to the Church, the experiences of the saints, which are quite inexplicable except

deeply indebted Balthasar's theology of Holy Saturday is to John of the Cross's spirituality of the "dark night."[3] Reading Balthasar's descent theology with the help of Constance Fitzgerald's interpretation of "dark night" as *impasse* reveals Balthasar's contemplation of two "dark nights"—namely, Christ's and the theologian's.[4] Balthasar urges theologians to enter the initially intolerable and finally fruitful space of *impasse* where human beings are remade in Christ's image.

First, for Balthasar, there is a sense in which Christ experiences a "dark night" as he undergoes the descent into Hell. Secondly, there is a sense in which the theologian goes through a "dark night," because Balthasar's theology strips her of her presuppositions regarding Christ's triumphant demolition of Hell's gates. Balthasar submerges his reader in unsettling theological speculations in order for her to emerge with a clearer vision of the trinitarian logic of love that is essentially beyond human comprehension. Through the *impasse* of the theologian's "dark night," one progresses from a kataphatic awareness to a deeper apophatic wisdom that accepts the extent to which human systems cannot hold the mystery of God hostage to their expectations and desires.

Balthasar's theology of Christ's descent helps his readers understand more profoundly how God is transforming the darkness of sin and death—not as the unmistakable King of power and might that they might like to imagine, but as the King on the Cross who has descended into the depths of Hell to rise again from his own "dark night." This speculative immersion

---

as a participation in Christ's states. These experiences constitute the vast, limitless field of the 'dark nights'...." From "Theology and Sanctity," in *Word Made Flesh*, trans. A.V. Littledale with Alexander Dru (San Francisco: Ignatius Press, 1989), 199. See also Balthasar, "Spirituality," in ibid., 211–26.

3   This passage from forgetfulness to remembering should call to mind Cyril O'Regan's *The Anatomy of Misremembering: Von Balthasar's Response to Philosophical Modernity* (Chestnut Ridge, NY: Crossroad, 2014). Balthasar directly refers to John of the Cross's influence in *Mysterium Paschale*, trans. Aidan Nichols (Grand Rapids, MI: Eerdmans, 1993), 76. See John of the Cross's "The Dark Night," in *John of the Cross: Selected Writings*, ed. Kieran Kavanaugh (New York: Paulist Press, 1987), 155–210.

4   See Constance Fitzgerald, O.C.D., "Impasse and Dark Night," in *Living with Apocalypse: Spiritual Resources for Social Compassion* (San Francisco: Harper and Row, 1984), 93–116.

in Christ's "dark night" is designed to inspire Christians' active imitation of christic *impasse*, during which they come to terms with their own personal sin and with the societal evils that threaten to darken the light of God's kenotic love.

Analogy of *Impasse* on the Christological Plane

Balthasar's theology as a whole—and in particular *Mysterium Paschale*, where he more specifically deals with Christ's descent—functions on the premise that a christological and trinitarian starting point yields both theo-logical and anthropo-logical fruit. This suggestion was intimated above when discussing the Christian's imitation of christic *impasse*. For Balthasar, there will always be a correspondence—not an identity—between divine life and human life, because of the Creator/creature relationship and distinction that establishes the *analogia entis*.[5] Due to the premise of analogy, the theologian is forever using concepts that function in multiple senses of similarity and difference. Chief among these concepts, for Balthasar, is that of kenosis. He masterfully distinguishes between divine kenosis and the human perception of kenosis through the experience of suffering. There are three levels of interpretation at work here: (1) the Son's kenotic mode of being in Incarnation, Cross, and descent into Hell; (2) the inter-trinitarian kenotic distance of love; and (3) the Christian vocation of a kenotic existence that imitates Christ's example.[6] Epistemologically speaking, one arrives at the second and third forms of kenosis by contemplating Christ's kenosis in the economy. Given the trinitarian axiom that the "immanent trinity is the economic trinity," one can move from what one sees in the economy to its analogate in the immanent trinity. In an analogous fashion, one can transition from a vision of Christ's kenosis to the similar yet different kenosis to which human beings are called through the grace of redemption and new life in Christ. Ontologically speaking, however, the inter-trinitarian kenotic distance of

---

5 See "The Analogy of Being," in Nicholas J. Healy, *The Eschatology of Hans Urs von Balthasar: Being as Communion* (Oxford: Oxford University Press, 2005), 19–90.

6 Balthasar, *The Action*, Vol. 4, *Theo-Drama*, trans. Graham Harrison (San Francisco: Ignatius Press, 1994), 325–28. See also Balthasar, *The New Covenant*, Vol. 7, *The Glory of the Lord: A Theological Aesthetics*, trans. Brian McNeil, ed. John Riches (San Francisco: Ignatius Press, 1984), 294, 305, 331.

love has first priority, because it is what undergirds its economic manifestation in Christ's kenotic mode of being. Though the theologian can point to the ontological ground for what is revealed in the economy, the words that one uses to make such a gesture never exhaust the Mystery that they reflect. Balthasar is always attentive to this point, even when he may seem to speak many words about what must, in the end, remain unsaid.

For Balthasar, Christ's Cross discloses the triune, kenotic love of eternal self-abandonment but is not identical to it. Christ uniquely and concretely embodies the *analogia entis*, as he is the perfect union between human and divine, wherein the human lives according to its pure, created nature of being ever wedded to divine intention.[7] The Savior Christ's pristine human existence in the being of the Word must come up against humanity's deformation of its true nature through disobedience and sin. Christ is obedient to the Father's will through the kenotic passion of the Cross according to the divine mode of existence that is everlastingly kenotic in giving itself away in the superabundance of triune love. Christ's giving up of his life on the Cross takes place within the divine being of perpetual agapic self-gift, which accords human death an entirely new meaning, purpose, and outcome.[8]

The exclusive meaning of Christ's death is a salvific one, because he alone performs the supreme act of giving humanity over to God, thereby reconstituting the fullness of human life. The salvific purpose of Christ's death is realized, because his human handing over of life to God is happening within God's own perpetual act of self-giving love that is the foundation of all created being.[9] Balthasar suggests that the Incarnation in its marriage of human and divine was always moving toward the Cross, where the human kenosis of death would be fully united to the trinitarian kenosis of divine life. The spotless Lamb takes upon himself humanity's sinful state of loss of intimacy with God, and he redeems humanity by giving humanity back to God precisely through the kenotic mode of suffering and death that sin has caused. Suffering and death themselves have been transformed, because they have been reformed according to divine, kenotic love. In Christ, the loss

---

[7] Balthasar, *Epilogue*, trans. Graham Harrison (San Francisco: Ignatius Press, 1991), 91.

[8] Balthasar, *The New Covenant*, 395.

[9] Balthasar, *The Action*, 323.

of life in death that was the result of sin is now a relinquishing of life that overcomes sin by becoming a self-giving love that occurs in freedom and obedience to the Father's will.

This is the gist of Balthasar's theology of the Cross that he expresses in the form of a theological aesthetics: God reforms the human form from within the human deformation of that form.[10] Christ reforms sin and death by transforming them into a kenosis analogous to the divine self-giving that is the love of the Trinity. Humanity's sinful turning away from God had always meant a forfeiture of the God-given life that was humanity's inheritance. Now, the suffering and death that bespoke this maximal loss speaks something new through the person of the Word. The Word rejects humanity's sin when Christ "dies to sin" and forsakes humanity's disobedience in order to hand it over in death to be reborn in the Spirit. In this way, Christ's passion and death speak the words of eternal life.

Though the Crucified has accomplished humanity's redemption and already spoken the words of eternal life, Balthasar insists there are more words to say regarding the consequences of Christ's salvific embrace of death on the Cross. This contention does not imply that Holy Saturday is the bona fide Good Friday. Rather, Holy Saturday is about the experience of death that is the Cross's outcome and that is still in the process of being transformed into the new life of Resurrection on Easter Sunday.[11] Seen in this light, Holy Saturday cannot simply be comprehended according to the kataphatic conception of the victorious defeat of sin and death through a harrowing of Hell that may prematurely anticipate the Resurrection if taken to an extreme. All good kataphasis is complemented by apophasis such that the kataphatic might be properly clarified in the blinding light of divine Mystery.[12] The kataphatic imagery of the warrior king storming the gates of Hell gives way to the apophatic sensibility for the Word's revelation in the silence and passivity of the womb of death. This apophatic dimension is borne out in Balthasar's reflections upon the mystical tradition's sense of Holy Saturday as "wordless," a time when speech about or with God is reformed and renewed through

---

10   Balthasar, *Seeing the Form*, Vol. 1, *The Glory of the Lord: A Theological Aesthetics*, trans. Erasmo Leiva-Merikakis, ed. Joseph Fessio, S.J., and John Riches (San Francisco: Ignatius Press, 1982), 454–55.

11   Balthasar, *The New Covenant*, 29–31.

12   Balthasar, *Seeing the Form*, 448.

the suffering and death of the Incarnate one.[13] This is also consistent with Balthasar's deployment of the Johannine expression of the divine glory that is revealed directly through its hiddenness on the Cross.[14]

Balthasar extends this Johannine hermeneutic to the Son's descent into Hell, which involves a *visio mortis* on the part of Christ's human soul: a vision of sin and death as it truly is in its absolute distance from the Father that results in God-forsakenness.[15] Whereas Christ's Cross occasioned the active passion of the body and soul, now the body remains in the tomb and the soul of Christ is passive in death.[16] After all, human death is not an active affair. If it were, Christ would still be alive. In such passivity, the darkness of sin and death and their resulting separation from God take over, to the extent that this reality is all that Christ sees with the eyes of his soul. As with the foregoing discussion of Christ's kenosis on the Cross, Christ's kenosis in the bowels of Sheol takes place within the context of the divine kenotic distance of the trinitarian persons' mutual abandonment to each other in love.

Knowing Balthasar's adherence to the unity between spiritual life and vision and theological *sciencia*, it should not be surprising that John of the Cross's dark night can elucidate Balthasar's theology of Holy Saturday. Especially helpful in this regard is Constance Fitzgerald's reading of John of the Cross's dark night as *impasse*. Fitzgerald's *impasse* can illumine the importance of Christ's passivity in the *visio mortis*, as his soul is completely conscious of the reality of sin all around him. Fitzgerald writes that

---

13 Balthasar writes that "not only the sensual man, but the mental and noumenal, must be buried.... God's word in the world has fallen silent.... It is not a silence pregnant with a thousand secrets of love that come from the sensed presence of the beloved, but the silence of absence.... And so there is the dull emptiness of purely human talking and thinking about God. Such talking has become a mere clatter of formal logic, empty syllogisms, because the breath of faith, hope, and charity no longer blows through it." From *A Theological Anthropology* (New York: Sheed and Ward, 1967), 284. This suspension of human thought and expression follows upon Christ's death. It is lifted when he is resurrected, as the Spirit patterns the speech and actions of Jesus's disciples after him.

14 Balthasar, *The Final Act*, 362.

15 Balthasar, *Mysterium Paschale*, 173.

16 Ibid., 172.

impasse can be the condition for creative growth and transformation *if* the experience of impasse is fully appropriated within one's heart and flesh with consciousness and consent; *if* the limitations of one's humanity and human condition are squarely faced and the sorrow of finitude allowed to invade the human spirit with real, existential powerlessness: *if* the ego does not demand understanding in the name of control and predictability but is willing to admit the mystery of its own being and surrender itself to this mystery; *if* the path into the unknown, into the uncontrolled and unpredictable margins of life, is freely taken when the path of deadly clarity fades.[17]

Of course, this passage refers to a human person who is faced with such an impasse during her lifetime, requiring that she head into the unknown and passively accept her finitude. Her unabashed recognition of her abandonment to the unknown is the condition for the possibility of the authentic knowing that occurs when God's Spirit is allowed to fill the space left open by her candid acceptance of weakness and vulnerability. This anthropological transformation through *impasse* is analogous to the christological *impasse* of the descent into Hell, where Christ's journey through the *impasse* includes the transformation of humanity's sinful disobedience into the active passivity of obedient participation in triune life. Like the human being who "squarely faces the sorrow of finitude," Christ enters the *impasse* of death's realm and consents to facing not only the created limitation of humanity but also humanity's self-imposed barrier of sin and detachment from divine sustenance.[18] Christ accepts his human vulnerability in the stead of human beings who have claimed power over God in their sin by choosing to remove themselves from God's love. He discerns that he is on the margins imposed

---

17 Fitzgerald, "Impasse and Dark Night," 96.

18 For Fitzgerald, one "squarely faces the sorrow of finitude" by passively dwelling precisely in the emptiness of a devastating situation that cannot be repaired by human striving. In this sense, it is an acquiescence to one's inability to save oneself or others from sin and death, an acknowledgment that one can never take the place of God. It is likewise, then, a handing over of oneself to the mystery of God. One's passive "dwelling in the emptiness" makes way for God's salvific action that awakens graced, transformative human responses to sin's ongoing effects in the world.

by death where sin uncovers the defeat of all human rationality that performs its thinking outside the boundaries of the human's relationship to God. Only Christ can passively undergo this kind of *impasse*, because only Christ as human and as Son of God can take on the overwhelming sorrow of all of human sin and consciously recognize it for what it is. The Word alone knows the intimacy of God's love that sinful humanity has willfully forsaken.[19]

As John of the Cross relates the travails of the soul's "dark night" using the poetic imagery of the lover who has lost her beloved, so too is Christ's "dark night" the story of the loving Son who has been separated from the beloved Father. The lover is the only one who can thoroughly taste the bitterness of separation from her love, because she alone has known what it means to be unconditionally loved by the beloved. In the same way, the Son is the only one who knows what it means for sinful humanity to be deprived of participation in divine love, because he alone is one in being with the absolute and unreserved love of the Father. Christ's *visio mortis* is the meditation upon sin in death's *impasse* that is witness to the negative reality that sin has created: a darkness replete with the sins themselves that have caused total separation from the God against whom these sins have been ultimately committed.[20] The purity of Christ's sinless meditation upon humanity's separation from God sees so clearly the false path that egotistical, misapplied human logic has trod whenever it has rationalized its choices to destroy the "other," who is God's beloved. There is no way out of the abyss that can be achieved on human terms alone, for humanity's choice to be on its own has caused the sinful situation in the first place. Christ experiences the hopelessness of humanity's sinful state at an intensity beyond human imagination, since his essential unity with God enables him to comprehend what has been lost.

What sets Christ's humanity apart is his union with the divine will, such that he has freely chosen to endure the full magnitude of sin's consequences so as to repair the damage by working through the wreckage itself. Once again, Balthasar sees the God who reforms the human form by entering into the human being's deformation of that form. Like Fitzgerald's mature human person who responsibly faces the threat of *impasse*,

---

19   Balthasar, *The New Covenant*, 231.
20   Balthasar, *Mysterium Paschale*, 173.

the Son of God does not run from the darkness that human beings have created through their sinfulness. This is an extreme form of kenosis that is akin to the kenosis of the Incarnation itself, the exact opposite of a power that would evade human experience when destroying the darkness of sin. By taking humanity unto himself in the Incarnation, the Son has willfully agreed to experience everything that lost humanity entails, even though he himself is not lost.

Christ passively waits in the plight of *impasse*, just as any other human soul would be forced to do in this state of death and separation from God. However, he does so as the human soul united to the divine Word who is being revealed even in this *impasse*, not as the mighty warrior who strides forth into Hell's citadel and breaks down its doors to liberate the righteous from their chains. Rather, this is the same Son of God who pours himself out in the love that is shared between Father, Son, and Spirit within the life of the immanent Trinity. In the finite context of sin and death, this outpouring of love has taken on the shape of *impasse*. Squarely facing sinful humanity's separation from God, Christ's kenotic obedience seems incapable of accomplishing its goal of reuniting humanity to God, especially since God the Father is entirely absent. The distance between Father and Son encompasses the human soul of Christ, who rests in the confines of Hell's elimination of God's presence. Within this unique *impasse* there lies the greatest potential for new life, given that Christ's faithful surrender to the distant Father is the humble power that deposes sin and its eradication of divine love in human self and society. The Son's faith-filled handing over of his spirit to the Father is the source and model for the human posture of self-offering enabled by the Spirit's gifts of faith and hope in God's creative and redemptive activity.

To illustrate further what happens to the human person submitting to *impasse*, Fitzgerald explains the necessary transition from fear to self-surrender in faith:

> Since dark night is a limit experience, and since it does expose human fragility, brokenness, neurotic dependence, and lack of integration, it is understandable that it undermines a person's self-esteem and activates anxious self-analysis. The only way to break out of this desperate circle of insoluble self-questioning is to surrender in

faith and trust to the unfathomable Mystery that beckons onward and inward beyond calculation, order, self-justification, and fear.[21]

This transposition of self-justification to self-abandonment is a supreme challenge, because there is no proof that such self-sacrifice will yield anything other than a continuation of the current condition of darkness and loss. It does not allow for a contrary vision of something brighter, since self-surrender is a passive procedure that is the "letting-be" of the darkness. If anything, it makes for an even more paralyzing entry into the abyss now that its gravity is being acknowledged rather than rationalized away. Gone are the illusions that the darkness was just a mirage and that obedience to God's will was the surest way to make one's self vanish into nothingness. In the case of Christ's descent into Hell, Christ as God's Son is the only human being who is without self-deception. Therefore, he can make the most complete entry into the darkness of sin and death due to the fact that he alone can passively let the darkness be darkness by accepting the powerlessness and inadequacy of humanity's logic and its machinations of self-justification; he knows that such surrender on the part of humanity is exactly what must happen in order for God's self-abandoning love to restore and renew it. Only Christ can enter into the mystery of the unknown, because he is that Mystery. When he entrusts his humanity to the Father, he is consigning all of humanity to the Father. The giving over of Christ's humanity in the *impasse* of death is held within the Son's giving over of himself to the Father that is constitutive of the Triune God's eternal kenosis of love.

Speaking of divine kenosis in the realm of the immanent Trinity is another way of expressing the Father's eternal generation of the Son that is an outpouring of love that continues with the Father and the Son's mutual spiration of the Holy Spirit. Balthasar further describes the interactions between Father, Son, and Spirit on the basis of the "distance" between them that accounts for their distinction from each other and the loving reciprocity of trinitarian relationship that takes place because of such a unity-in-difference. The Father's abandonment of the Son in the death of Hell's *impasse* is the economic shape that this trinitarian "distance of love" takes within the dire circumstances of human sin and death; the Father's love for the Son

---

21 Fitzgerald, "Impasse and Dark Night," 103.

and the Son's for the Father is now taking place through their mutual act of self-abandonment on behalf of humanity's restoration to participation in Triune life. The loving distance between Father and Son is now such that it encircles the space of death's *impasse* so that the grave might become the open tomb. Christ passively allows himself to be thrown into the *impasse* of humanity's sin and death, because this passivity leaves humanity wide open for the breadth of God's creative and salvific activity. Christ must be the human who takes lifeless humanity back to God the Father through the power of the Son that is always the strength of self-abandoning love.

Balthasar avoids the danger of ascribing suffering in human terms to the Godhead by supporting an analogy in ever-greater difference between the economic kenosis of the Son's abandonment by the Father and the eternal divine kenosis of trinitarian love; the mystery of inter-trinitarian kenosis is both revealed and hidden by the economic form of kenosis in the Son's abandonment. The eternal distance of love between Father and Son takes on a particular cast through the Son's acceptance of the human lot to the extent of Christ's becoming sin in order to save humanity from that sin. The Son does not experience *impasse* by admitting his weakness as Word; he submits to the *impasse* by having taken on the fullness of humanity's current condition, including humanity's dissent against God in sin. The Son carries humanity through the *impasse* when Christ acknowledges human disobedience on behalf of all of humanity and undergoes exactly what humanity must—a passage through the darkness that can only be illuminated by the Father.

Through the Son's descent into Hell, he does not change but rather exists according to the eternal truth that is the Son's relationship to the Father: that his life belongs to the Father as the result of the Father's infinite, self-giving love. In this economic instance, the Son who is generated through the Father's endless outpouring of love expresses himself by ushering human beings into an acceptance of their created dependence upon the generosity of triune love that is analogous to the Son's eternal procession from the Father. Humanity can only arrive at this kind of acquiescence through the conversion that *impasse* necessitates: a transition from dread and helplessness to empowerment through the grace of God. The Son undertakes this movement in the sense that he holds the human soul's authentic fear and trembling in the Father's absence. He then takes it through the negative distance of sin and death into the positive distance of loving kenosis between the persons of the Trinity. The Son accomplishes this feat because as the Christ he meditates upon the sinful distance of humanity from the Father and traverses the *impasse* to arrive at Easter Sunday; this is the day when the Incarnate One is resurrected by the Father to the superabundant life of the Son that was always held in the distance of divine love.

In his essay "Hell and Descent," Balthasar summarizes the Incarnate One's unrepeatable *impasse* that reveals the Son's kenotic posture of selfless abandonment to the Father's will:

> And in his being dead with the dead, the attitude and stance of the divine Logos has been stripped away, as it were. For it was in the extremities of this death that the Logos found the adequate expression of this divine stance: letting himself remain available for the Father in everything, even in ultimate alienation. The stripping away of the man Jesus is the laying bare not only of Sheol but also of the trinitarian relationship in which the Son is entirely the one who springs forth from the Father. Holy Saturday is thus a kind of suspension, as it were, of the Incarnation, whose result is given back to the hands of the Father and which the Father will renew and definitively confirm by the Easter Resurrection.[22]

The Son has left himself open to be used by the Father for the sake of humanity's salvation, through Christ's passive submission to death's separation of the soul from the body, through his meditation upon sin and all its ramifications, and through his contemplative steadfastness within the darkness in order to reunite humanity with God in the crucible of Hell's *impasse*. In this economic instance, the Son's obedience to the Father involves being left alone in humanity's deadly reality of sin and ultimate isolation, waiting for the Father to restore his Incarnate life with the reunification of his body and soul in the event of the Resurrection. Balthasar suggests that the Incarnation has been suspended during Christ's reckoning with death, in order to call attention to the fact that Christ's sacrifice on the Cross meant the tearing apart of the flesh of the Incarnate One, its severing from the soul of Christ, and

---

22 Balthasar, "The Descent into Hell," in *Spirit and Institution*, trans. Edward T. Oakes, S.J. (San Francisco: Ignatius Press, 1995), 411–12.

therefore the seeming undoing of the effects of the Incarnation in the depths of Sheol—all in order that the purpose of the Incarnation might be fulfilled. The glory of God's victory in Christ's Incarnation is paradoxically hidden in death's undoing of the flesh and Hell's forcing of the soul into *impasse*—the portal to Resurrection for both Christ and his disciples.

Analogy of Impasse on the Theologian's Plane

Balthasar inspires theologians to strip away their theological calculations. As theologians accompanying Balthasar in his speculative "descent," we cannot help but be initially confused when we relinquish the traditional way of looking at things. Our limited suppositions must give way to the boundless logic of love in Christ, and this surrender threatens us and makes us feel as if the darkness of *impasse* is an indication that our speculations are moving in the wrong direction. The apophatic *impasse*, where our rationality does not hold ultimate sway, affords a more profound understanding of God's loving triumph in Christ than the kataphatic accounting of the victorious, almost already risen Christ who gloriously frees the righteous for their heavenly reward. We are not, however, entirely forsaking the kataphatic dimension. Rather, we are allowing it to be illumined by the darkness of unknowing that is the heart of apophatic prayer and contemplation.

The theologian's *impasse* is something akin to Christ's "dark night": the possibility for union with God by moving through the darkness as the space through which God's light emerges. The light that is shining in the darkness indicates that the darkness itself has been transformed so as to reflect the light. Nothing that God impacts is left unchanged, even our preconceived notions of how God touches us and makes us to live again in the triumph over sin and death. When the theologian uses Balthasar's lens of *impasse* to encounter the more traditional theology of Christ's descent, she finds theology alive again with renewed vigor in a way that she could not have imagined if she had remained satisfied with her previous assumptions.

The theologian's "dark night" is reminiscent of the universal call to all Christians to brave a progression from meditation to contemplation that requires the denuding of one's expectations on the individual physical, psychological, emotional, and spiritual levels. It must not stop there but rather continue onward to include the individual's interactions with others within the Christian community and in society at large so that we and all those we encounter might be transformed by the Spirit into God's expectations for us. We have traversed, then, from Fitzgerald's (and John of the Cross's) anthropological plane to the christological, to the theologian's contemplation of the christological, and have finally returned to the anthropological plane transformed in Christ.

Balthasar's descent theology functions on all three of these levels and is therefore a microcosm of his entire theological project. Only in Christ's disclosure of divine life do we see the triumph of love for what it really is: a willingness to overcome its opposite by embracing it so completely that sin cannot help but be healed by the love that is its antidote. This is a God who does not express his love by administering sin's remedy to human beings as if it were a medicine that could be applied topically to heal the wound that sin has caused. This would only be a superficial approach that would allow the wound of sin to continue to fester, under the illusion that it had been attended to thoroughly. Instead, God performs a complete transformation of the human person from the inside out; in Christ, God reforms the human form from within the human form itself.

Balthasar's theological aesthetics of the Christ-form underlies all of his theology as he narrates salvation history from the perspective of the almighty God who glories in transforming God's creation into God's image and likeness through the Incarnation and the Paschal Mystery of Christ's suffering, death, and resurrection. This Christ-form is God's design for all human beings, and it is meant to inform the way we think, speak, act, and engage in relationships with each other in both Church and society. Unfortunately, we are often not malleable enough to let the creative Spirit in to set the seal of Christ's kenotic love on our hearts, because we are bound and determined to live according to our own lights. Therefore, Balthasar introduces us to the christological *impasse* and "dark night" in the hope that we Christians might become aware of the folly of ignoring the roadblocks toward which our ill-advised individual and social programs steer us. Perhaps, then, we will be willing to wholeheartedly accept our daily opportunities for *impasse* so that we might begin to live out our inheritance of participation in the eternal, kenotic love of triune life.

When read in light of John of the Cross's dark night as *impasse*, Balthasar's theology of Holy Saturday can be an opportunity for theologians to contemplate Christ's passage through death's *impasse* and their participation in it. Cyril O'Regan recognizes that this apophatic, hermeneutical turn necessitates a theologian's imitation of the practices and forms of life of the saints, principally their embodiment of scripture that adopts Christ's self-emptying posture. Appreciating Balthasar's perspective on this, O'Regan opines that "the saint enacts the wildness of scripture, which is the wildness of love, and as she does, she defeats the all-knowingness of any and all systems."[23] Likewise, along with Balthasar, he asserts that to be a Christian means to be a saint in this regard: "… a subject that cannot empty itself and surrender in ecstasy is not a Christian subject."[24] In his scholarly output and in his teaching and mentorship, Cyril O'Regan embodies his words by practicing a theology of "ecstatic surrender" that inspires his readers and students to do the same. For this reason, he is the guiding influence behind this study's approach to Balthasar's Holy Saturday that affirms the mutually enriching relationship between spirituality and theology. It is fitting, therefore, to close by echoing his words that attest to theology's spiritual core as a discipline committed to enlivening an already Spirit-filled world: "As 'academic' theology has a source that is not itself, a tradition to which it is faithful, it also has an ecstatic aspect: the incarnation of a vision in a world that requires it be regarded as precious, but also groaning towards transformation."[25] May we follow in Cyril O'Regan's footsteps, with the humility to recognize our theological efforts as a participation in creation's "groaning toward transformation."

---

23 O'Regan, *Anatomy of Misremembering*, 148.

24 Cyril O'Regan, "Von Balthasar's Valorization and Critique of Heidegger's Genealogy of Modernity," in *Christian Spirituality and the Culture of Modernity: The Thought of Louis Dupré*, eds. Peter J. Casarella and George P. Schner, S.J. (Grand Rapids, MI: Eerdmans, 1998), 158.

25 Cyril O' Regan, "Review of Rowan Williams, *Wrestling with Angels: Conversations in Modern Theology*," *Modern Theology* 26 (2010): 152.

CHAPTER FOUR

Theology in the Middle Voice

Thomas Aquinas and Immanuel Kant on Natural Ends

Corey L. Barnes

Reflections on final causality can broadly reveal fundamental dispositions of diverse historical periods while also indicating fundamental continuities among the diverse dispositions. This poses a challenge to historically and systematically invested treatments of final causality, but it is not the only challenge. The very meaning of a cause has changed throughout the course of western thought, which makes difficult the task of tracing or deciphering the relationship between Aristotle's four types of explanations and modern notions of cause as event. Part of these changes involved a reduction of causality to efficiency (perhaps beginning with Avicenna), but these changes also emerged from developing understandings of nature and finality. Such changes have shaped our basic assumptions regarding causality. Recognizing diversity between modern and ancient conceptions of final causality (or causality more generally) does not ensure that we can conceptually overcome them. Awareness of the difficulty might be necessary for solving the difficulty without itself constituting a solution. Though the problem might seem restricted to investigations of pre-modern thought, it can also obscure understandings of modern thought.

Recent treatments of final causality or teleology have held together Kant and Aristotle, though often for different reasons or aims.[1] Monte Johnson has argued that approaches to final causality in Aristotle have been unduly shaped by conceptual categories derived from Kant's teleology.[2] Several interpreters of Kant have indicated or even stressed parallels between Kantian teleology and Aristotelian final causality, though they by no means presume to minimize the differences.[3] These various scholars approach this pairing from diverse vantages and include a range of emphases and opinions, but they tend to agree on certain omissions. One striking similarity between investigations of final causality by specialists in ancient philosophy and in modern philosophy is their benign neglect or collective condemnation of scholastic thought.[4] Others, especially those interested in genealogies of modernity, often share the desire to identify a historical villain and resist blanket condemnations of scholasticism by singling out some figures for rebuke (typically Scotus or Ockham) and others for praise (typically Aquinas).[5] Attempting to rectify these problematic approaches while confronting the general difficulties facing historical and systematic study of final causality requires a different approach or perspective. Walter Benjamin's idea

---

1   Some recent discussions focus exclusively on notions of function and how functional language has persisted in certain scientific disciplines and philosophical discourses. See Mark Perlman, "The Modern Philosophical Resurrection of Teleology," *The Monist* 87 (2004): 3–51.

2   Monte R. Johnson, *Aristotle on Teleology* (Oxford: Clarendon Press, 2005).

3   Hannah Ginsborg, *The Normativity of Nature: Essays on Kant's* Critique of Judgment (Oxford: Oxford University Press, 2015); Angela Breitenbach, "Two Views on Nature: A Solution to Kant's Antinomy of Mechanism and Teleology," *British Journal for the History of Philosophy* 16 (2008): 351–69. For a comprehensive examination of teleology within Kant's thought, see Courtney Fugate, *The Teleology of Reason: A Study of the Structure of Kant's Critical Philosophy* (Berlin: Walter de Gruyter, 2014).

4   John Carriero serves as a notable exception. See his excellent "Spinoza on Final Causality," in *Oxford Studies in Early Modern Philosophy*, Vol. 2, ed. D. Garber and S. Nadler (Oxford: Clarendon Press, 2006), 105–47.

5   For a criticism of this trend with respect to John Duns Scotus, see Cyril O'Regan, "Scotus the Nefarious: Uncovering Genealogical Sophistications," in *The Newman-Scotus Reader: Contexts and Commonalities*, ed. E.J. Ondrako (New Bedford, MA: Academy of the Immaculate, 2015), 611–36.

of constellated historical eras and Cyril O'Regan's project of middle-voice genealogy offer guidance for an alternative and fruitful approach.

Informed by these two perspectives, we can read Kantian natural teleology and Thomistic natural final causality together. A middle-voice reading of this historical constellation serves at least three purposes: first, it enriches the conceptual scheme for interpreting Kant and the basic problematic confronted in the *Critique of the Power of Judgment*; second, it offers new insights into the tensions underlying Thomas Aquinas's endeavor to integrate diverse strands of reflection on final causality; and third, it contributes to genealogies of modernity and broader concerns of intellectual history.

Methodological Inspirations

Work in historical theology or scholarship identified with historical theology follows no strict definition, ranging in purpose along a spectrum of concerns historical, systematic, and comparative, and ranging in period from late antiquity through modernity.[6] It typically attends closely to historical, social, and intellectual contexts through careful textual analysis, often attempting to correct anachronistic (mis)readings. Regardless, the emphasis on contextualized textual analysis functions as a standard (and perhaps necessary) feature of historical theology, yet it can present a danger if employed myopically. An extreme emphasis on context can function as a limiting factor, restricting past figures and texts to a bygone historical moment and implicitly criticizing all subsequent uses of these figures, texts, or ideas as inherent misuses. If we aim for the richest (or even the most charitable) reading of a text, we must articulate close contextual readings as points of departure rather than arrival. Benjamin's notion of constellated eras and O'Regan's idea of middle-voice genealogies can guide all those operating within a broad framework of historical theology, even those whose interests in intellectual archaeology or genealogy are strictly limited. Original meanings are not preserved intact and unchanging in a (platonic) realm accessible only to those committed to contextual immersion. Rather, every attempt to examine these past texts and thinkers relates in some way to genealogical projects.

Walter Benjamin's image of constellated eras is best introduced in his own words:

---

6   It is a separate question what makes something count as historical.

> Historicism contents itself with establishing a causal connection between various moments in history. But no fact that is a cause is for that very reason historical. It became historical posthumously, as it were, through events that may be separated from it by thousands of years. A historian who takes this as his point of departure stops telling the sequence of events like the beads of a rosary. Instead, he grasps the constellation which his own era has formed with a definite earlier one. Thus he establishes a conception of the present as the "time of the now" which is shot through with chips of Messianic time.[7]

Benjamin writes here of constellating the present with earlier eras, but the lesson for historical theology works in multiple directions. That is, historical theology can genealogically enrich our understanding of the present and can use Benjamin's basic lesson in viewing earlier eras, movements, thinkers, texts, and ideas, as possible participants in various constellations, all of which can alter the meaning of each term so constellated. So, for example, ideas of medieval scholasticism could be constellated with earlier periods or thinkers (e.g., classical philosophy) to form a new shape, or they could be constellated with figures from modernity to explore mutual tensions or patterns of thought. Examining in parallel such patterns can offer insight into both eras or figures, though this does not warrant any reading or use as equally permissible, effective, or informative.

A second notion helpfully illustrates aspects of Benjamin's sentiment while also guarding against possible misuses or dangers. That notion is O'Regan's middle-voice genealogy, a concept adapted from middle-voice rhetoric. O'Regan distinguishes this from low genealogy, which purports to offer a disinterested history of ideas, and from high genealogy, which equates truth claims with discourses of power and so refuses to judge them. By contrast, middle-voice genealogy acknowledges its subjective position and values without granting those positions and values the power to overwhelm the analysis and all of its truth claims.[8] Middle-voice genealogy re-

---

7   Walter Benjamin, *On the Concept of History*, XVIII.A, in *Selected Writings: Volume 4, 1938–1940*, ed. H. Eiland and M. Jennings (Cambridge: The Belknap Press of Harvard University Press, 2003), 397.

8   Cyril O'Regan, *Gnostic Return in Modernity* (Albany: State University of New York Press, 2001), 15–16.

sists the limiting temptation of characterizing intellectual history as a series of epochal ruptures or as a series of accidental modifications predicated upon a substantially continuous ground.

Given the methodological principles indicated above, the pairing of Thomas Aquinas and Immanuel Kant should appear less improbable than it might otherwise, yet some justification is warranted nonetheless. Thomas Aquinas stands as one of the great medieval scholastics, continuing and advancing the scholastic project of integrating Aristotelian and Neoplatonic impulses within a Christian framework. Aquinas achieves that integration smoothly but not seamlessly, as is apparent in his considerations of nature. Scholastic treatments of nature, and even specifically Thomistic understandings, raise a host of vexed questions, leading to extensive and strikingly divided interpretations. One compelling explanation for polarizing interpretations of a careful, irenic philosophical synthesis looks to internal tensions that, while manageable within the whole, seemingly introduce fractures threatening particular structural elements within that whole. Thomas's engagements with natural final causality offer an example.

Kant's defense of natural teleology continually generates a similar polarity of interpretations. Vast historical and intellectual gaps separate Kant from Thomas, yet they both address cognate topics and questions without flattening the depth of their thought in the interest of uniformity masquerading as consistency. Kant's antinomy of judgment related to organisms preserves fundamental tensions not entirely dissimilar to tensions built into Thomas's approach to natural final causality. Despite the numerous and substantial divergences, Thomas and Kant nourish parallel tensions such that their coincidences are no less significant than the abundance of their differences. To draw this conclusion out, I will provide selective examinations of Kantian natural teleology and then of Thomistic natural final causality.[9] These summary sketches will allow a fuller—though still concise—consideration of parallel tensions within these systems of thought. The parallels will not be formulated to suggest a concrete historical connection—for example, a relationship of dependence, however mediated—but rather to constellate these thinkers in a mutually illuminating formation that avoids epochalism and resists the dangers of certain genealogies of modernity. The analysis

---

9 For an introduction to Thomas on final causality, see Simon Oliver, "Aquinas and Aristotle's Teleology," *Nova et Vetera* 11 (2013): 849–70.

offered here will look backward from Kant to Thomas and forward from Thomas to Kant.[10]

Kantian Natural Teleology

Late in his *Critique of the Power of Judgment*, Kant introduces antinomies related to judgment and concerning explanations for organisms. He presents two formulations bearing subtle but crucial differences. One formulation involves a contradiction; the other does not. Clarifying the differences assists in the often-arduous process of discerning Kant's meaning or even line of argumentation within the *Critique of the Power of Judgment* regarding teleology, and many scholars have devoted extensive energies to such clarifications. The aim here will decidedly not involve arbitrating the various interpretive proposals. Rather, the presentation will simply consider the tensions dissected by Kant in preparation for comparison with Thomas Aquinas's understanding of natural final causality.

The two forms of antinomy differ in considering regulative versus constitutive principles "of the possibility of the objects themselves."[11] Presenting the antinomies in reverse order guards against a misperception of natural teleology, according to which Kant asymmetrically affirms the universal validity and sufficiency of mechanical laws but affirms a purely heuristic validity and sufficiency for natural teleology. For the second antinomy, Kant presents as contradictory the thesis that "[a]ll generation of material things is possible in accordance with merely mechanical laws" and the antithesis that "[s]ome generation of such things is not possible in accordance with merely mechanical laws."[12] These maxims are formulated as universal laws requiring no "special principle of reflection" and pertain to the determining power of

---

10 The approach recognizes John Henry Newman's remark that "the present is a text, and the past its interpretation," while also holding that the past is a text, and the present one of its interpretations. The quotation originally derives from Newman's "Reformation of the Eleventh Century" and is repeated here in a preliminary unnumbered page in Thomas Pfau, *Minding the Modern: Human Agency, Intellectual Traditions, and Responsible Knowledge* (Notre Dame, IN: University of Notre Dame Press, 2013).

11 Immanuel Kant, *Critique of the Power of Judgment*, trans. P. Guyer (Cambridge: Cambridge University Press, 2000), §70, p. 259.

12 Kant, *Critique of the Power of Judgment*, §70, p. 259.

judgment. Such an antinomy would represent a fundamental contradiction of universal laws, but Kant resolves the worry easily, arguing that "reason can prove neither the one nor the other of these fundamental principles, because we can have no determining principle *a priori* of the possibility of things in accordance with merely empirical laws of nature."[13] Formulating an antinomy of universal principles oversteps and misinterprets the epistemic warrants. Kant's rejection of universal constitutive principles as epistemically unwaranted forestalls the temptation to "modernize" Kant such that the mechanical explicability of all material generation can be regarded as a universal law, while the need for teleological thinking simply emerges from the limitations of human cognitive structures.[14] With this rejection in mind, we can turn to his formulation of the first antinomy. Kant writes:

> The first maxim of the power of judgment is the thesis: All generation of material things and their forms must be judged as possible in accordance with merely mechanical laws.
>
> The second maxim is the antithesis: Some products of material nature cannot be judged as possible according to merely mechanical laws (judging them requires an entirely different law of causality, namely that of final causality).[15]

Regarding these maxims, Kant insists there is no contradiction.[16] The injunction to judge all things in accordance with merely mechanical laws differs from claiming conditions for the possibility of the things themselves. Failure to grasp the distinction involves a category mistake between the reflective power and the determining power of judgment and their respective

---

13 Ibid.

14 Breitenbach helpfully illustrates this in "Two Views of Nature."

15 Kant, *Critique of the Power of Judgment*, §70, pp. 258–59.

16 Exactly why this is the case is sufficiently unclear as to generate a host of differing interpretations. In addition to Ginsborg, *The Normativity of Nature*, and Breitenbach, "Two Views on Nature," see Thomas Gfeller, "Wie tragfähig ist der teleologische Brückenschlag?" *Zeitschrift für philosophische Forschung* 52 (1998): 215–36, and Peter McLaughlin, *Kant's Critique of Teleology in Biological Explanation* (Lewiston, NY: Edwin Mellen Press, 1990).

scopes.¹⁷ Within the proper regulative scope, how does Kant conceive of natural teleology? Kant provisionally proposes:

> [A] thing exists as a natural end if it is cause and effect of itself (although in a twofold sense); for in this there lies a causality the likes of which cannot be connected with the mere concept of a nature without ascribing an end to it, but which in that case also can be conceived without contradiction but cannot be comprehended.¹⁸

Though this entire quotation merits careful study, the most curious point concerns something being a cause and effect of itself. One aspect of something being a cause and effect of itself seems to be perpetuation of the species through individual generation of like from like. Individuals of the species are effects of previous individuals of the species and cause of subsequent individuals of the species. Another aspect, and one not limited to generation, could be termed the reciprocal causality of parts and whole within an organism.¹⁹ Furthermore, thinking the organism as a reciprocally caused whole itself serves as ground for examining organisms teleologically. Kant

---

17 Kant argues that any ascription of contradiction here "rests on confusing a fundamental principle of the reflecting with that of the determining power of judgment, and on confusing the autonomy of the former (which is valid merely subjectively for the use of our reason in regard to the particular laws of experience) with the heteronomy of the later, which has to conform to the laws given by the understanding (whether general or particular)" (*Critique of the Power of Judgment*, §71, p. 261). Kantian teleology is generally described as heuristic, and though correct, this description can yield the false sense that Kant views nature as truly operating according to merely mechanical laws and that ascriptions of teleology relate to human cognitive structures rather than to the natural world.

18 Kant, *Critique of the Power of Judgment*, §64, p. 243.

19 "For a body, therefore, which is to be judged as a natural end in itself and in accordance with its internal possibility, it is required that its parts reciprocally produce each other, as far as both their form and their combination is concerned, and thus produce a whole out of their own causality, the concept of which, conversely, is in turn the cause (in a being that would possess the causality according to concepts appropriate for such a product) of it in accordance with a principle; consequently the connection of efficient causes could at the same time be judged as an effect through final causes" (*Critique of the Power of Judgment*, §65, p. 245).

concludes that "[o]rganized beings are thus the only ones in nature which, even if considered in themselves and without a relation to other things, must nevertheless be thought of as possible only as its ends."[20] The mechanical inexplicability of organisms is not limited to their production or generation and extends as well to the mutual dependence of their parts and to the functions of the organisms. In terms of production, Kant regards as absurd the notion that unorganized matter could produce organization.[21] The fundamental powers of matter alone (e.g., attraction, repulsion, and so on) cannot account for organisms.[22] This, however, is true not simply for production but also for general regularities of organisms.[23] Such regularities are apparent in artifacts. Following a long line of reflection, Kant employs strategic parallels between artifacts and organisms to bolster judgments and even necessary judgments, for scientifically investigating organisms teleological-

---

20   Ibid., §65, p. 247. For Kant, this provides sufficient warrant for assuming natural teleology within natural science. This is important as a counter to any interpretation that reads Kant as linking mechanical explanations of nature with science and teleology with cultural and religious residues or with cognitive structures. One could compare aspects of Kant's approach to Robert Boyle, *A Free Inquiry into the Vulgarly Received Notion of Nature*, ed. E. Davis and M. Hunter (Cambridge: Cambridge University Press, 1996).

21   See *Critique of the Power of Judgment*, §80, p. 288, and Ginsborg, *The Normativity of Nature*, 291.

22   On Kant's understanding of mechanical laws and the fundamental forces of matter, see Ginsborg, *The Normativity of Nature*, 281–315, and Cinzia Ferrini, "Testing the Limits of Mechanical Explanation in Kant's Pre-Critical Writings," *Archiv for Geschichte der Philosophie* 82 (2000): 297–331.

23   Ginsborg writes that it "is the regularity exhibited by organisms, not just the mere fact that they correspond to a statistically improbable arrangement of matter, which calls for an explanation above and beyond appeal to the powers of matter as such" (Ginsborg, *The Normativity of Nature*, 301). Based upon careful analysis of both parts of the *Critique of the Power of Judgment*, Ginsborg argues that the key to interpreting Kant on aesthetic and teleological judgments concerns regularity and normativity. Ginsborg writes that to "regard something as a purpose without regarding it as an artefact is to read it as governed by normative rules without regarding these rules as concepts in the mind of a designer" (Ginsborg, *The Normativity of Nature*, 277). The normative rules indicate what is "supposed to happen." Ginsborg's emphasis on regularity draws attention to one crucial aspect in the history of reflection on natural final causality, and her presentation of normativity has much to recommend it.

ly. This move does not, however, suggest perfect similitude between organisms and artifacts. Discerning the particularities and the degree of similitude consistently generates polarizing debates and ultimately bears directly on approaches to and conceptions of natural integrity.

Kant complicates the scenario in viewing nature as a teleologically ordered whole, and this goes beyond some of the particular comparisons between nature and artifacts and between organisms and inorganic matter. Scholars have noted the theological matrix for Kant's entire system of thought. Fugate notes that it "should come as no surprise to find that Kant's pre-critical philosophy shares this very same commitment to a metaphysically teleological worldview, indeed that all of his major writings between 1755 and 1765 seek to articulate a specific version of a telically unified world whose foundation lies entirely in the will of God."[24] Orr similarly stresses the theological grounding for Kant's pre-critical discussions of natural teleology, writing that "Kant not only emphasizes the heuristic benefits that his reformulated teleology of nature opens up for the natural sciences. He also expressly argues that theoretical demonstrations of purposiveness in nature presuppose a theocentric perspective inaccessible to human reason."[25] The inaccessibility of such a perspective to human reason serves as an important reminder for the two forms of antinomy that Kant discusses.

Thomistic Natural Final Causality

Thomas's perspective on nature, while preserving a stable core of basic theological and philosophical commitments, varies somewhat among his diverse works. The stable core of commitments holds greater interest for the present purposes than the variations, principally insofar as the stable commitments are not themselves without internal stresses related to the breadth of sources standardly received as authoritative in the medieval universities and to the dissimilarity of assumptions and perspectives reflected in those authorities. Aristotle looms large over any and all scholastic iterations of final causality, yet Aristotle's shadow is not so dark or foreboding as to occlude the influence of Pseudo-Dionysius and a host of other Neoplatonic authors and texts.[26]

---

24 Fugate, *The Teleology of Reason*, 27.

25 James Orr, "Teleology as Theological Problem in Kant's Pre-Critical Thought," *Modern Theology* 32 (2016): 522–43.

26 For discussions of Thomas's uses of Aristotle, see Rudi te Velde, "Aquinas's

The Aristotelian and Neoplatonic perspectives on nature, though not necessarily mutually exclusive or even incompatible, differ in fundamental ways such that any simultaneous allegiance to both necessitates harmonizing the dissonance. Within his *Physics* commentary, Thomas presents nature according to both perspectives. Early on he affirms Aristotle's position on nature as "nothing other than a *principle of motion and rest in that in which it is first and* per se *and not* secundum accidens."[27] Commenting later in Book II, Thomas defends a Neoplatonic and seemingly divergent conception of nature: "nature is nothing other than some art, namely the divine, implanted in things by which they are moved to their determinate ends."[28] Reconciling these two definitions—if reconciliation is indeed what they require—hinges upon the fundamental gap between divine transcendental causality and the workings of created secondary causality, a distinction that explains why nature is not simply art, even if it can be understood in some respects according to the model of art. Before delving into such reconciliation, some comments regarding each perspective individually are in order. The comments here are far from exhaustive and are decidedly targeted for conversation with Kantian natural teleology.

When discussing natural ends, Thomas oscillates between two pairs of contrasting ideas: the natural and the artificial, on the one hand, and the natural and the voluntary, on the other. Keeping both pairs in mind isolates the fundamental difficulties surrounding natural final causality and thus specifies the question with which Thomas is principally occupied. Natures are internally oriented toward intrinsic ends, whereas artifacts are externally ordered toward intrinsic ends, with this external ordering itself in some

---

Aristotelian Science of Metaphysics and Its Revised Platonism," *Nova et Vetera* 13 (2015): 743–64, and Mark D. Jordan, *The Alleged Aristotelianism of Thomas Aquinas* (Toronto: Pontifical Institute of Medieval Studies, 1992).

27   Thomas Aquinas, *In Physic.* II, c. 1, l. 1, p. 56 (*In Octos Libros Physicorum Aristotelis Expositio, Opera omnia*, t. 2 [Rome: Ex Typografia Polyglotta, 1884]). Thomas clarifies the *per se*/*secundum accidens* distinction in *De principiis naturae*. A builder serves as a *per se* cause of the house she builds. Should this builder also be a grammarian, the grammarian would serve as a *per accidens* cause of the house because she builds the house insofar as she is a builder rather than insofar as she is a grammarian. See *De principiis naturae*, c. 5, p. 126, (*Opuscula philosophica*, ed. R. Spiazzi [Taurini and Romae: Marietti, 1954]).

28   Thomas Aquinas, *In Physic.* II, l. 14, n. 8, p. 96.

sense constituting the artificiality of the artifacts.[29] Thomas also distinguishes between the natural and the voluntary. One challenge to the basic notion of natural final causality concerns the necessary conditions for intending an end. Some would limit any meaningful use of final causality to intentional or voluntary agents. Thomas rejects this limitation. The rejection interestingly returns to the natural and artificial distinction in arguing that artists confirmed in their art often execute that art without any deliberation, clarifying that deliberation is at most a sufficient condition for intending an end. Deliberation ceases to be necessary where an artist is confirmed in acting through artistry toward a determinate end, just as natures include an internal orientation toward determinate ends without deliberation.[30]

Combining the two pairs reveals Thomas's fundamental understanding of natural final causality as pertaining to determinate ends intrinsic to natures such that the nature intends an end without deliberation and as an internal ordering. This core understanding of natural final causality, that natures act or rest for determinate ends intrinsic to what they are, must withstand countervailing forces within Thomas's own system of thought. Thomas insists that natures possess intrinsic ends, and yet these ends were divinely bestowed and serve the end of nature as a whole.

Reciprocal Interpretations

Kant's natural teleology forcefully addresses a tension between two necessary judgments regarding nature, judgments that inform the study of nature. Thomas Aquinas's natural final causality forcefully addresses a tension between Aristotelian and Neoplatonic accounts of natural ends. Though significant differences and distances separate these thinkers, the tensions addressed by each are not without interesting parallels. Constellating these thinkers based upon these parallels fosters a richer appreciation of each

---

29   Witt argues that in an Aristotelian scheme it is more accurate to assign intrinsic ends both to natures and to artifacts and to mark the difference in terms of origin. The intrinsic ends of natures have an internal origin, while the intrinsic ends of artifacts have an external origin. See Charlotte Witt, "In Defense of the Craft Analogy: Artifacts and Natural Teleology," in *Aristotle's* Physics: *A Critical Guide*, ed. Mariska Leunissen (Cambridge: Cambridge University Press, 2015), 107–20.

30   *De principiis naturae*, c. 3, p. 124: "It is therefore possible for a natural agent to intend an end without deliberation, and this intending is nothing other than having a natural inclination to something."

author, combats epochalism as a barrier to considering linkages or connections between periods, and reveals persistent concerns in discussions of nature and finality. Scholastic thinkers are often enough treated together and over and against classical (Aristotelian) expressions of final causality, on the one hand, and against early modern rejections of final causality in light of mechanistic approaches to nature, on the other. Kant is often enough treated as if the development and prominence of mechanistic approaches to nature exhaustively explains one major condition for his thought, as well as the conditions for his radical difference from scholastic considerations of final causality. Reading Thomas Aquinas and Immanuel Kant together reveals an unexpected depth of commonality, through or according to which we can discern perduring questions and concerns in attempts to study and explain nature and natural integrity.

Each thinker complicates the picture of natural integrity by insisting that preserving such integrity requires appeal to ends, which raises the question of how each conceives of natural integrity. Though Thomas and Kant differ on the specific forces pulling against each other in their defenses of natural integrity, they agree that preserving natural integrity requires negotiating a basic tension or harmonizing dissonant notes. Kant's first antinomy of regulative judgment negotiates this basic tension by simultaneously defending its two maxims and by insisting that both maxims prove necessary assumptions for the scientific investigation of nature. For Kant, natural integrity demands conceiving every natural thing as fully explicable according to merely mechanical laws and conceiving organisms as inexplicable without appeal to teleology beyond mechanical laws. Employing the negotiation of a basic tension as an interpretive principle yields interesting results when applied to Thomas. The multiple perspectives at play in Thomas on natural final causality can thus be read not only as the interplay of various philosophical systems joined together under the influence of Christian theological commitments, but also as a particular instantiation of this basic and perennial tension, a tension that survives alterations and developments in science, philosophy, and theology. Reading Thomas informed by Kant reveals as much as it imposes.

At the same time, Thomas can also offer a new perspective on Kant. Thomas labors to harmonize divergent systems, perspectives, and commitments not simply because they reflect inherited authorities but because he understands preserving natural integrity to require a full range of divergent views. His contrasting pairs (natures-artifacts, natural-volitional) illustrate this understanding. Nature is best approached through contrasts, though no contrast alone sufficiently explains or isolates nature. Employing this notion is useful in reading Kant, whose antinomy of regulative judgment precisely illustrates an attempt to understand nature through contrasts. Both maxims express necessary judgments for scientific inquiry into nature, and preserving natural integrity requires both without the burden of perfect reconciliation.

Having indicated a common underlying tension in Kant and Thomas regarding natural integrity, we can further specify that tension based upon parallels or points of similarity. Noting these parallels certainly does not advocate for the virtual identity of Kantian natural teleology and Thomistic natural final causality. Serious differences distinguish Kant and Thomas. The language of parallels does not substitute continuities for ruptures but strives to discern the continuities embedded within the ruptures and the ruptures embedded within continuities as reciprocally enriching and illuminating.

Kant identifies things as natural ends when they are the cause and effect of themselves, a principle that seemingly includes generation and the reciprocal arrangement of parts within the whole. Kant develops this reciprocal production through language most telling for this comparison. The parts of organisms produce a whole "out of their own causality," while the concept of this whole serves through its own causality as the principle for this production, and "consequently the connection of efficient causes could at the same time be judged as an effect through final causes."[31] Thomas formulates striking parallels in insisting that something can be both cause and effect of the same thing in different ways and that a natural end is twofold, of the generation and of the thing generated. Regarding the former, Thomas holds that "it is not impossible that the very same thing is cause and caused in respect of the same but diversely, as walking is sometimes the efficient cause of health, and health is the final cause of walking."[32] Regarding the latter, he illustrates the point with an artificial example: making a knife. "The form of the knife," Thomas argues, "is the end of generation, but cutting, which

---

31 Kant, *Critique of the Power of Judgment*, §65, p. 245.

32 Thomas Aquinas, *De principiis naturae*, c. 4, p. 125. See also *In Meta.* V, l. 2, n. 775, p. 213 (*In Duodecimo Libros Metaphysicorum Aristotelis Expositio*, ed. M.-R. Catéala and R.M. Spiazzi [Taurini and Romae: Marietti, 1964]).

is the operation of the knife itself, is the end of the generated, namely of the knife."[33]

We can note two further related points with parallels in Thomas and Kant. Neither point represents a singular or surprising view, though general acceptance of these points need not undermine the significance of the parallels. The first point holds there to be an end of nature itself or as a whole. Though in theory an end to nature itself or as a whole neither depends upon nor entails ends to particular natures, for Kant and Thomas the particular ends of natures relate to and are grounded in the end of nature itself or as a whole.[34] Such affirmations trouble many, but they must be read in context. Thomas and Kant both affirm an end to nature but do not require, assume, or allow that human intellection or human cognitive structures suffice for knowing that end. Thomas defends the unknowability of providence and so of the providential ordering of nature beyond what can be discerned through revelation. A hallmark of Kantian philosophy concerns the distinction between phenomena and noumena and the restriction of our knowledge to the former. These parallel affirmations should not be regarded as equivalent, but they do indicate a dispositional similarity in approaches to nature.[35]

Though there is not simply one tension or disharmony at play here, we can note that cognate tensions animate Thomas and Kant on natural ends without reducing the differences either to the accidental or the incidental. Kant and Thomas both struggle to preserve the integrity of nature without

---

33 Thomas Aquinas, *De principiis naturae*, c. 4, p. 125.

34 Thomas explicitly addresses the end of nature most often in systematic theological works rather than in his *Physics* commentary, which supports the general trend of harmonizing the providential ordering of creation with natural integrity. See *Summa contra Gentiles*, 3.99.10 and 4.97.3, and *Summa theologiae* I, q. 62, a. 1, and I–II, q. 49, a. 3. In *ST* I, q. 62, a. 1, Thomas presents beatitude as the end of nature and, because the end of nature, not something of nature. For a most insightful analysis of this and many other related ideas in Kant, see Fugate, *The Teleology of Reason*.

35 Other medieval and early modern thinkers employ this principle to discount the relevance of final causality for inquiries into nature. For a discussion of this phenomenon in early modern thinkers, see Pierre Hadot, *The Veil of Isis: An Essay on the History of the Idea of Nature*, trans. M. Chase (Cambridge: The Belknap Press of Harvard University Press, 2006), 118–37.

accepting some form of epicurianism, atomism, Deism, or physico-theology/physico-teleology. Admitting nature's integrity seems hardly difficult until other convictions test that integrity or our understandings of it such that the deeper challenge of maintaining nature's integrity emerges. Thomas and Kant specify the integrity of nature differently, yet this difference should not obscure the similarity of both thinkers in defending fundamental natural integrity in the service of knowledge.

This essay took its methodological inspiration from Benjamin's notion of constellated historical eras and O'Regan's project of middle-voice genealogy. Taken together, these methodological perspectives offer substantial and programmatic guidance for historical theology. Constellating Kant and Thomas can illuminate the past as much as the present. Reading this constellation in a middle voice allows the analysis to investigate similarities and differences between Thomas and Kant, aware of—but not determined by—our own subjective position with respect to this constellation. Middle-voice historical theology focused on Thomas and Kant enriches our understanding of the history of final causality and furthers genealogies of modernity.

CHAPTER FIVE

Haunted by Heteronomy

Cyril O'Regan, Hegelian Misremembering, and the Counterfeit Doubles of God

WILLIAM DESMOND

IN THE FOLLOWING ESSAY I want to honor Cyril O'Regan's work on Hegel, especially his philosophy of religion. In my view, O'Regan's work is at the summit of recent Hegel scholarship. It is marked by philological precision vis-à-vis Hegel's own writings. It is impressively informed by a magisterial command of significant secondary commentary. It is fair to Hegel to a fault, and yet it is marked by a philosophical and theological finesse that penetrates to the heart of Hegelian matters. Nor is O'Regan taken in naively by the speculative rhetoric of Hegel when he speaks of God. O'Regan reads Hegel with hermeneutical finesse, attentive to significant equivocities in his dialectical-speculative rendition of God and the relation between God and humans. I have asked the question of Hegel as to whether his "God" is a counterfeit double of God, and I find significant corroboration of this view in the impressive work of O'Regan. I find this in many places, but it is evident recently in his notion of misremembering in his magisterial *Anatomy of Misremembering*.[1] I will propose that crucial in the overlap of misremem-

---

1 Cyril O'Regan, *Anatomy of Misremembering: Von Balthasar's Response to Phil-

bering and the counterfeit double is the issue of divine transcendence, its religious figuration and philosophical reconfiguration. Hegel's philosophy of holistic immanence takes its leave from all forms of dualistic transcendence, and yet, I will argue, it is haunted by heteronomy. I do not mean heteronomy in a necessarily invidious sense. That we tend to think heteronomy has an invidious sense only shows how much we still remain anonymous Hegelians. As bearing on the *nomos* of *to heteron*, heteronomy can be benignly related to a truer figuration of divine transcendence.

Let me first say a few things about O'Regan's extensive writings on Hegel, which pay particular attention to his philosophy of religion, indeed to the relationship between religion and philosophy. His book *The Heterodox Hegel* is an outstanding work, and one of the best books on Hegel's philosophy of religion to have appeared in English.[2] O'Regan has written many essays (some of them verging on being small monographs) on themes in Hegel's philosophy of religion. I am thinking particularly of his marvelous review essay of Henry Harris's book on Hegel's *Phenomenology of Spirit* which has the subtitle: "H.S. Harris on Hegel's Liquidation of Christianity."[3] Finally, it is worth mentioning that his most recent book, *Anatomy of Misremembering*, is an extended conversation between Balthasar and Hegel. It is a treasury of remarkable discussions, reaching back into the long tradition of theological reflection, as well as paying attention to major modern interlocutors with that tradition, Hegel most particularly. An intellectual cornucopia, it could be the basis for an extensive education in modern theology, as well as recuperative appropriations of major figures in western theological and philosophical traditions. In this first volume, Hegel is singled out as a major dialogue partner with the theological project of Balthasar. The volume to follow is one in which Heidegger will figure as major interlocutor with Balthasar. It should be noted that O'Regan's relation to Hegel figures importantly in his larger project concerning gnostic return

---

osophical Modernity. Volume 1: Hegel (Spring Valley, NY: Crossroad Publishing Company, 2014).

2 Cyril O'Regan, *The Heterodox Hegel* (Albany: State University of New York Press, 1994).

3 Cyril O'Regan, "The Impossibility of a Christian Reading of the *Phenomenology of Spirit*: H.S. Harris on Hegel's Liquidation of Christianity," *The Owl of Minerva* 33, no. 1 (Fall/Winter 2001–02): 45–95.

in modernity, and will in due course be the subject of a projected volume.[4]

Take note of the titles and subtitle: *The Heterodox Hegel*, "H.S. Harris on Hegel's Liquidation of Christianity," *Anatomy of Misremembering*. The first title intimates an important equivocity: is Hegel the philosopher who sums up in his system western Christianity, and hence the last Christian philosopher? Or is there something more recessed in his work that is indicative of a deviation; and hence the first philosopher who so conceptually colonizes Christianity that its remote death warrant qua religion is signed? In the first instance, we have a sign of fulfillment and completion; in the second instance, we have a watershed of transition in which the new orientation emerges on the basis of the overcoming of a long, speculative development. O'Regan's book was very warmly received by Hegel scholars, not least by those whom one might call the pious Hegelians. The deviation of Hegel that O'Regan narrates did not always get the attention it deserved. The heterodox Hegel was close, and yet not close, to Christianity. A narrative was being re-narrated, in line with the grammatical protocols laid down by Hegel's philosophical concept. These pious Hegelians did not always pay enough attention to O'Regan's invocation of Irenaeus and Ferdinand Christian Baur, the first as the first great heresiologist of Christianity, the second as a severe nineteenth-century critic of Hegel's take on Christianity, Hegel's speculative takeover, his conceptual overtaking of Christianity.

The second title carries a perhaps more negative connotation: liquidation. Liquidation, of course, can mean the killing, the rubbing out of, the assassination of Christianity. In any event, a transition is at work that indicates the doing away with something. Liquidation can also call to mind the economic activity of liquidating one's assets, and hence potentially making them available for new uses. Once one liquidates one's assets and does not negate them, one makes them take a form that allows reuse, that itself allows perhaps the generation of new value impossible to achieve in the older form of these assets prior to liquidation. Finally, liquidation carries the metaphorical sense of fluidity: something is now more mobile, something is now more malleable. Something now can become the magma, to change metaphors, out of which once again new buildings, undreamt of before,

---

4 Cyril O'Regan, *Gnostic Return in Modernity* (Albany: State University of New York Press, 2001); *Gnostic Apocalypse: Jacob Boehme's Haunted Narrative* (Albany: State University of New York Press, 2002).

can come to be built. I think one can see all of these possibilities at work in post-Hegelian uses of Hegel: we often find liquidation as a violent negation of Christianity, a violent negation that often is dependent upon the very Christianity being negated—think only of Nietzsche, the assassin of the millennia, and his curse on Christianity (the subtitle of his *Anti-Christ*, crossed out in the manuscript, but not rubbed out in the spiritual effect of the work).

The second sense of liquidation as liquefying one's assets in the interests of reusing them brings to mind the possibility that the philosophical concept rather than the religious representation is the true measure of worth according to which such spiritual assets are to be (re-)invested. The second sense of liquidation points toward more than a philosophical overcoming of religion, more than just the overtaking of religion and its transposition into a rational concept of philosophy, and perhaps in a form not recognizable to those who continue to believe in the old currencies. Something new is being insinuated, a birth beyond the death of the old Christianity. We witness examples of this general strategy where the overtaking of Christianity is justified by the new post-Christian form, now said to be the real truth of Christianity, all along hidden by the representations that encrust the inner truth.

Finally, the third sense of liquidation, where everything is potentially in motion, where everything is fluid, allows of a more pervasive plasticity in the use and appropriation of the Hegelian categories. I am thinking of the remark that Maurice Merleau-Ponty made: there is hardly a position in post-Hegelian philosophy that does not owe its basis to Hegel's dialectic. I am thinking of Hegel's own return to favor in (post-)deconstructionist thinkers like Catherine Malabou, who speaks of plasticity in connection with Hegel.[5] I am thinking also how easy it is on the part of post-Hegelians to ventriloquize through Hegel. They make him say what they themselves want to say, as if he were a plastic puppet out of whom a voice comes that does not always bear resemblance to the voice we hear when we read Hegel's own texts.

In any case, this marvelous review article by O'Regan is uncompromising in not allowing pious Hegelians to continue to promulgate the myth that Hegelian speculative reason is seamlessly compatible with Christianity. A meticulous reading of Hegel's take on religion as penultimate to philosophy

---

5 Catherine Malabou, *The Future of Hegel: Plasticity, Temporality and Dialectic*, trans. Lisabeth During (London and New York: Routledge, 2005).

as absolute knowing makes the point unequivocally. That said, there is no implication that Hegel is to be criticized simply as a crude atheist. The complexities of the question are already evident in the title *Heterodox Hegel*, namely, that a form of Christianity continues to be defended by Hegel, and said to be confirmed by his speculative concept. The heterodox Hegel gives articulation to a very subtle recurrence of the Valentinian Gnostic grammar in the speculative system of Hegelian thoughts. This is not unconnected with my own question to Hegel as to whether his philosophical appropriation of religion in general and Christianity in particular offers us a counterfeit double of God.

To turn to the third text mentioned, *Anatomy of Misremembering*, the title is also marvelously suggestive. An anatomy, at least in the medical dissection carried out in earlier medical history, is performed on a body that is dead. I do not think O'Regan wants to imply that the body of Hegel is dead simply. There is a haunting at work (as we see also if we look at his exploration of Jacob Boehme relative to Gnostic return in modernity). Haunting has to do with something that is dead, a ghost, a *Geist*, not alive and still alive, in life and beyond life, taking forms, often unnatural if we go by the measure of given being. A revenant: someone who returns (from the dead). The theme is not far from the Christian notion of resurrection, though not the same as it. And yet this pervasively haunts Hegel's system as a whole: the returning ghost, the ever-returning *Geist*, the always-self-returning Holy Ghost.

I would put the primary stress on the word "misremembering." Hegel's *Phenomenology* ends with the claim that the absolute knowing of true philosophy is a recollection, an *Erinnerung* in which spirit runs through its myriad forms and now at this point of culmination *finds always itself*, even in those forms it had previously taken to be related to something other than itself. Now in the final self-recollection, it is the self of absolute *Geist* that finds itself in all of these others. In a way, this is a claim of absolute philosophical memory. We might recall, of course, the doctrine of anamnesis in the Platonic way of thinking, but anamnesis can never be absolutely accomplished in this life, again according to the Platonic way of thinking. The Hegelian claim seems to be that absolute knowing is itself the accomplishment of this completed *Erinnerung*. In this, finally, there is nothing other than knowing itself, which now can come to be at home entirely with itself, since it knows it no longer needs to go beyond itself. This is, in effect, the claim entirely to overcome any "beyond," any transcendence that only seemingly remains other to the process of philosophical knowing itself.

It is also the liquidation of the sense of insuperable mystery marking the divine in its asymmetrical transcendence. The originality of O'Regan's suggestion here is that this project of complete *Erinnerung* is not the completion of Platonic anamnesis at all, nor any other philosophical remembering, but a crucial mis-remembering. It remembers, and its memory might seem to be accurate, but this turns out not to be true. It is an extraordinary engagement with the diversity of forms that have been assumed previously by the spirit, but because the form of remembering is itself marked by a kind of forgetting, it is an extraordinary misremembering of something that, above all else, should not be forgotten.

Crucial to the misremembering is the memory of the asymmetrical otherness of the divine, even when the divine is intimate in all creation. The case is all the more complex when Hegel claims to be speculatively remembering Christianity. Christianity is not a doctrine of divine transcendence; it is a proclamation of an event in which the divine becomes immanent. Hegel is not wrong about the latter, but his remembering of this is the forgetting of the former. Remembering becomes misremembering. This is a central theme that O'Regan engages with respect to the extraordinarily extensive work of Balthasar, but it is also present throughout his reflections and researches on Hegel as a whole.

I want to say that this understanding of misremembering can be connected with my own notion of the counterfeit double.[6] Before coming to this point, I want to comment on how O'Regan is acutely aware of the contribution of religion to the very formation of Hegel's philosophy as a whole. The intimate interplay of religion and philosophy also has an important relation to the modernity that Hegel was keen to endorse, a modernity defined by an ethos of freedom, and crowned by human self-determination. Unlike many modern philosophers, Hegel takes Christianity into account in his philosophizing about self-determination. He pays attention to other religions, but makes a strong claim about the affinity between his own philosophy and the Christian religion. And yet there are dialectical equivocities here. As suggested above, Hegel has been seen as the last great philosopher of Chris-

---

6 Some of the ideas presented here are more fully elaborated in William Desmond, *Hegel's God: A Counterfeit Double?* (Burlington, VT: Ashgate Publishing, 2003).

tendom, and yet there are striking ironies about how he has been interpreted: extraordinarily ambitious for philosophical reason, yet seen by some as a source of the self-deconstruction of philosophical reason; supremely complementary to art and religion, which he places with philosophy at the highest standpoint of absolute spirit, and yet identified with the so-called "end of art"; and as a major influence on modern atheism, especially in in its left-Hegelian line of inheritance. At the heart of this, I think, is dialectical equivocation about divine transcendence.

"Transcendence" is not a Hegelian word. Hegel, like Spinoza before him and post-Hegelian philosophers after him, endorsed what was essentially a philosophy of immanence. The human being is capable of a kind of self-transcendence, a self-surpassing, say in art, religion, and philosophy, but this self-surpassing is coupled with a critique of any God who is unsurpassably "beyond." Being unsurpassably beyond is for Hegel a problem rather than any answer. His own answer is a speculative philosophy of holistic immanence. The relation of human self-transcendence and God as transcendence that is *other* to human self-transcendence provides a central consideration shaping that result, and around which Hegel formed and reformed his understanding of God.

What of this reformation? What we see in Hegel is not quite a simple repudiation or evasion of divine transcendence as other, but rather a reconfiguration of its meaning such that its ultimacy is relativized. Hegel enacts a philosophical *project* in reconstructing God. His conceptual construction of "God" is a project deriving from religious sources, but also diverging from them in a decisive reconfiguration of divine transcendence. Here I would introduce the notion of the counterfeit double and pose the question as to whether in speculatively "overcoming" the God of religious transcendence Hegel offers a "God" who is such a counterfeit double. Hegel does stress a self-surpassing, a self-transcendence in which there is a *relating* to the other, but in that relating to the other, a *fuller self-relating* comes to be. Transcendence as other to our self-surpassing is reformulated in terms of a self-completing of self-transcendence. Taken overall, the movement of transcending is from self to other to self again, and finally there is no ultimate *transcendence* as other, only self-completing immanence. Put in terms of God, this movement would be: transcendence from Godself to God as self-othered to Godself again as consummately self-intermediated, such that finally there is no ultimate transcendence as other, only God's self-completing immanence.

Hegel's God is beyond any dualism of objective and subjective in terms of an absolute subjectivity that includes in its immanence the relation of subject and object, such that even divine intersubjectivity is, in the end, a self-relation between God and itself.

While this project may claim to overcome transcendence speculatively in the name of a self-completing self-determination in immanence, does it find itself haunted by heteronomy? Rejecting or reconfiguring a robust sense of divine transcendence, does it produce a "God" who is not God? If we take seriously the understanding of God inherited from the tradition of biblical monotheism, we certainly are given to pause. God is God, and only God is God; God is not finite creation or nature; God is not humanity, not history. This "not" signals a qualitative difference that does not obviate the possibility of communication *between* God and created others, natural and human. But this communication is not a matter of "overcoming" the difference in a dialectical-speculative whole. One is led to worry if there is here a speculative-dialectical equivocity that purports to answer equivocities in the relation between God and humans, or religion and philosophy, only to hide *new equivocations* in its purported answer.

In line with Hegel's endorsement of the modern sense of freedom, a logic of *self-determination* insinuates itself into all this thinking, such that divine transcendence as other becomes endowed with an equivocal position. I suggest that there is not only a tension but a certain antinomy between autonomy and transcendence. By antinomy I mean not just a contradiction, but a position of stress that articulates an equivocal space of spirit full of tension wherein we have to confront different basic options. How ought we to think autonomy and transcendence together, when something about each seems to strain against the other? Autonomy stresses self-determining power, while transcendence stresses the importance of some otherness, whether our own or that of the divine, or indeed that of nature, otherness not reducible to our self-determining. This is then the antinomy: if autonomy is absolute, transcendence as other has to be relativized; if transcendence as other is absolute, autonomy must be relativized. In the equivocal space of this antinomy, the traditional religious respect for the stronger sense of transcendence as other comes under critique in modernity generally and in Hegel in particular. Into this equivocal space claims of self-determination are inserted, as answering this antinomy of autonomy and transcendence. Hegel follows one of the dominant trends in western modernity in opting for this alternative, namely the relativization of transcendence as other in favor of autonomy as self-determination. And while he does not do away with God, his option has momentous repercussions in relation to the God of transcendence as other.

One of these repercussions is the following: the exigency of transcendence does not die, but rather human autonomy assumes for itself the energies of transcending. We will claim to be *immanent* transcending power, where we purport to have both autonomy and immanent transcendence, without any need for an *other* transcendence. If we must speak of transcendence at all in Hegel's case, this must be relativized by reference to the Christian claim that God enters time, hence abrogating its own transcendence. God, as much as humanity, it will be said, is given over to immanence. The process of immanence is the very process of both God's and humanity's self-becoming. True self-determination relativizes all relations to transcendence as other by including them within its own self-completing absoluteness.

In this light, Hegel epitomizes the privilege given to self-determination in modernity. I have wondered if the equivocity in his speculative dialectic is signaled by the fact that his claim to the completion of self-determining being is almost simultaneously followed by a *dialectical reversal* of that completion. Hegel's discourse is saturated with the language of God, but his rebel—if not revolutionary—sons on the left claimed to reveal exoterically what Hegel kept too esoteric, namely, that the speculative unity of humanity and divinity, in fact, means there is no divinity but humanity. These inheritors of Hegel might make cruder uses of dialectic than Hegel himself, but they were not entirely untrue to this dialectical equivocity. While many readers of Hegel take him too much at face value on the unity of the human and divine, O'Regan is not one of them. Indeed, he is superbly attuned to these dialectical equivocities nesting in the speculative sublation of the Christian religion. His treatment of Hegel's transition (at the culmination of the *Phenomenology of Spirit*) from religion to philosophy as absolute knowing is a brilliant example of this liquidation of Christianity. He is not a foolish virgin but has oil in his lamps in preparation for the coming of a different God.

Hegel remains haunted by the heteronomy that he claims to transcend speculatively. As O'Regan has impressively indicated, Hegel is haunted by a recurrence of a form of Gnosticism, just so defined by its production of equivocal doubles of the divine. Hegel himself thought he had exorcised the ghosts of dualistic transcendence perhaps, but his own *Geist* is haunted by the original God who can never be exorcised. We see the haunting and attempted exorcism in quite a few of his successors. While Hegel absolutizes the claim of self-determining reason, these successors relativize reason, though they do not entirely abandon self-determination. Hegel makes absolute claims about his "God," but his successors debunk such claims: we swing between inflation and deflation. Hegel's system looks like the high noon of thought thinking itself, modern rational self-determination, but only consider Schopenhauer's Will as the descent matching its ascent, now downward, turned into the irrationality of a darker origin. Hegel's *Science of Logic* was composed almost *contemporaneously* to Schopenhauer's *The World as Will and Representation*, its dark twin, so to say. This dark twin is redolent of the dismal creator of gnostic narratives. There is no good to the "to be" of given creation. Can we separate the ascent of one from the descent of the other? Do we still live out of the consequences of that ascent and descent? To speak of being haunted by heteronomy means that the thought thinking itself of one is shadowed by its reverse, namely, thought thinking what is *other* to thought itself. But the nature of that other is contested by many of Hegel's successors, and it is not the transcendent otherness of the agapeic origin that is accorded the honors. In its place come other doubles of divinity, even when no divinity is affirmed, even when the ultimate divinity is given the godless name of "nothing."

Recall that the atheistic otherness of the dark origin, in the case of someone like Schopenhauer, is identified with Will as a kind of *eros turannos*. It is important to remember that Hegel's absolute is also a version of an erotic absolute.[7] The origin in itself is lacking indeterminacy until it determines itself, determination that only seems other, for it is in fact the self-determination of the origin itself, which now at the completion is properly what it is. Hegel negates every "objectivized" beyond in favor of an immanent self-surpassing process of self-determination. We meet a "God" that has to *become itself*, determining itself in a process that begins in a kind

---

7 The contrast of an erotic and agapeic absolute is something I speak about throughout my own writings. See, for instance, William Desmond, *Being and the Between* (Albany: State University of New York Press, 1995), and *Perplexity and Ultimacy* (Albany: State University of New York Press, 1995).

of lacking indefiniteness that is overcome just in its self-becoming. Divine self-becoming is fulfilled only in the end that is the complete self-determination of what is merely implicit in the beginning. There is a triadic logic of indeterminate, determinate, and self-determinate that looks Trinitarian but is an erotic triadic self-mediating absolute rather than an agapeic Trinity. The God of biblical revelation has been spoken of as beyond humanity and beyond nature, though revealing itself from a superlative fullness (overdeterminate not indeterminate) named as agapeic rather than erotic. The agapeic origin and the immanent world are not devoid of communication or intermediation. In modernity there has been widespread opposition to this view of God, as much in Hegel, as in Nietzsche, and in other currents of thought. Yet some sense of transcendence as other to human self-transcendence and nature as a totality of finite beings is essentially entailed by the biblical God. Without some irreducible sense of divine transcendence, one wonders about inevitable equivocation in what we mean by God.[8]

The word "God" may be frequently on Hegel's lips, but there is a hollowness with respect to this irreducible transcendence. The hollowness is indulged by his religious admirers when they look to Hegel for succor in a godless world. The hollowness is exploited for cruder deconstructions by his anti-religious students when they look to him for a logic, a speculative-historical ABC, to further the self-apotheosis of secular man. Instead of just the Hegelian triad of the indeterminate, the determinate, the self-determining (corresponding to his triadic logic of universal, particular, singular), the agapeics of divine transcendence reveals God as overdeterminate. In excess of the determinacies of things and our self-determining, the agapeics of overdeterminate transcendence could not be defined as a merely *indefinite beyond* to finite being. If it were, its relation to and participation in the immanent world would be feeble. Speaking of transcendence in the context of biblical monotheism does require that we reconsider the *intimacy* of God with the immanent world. This is not a matter of dualistic opposition counterposed to holistic immanence. Divine transcendence as agapeic is not an empty indefinite but overdetermined in a surplus sense. Such divine transcendence could not be identified with any projection onto some ultimate other of our own self-transcendence or some sense of otherness we encounter in the given world of immanent creation. I

---

8 William Desmond, *God and the Between* (Oxford: Blackwell-Wiley, 2008) attempts to take up the task of articulating a metaxological conception of God.

would speak of the *intimate universal* rather than Hegel's concrete universal[9]: the first saves this sense of transcendence without dualistically opposing it to what is immanently given; the second claims dialectically to reconcile the particular and the universal, but the surplus overdeterminacy of both the intimate and the radically transcendent are inadequately described in the language of the indeterminate. We live in an ambiguous intermediate world whose signs have to be discerned with finesse. Divine transcendence as other need not be compromised by this. Hegel lacks the relevant sense of the overdeterminate, a lack with consequences for divine transcendence as other.

While these considerations have repercussions extending in many directions, I want to conclude with something about the question of the counterfeit double. There is something plurivocal about our being religious; it resists reduction to one univocal meaning. If we recall the ambiguous doubleness of the equivocal, we might construe this as a defect to be treated with more rational univocity; or we might see it affirmatively as calling to mind the enigma of the divine with which we are never conceptually on par. Hegel claims to be conceptually on par with divinity. His resort to the *Begriff* in relation to the *Vorstellung* thus represents one philosophical response to this doubleness. Admittedly, philosophy's discernment must be attentive to what is shown, or not shown, in and through the religious image. Religion may play false; philosophy may also play false. We secrete idols, thinking them to be true images. These idols are the counterfeit doubles of God. Images recall us to our limits, and yet we cannot do without images.

The catch with the counterfeit double is that the image will mimic as well as show the original, and mimic by presenting itself as the original. It may seem so like the original that we have difficulty telling it is an image. If it usurps the original, how can we tell this, since it looks the same as the original? If we live in an ultimate relation *between* ourselves and God, a first middle, we also construct a *second middle* in the given middle. The images in the second middle may well be false doubles, say, doublings of ourselves and the circuit of self-transcendence clogged with itself. We traverse the middle space but now as only the medium of our own immanent transcending. What then can we claim as the true original in this second middle? A religious person will still claim the original as God; atheism will say there is

---

9   See William Desmond, *The Intimate Universal: The Hidden Porosity among Religion, Art, Philosophy, and Politics* (New York: Columbia University Press, 2016).

no divine original; post-modern thought will say there is no original at all. Are we then in the midst of images of nothing—except ourselves perhaps? Do we come to the ultimate parting: either God or nothing; religious trust or nihilism? But how mark the discrimination of this difference, given that all our efforts seem to circulate in the images of the second middle? Even in this equivocal middle, the biblical religions enjoin absolute trust in the unsurpassable absoluteness of God, even when in Christianity that God is fleshed as the agapeic servant. Despite all difficulties of discernment, some sense of transcendence as other is *finally not negotiable*.

Think of the counterfeit double this way. A counterfeit double is an image that is almost exactly like the original, but something has been altered that vitiates its claim to be true. I have a counterfeit banknote. It looks good, but there is something missing, or something added that is not quite right. A true note, with genuine reserves to back it up, has, say, a line of silver running from below upward, and this *vertical thread* can only be seen when it is held up to the light. But when I hold the counterfeit to the light, I do not see the vertical line, but, say, the watermark of a circle closed on itself. If I do not hold it to the light, I will not see—even suspect—the absence of the vertical line. More complexly yet: what if there is a banknote that mimics the vertical line, though the foregrounded line is backed by the watermark of a circle closed on itself? How then to identify a counterfeit? And what is *the light* up to which I hold each?

Discernment of spirit is needed, and more and more so, the *better* the counterfeit. The better a counterfeit, the more it is *true* to the original. Its *achieved falsity* is dependent on its *being true to the original*. This is a very paradoxical situation: *perfected falsity is a function of being true to what is not false*. The perfect counterfeit looks almost exactly like the true currency. But somehow (and much of the difficulty lies in this little word "somehow") the claim it makes, or the authority it claims, is not to be sustained. It may even be that the falsity of the counterfeit is that it is *too perfect*. There is a story told that during World War II the Germans dropped counterfeit twenty-pound notes in Great Britain, which caused some havoc for a while because they were taken for true notes. The counterfeit notes were eventually discovered to be such, but how? It was noted that the counterfeit notes were *always perfect*, while the genuine notes seemed to have *some blemish*! The counterfeit was a *perfected double*, but it was false to the original—just in its perfect mimicry of the true original.

This perfected doubling sometimes worries one about Hegel's system. Philosophy perfects religion but plays false in its conceptual perfection, false to religion, false to philosophy itself. The God of holistic immanence seems to outdo in dialectical-speculative self-completeness the merely representational God of monotheistic transcendence. Are we haunted by heteronomy again? Do we need an *original as other* to sustain the claim made by an image to be a genuine image? A genuine image not simply of itself—for then it would be only a self-referring image, a self-reflexive image, a self-creating original, or (as Nietzsche claimed for the world) a work of art giving birth to itself. Is it surprising that the exclusion or reconfiguration of God as the other original leads to the self-divinization of immanent finitude as its own self-original? But where do we get that sense of the original as other? And how do we discern claims that this or that is the original, since every such claim seems itself open to the suspicion of being a counterfeit double? And what if the original can never be identified with this or that, or even the totality of this, that, and the other? In such an equivocal situation, is there any finesse that will help? Where would that finesse come from?

There is no easy philosophical answer. The religious image itself, even if it is genuine, is here also tested by this perplexity of the counterfeit double. There may be internal instabilities, even incoherencies in Hegel, but fidelity to the "matter itself" is more important. Hegel is not lacking in significant openness to religion, but he combines it with a way of thinking that reconfigures what is being religiously communicated, leading ultimately to its being recast in a form that closes our porosity to the ultimate transcendence of the divine. Then revelation must submit to self-determining reason. There is no Godsend that reason receives from beyond itself, and there is no surprise of revelation.[10] Hegel is a philosopher who tries rationally to underwrite self-determining modernity. His commitment to rational self-determining humanity, in its modern form, is finally hard to disentangle completely from a religion of humanity, all dialectical-speculative complications notwithstanding. Is it not the case that Hegel himself, in connection with modern art, endorses the claim that Humanity is its new holy of holies (*Humanus heißt der Heilige*)? The point has relevance beyond modern art to modern life generally. Today members of the church invisible of the religion of hu-

---

10 See William Desmond, "Godsends: On the Surprise of Revelation," *Ephemerides Theologicae Lovanienses* 92, no. 1 (2016), 7–28.

manity might be embarrassed by the word "religion." In Hegel's time it was different: the religion of humanity often had to present itself as a philosophy of *Geist*, with surface dialectical equivocations about God, which masked the deeper substitution of a self-determining humanity for the religious God of Jewish-Christian revelation.

We need not subscribe to a hermeneutics of suspicion, but it is possible to interpret Hegel on religion in too innocent a way. If what O'Regan says about misremembering and if what is here said about the counterfeit double holds true, nothing that Hegel says about religion can be taken univocally at face value. It is not unknown to find Hegelians citing Hegel as if he were a good Christian preacher, and he is, in a sense. I think of O'Regan's hermeneutics as trying to find the right place to behold, say, a beautiful painting. If we come too close, we see many details, but we might see nothing of the whole. If we stand too far off, we might see a whole in the large but perhaps not the lines of detailed nuance. The better place for our beholding is *between* too near and too far. There is something metaxological about finding that place. It is true that in O'Regan's work there is also another beholding that is beyond the Hegelian vision, and this is dictated by fidelity to the surprise of revelation. This fidelity is a second fidelity beyond the need for fidelity in the hermeneutical reading of Hegel. There is a doubleness to this, perhaps, but it is in the service of remembering what is misremembered, of seeing through and seeing beyond, in a contemporary Irenaean spirit, the counterfeit doubles of the divine.

CHAPTER SIX

On Hegel

Sorcerers and Apprentices

DAVID WALSH

As a tribute to my friend Cyril O' Regan, I offer the following reflection on Eric Voegelin's relationship to Hegel. This will partly fulfill my assignment in the volume of addressing the general topic of Hegel, and it will do so in a way that does not bring me into disagreement with the honoree. Besides, after many pleasant discussions with one another, it is still not clear to me that we diverge all that substantially on the question of Hegel. We may have traded places over the years in our assessments of the great Idealist, Cyril moving from a less sharply negative estimate to one more highly critical, while I followed almost the opposite trajectory. Yet I could not be sure that this divergence was not attributable to the different narrative contexts in which our views of Hegel matured. Beginning with a remarkable convergence in our dissertation topics, on the Boehme-Hegel connection, we went on to inhabit different disciplinary settings. Yet we remain philosophical partners and, in that intriguing interplay, have discovered the impossibility of reaching a definitive judgment. Philosophy remains the pursuit of wisdom, not its possession. This means that even a flawed genius of the stature of Hegel contained and revealed endless perspectives we could not afford to dismiss. Indeed, it may well be the case that it is the deficits that Hegel exhibits that call attention most effectively to the remediations that are also so powerfully present.

As with Hans Urs von Balthasar, whose own relationship with Hegel is the subject of Cyril's recent magisterial treatment, we find ourselves engaged with a problematic that can neither be resolved nor dismissed. Hegel remains the pivotal figure for the self-understanding of our world. Any philosophical articulation of the way in which theology stands in relation to that world cannot afford to overlook the thinker for whom the Incarnation remained the pivot of history. For better or worse, the Hegelian synthesis of philosophy and revelation, along with his newly elevated prominence of art, simply could not be ignored. Hegel is the figure that cannot be overcome, or he can be overcome only by extending the direction in which he pointed. Thus it is in noting Balthasar's resistance to the infamous Hegelian apocalypse that Cyril observes, "far from ruling out apocalyptic inflection in Balthasar's thought, it effectively demands it."[1] Even the judgment of heterodoxy, to which Cyril was first inclined, is fraught with the ambivalence of the debt that all orthodoxy owes to the heterodox. It is to the further exploration of that complicated relationship that I would like to add a chapter by exploring the similar case of Eric Voegelin's unending absorption with Hegel. In many ways Voegelin is a parallel figure to Balthasar, not least because of the guidance he took from the latter, but most especially for the increasing prominence he accorded to the Hegelian philosophy of history. In what follows I will attempt to trace the transition from Voegelin's incendiary accusation of Hegel as a sorcerer to the calmer embrace of him as a partner in his own later meditation.[2]

The modulation evident in Voegelin's relationship with Hegel is of more than incidental concern to me. In many ways it tracks my own evolving assessment of the notorious sorcerer as I began to explore the esoteric origins of his philosophical thought. The connection with the Hermetic-Kabbal-

---

1 Cyril O' Regan, *The Anatomy of Misremembering: Von Balthasar's Response to Philosophical Modernity*, Vol. 1: *Hegel* (Spring Valley, NY: Crossroad Publishing Company, 2014), 419.

2 Eric Voegelin, "On Hegel: A Study in Sorcery," *Collected Works*, Vol. 12: *Published Essays, 1966–1985*, ed. Ellis Sandoz (Baton Rouge: Louisiana State University Press, 1990), 213–55. Originally published in *Studium Generale* 24 (1971): 335–68. A longer version of the paper was delivered at the First Conference of the International Society for the Study of Time, 1969.

ist axis, as it was transmitted through the speculative theosophy of Jacob Boehme and the continuing strands of the occult in Romanticism, seemed to be the most fruitful line of inquiry. Voegelin had done much to implant this interest when I consulted him about dissertation topics, so it took a considerable period of time for that initial fascination with what had seemed such a novel perspective on familiar philosophical material to wear off. Only then would it be possible to consider Hegel anew in a reading that left behind all preconceived contexts of interpretation. Read in his own light, and in relation to his immediate setting within the Kantian "Copernican revolution," it would become apparent that, apart from occasional rhetorical flourishes, Hegel was engaged in a radical realignment of philosophical reflection that would establish its modern relevance and confirm its long-standing intersection with Christianity.[3] As it turns out, that was more or less the circuit of Voegelin's own reconsiderations of Hegel that stretch from the notorious blasts of the Sorcery essay to the profound meditations of the final volume of *Order and History*. In what follows, we will trace his steps as we begin with the provocative accusation of Hegel as a sorcerer in the 1971 essay, then turn to the misgivings that initially strike us about it, followed by a more extended account of the principal charges of Hegel's consummation of history, and his surreptitious displacement of God, before turning to the far more positive assessment of Hegel that is included in *In Search of Order*. This will make it possible to shed light on the wider significance of Hegel as the thinker that Voegelin himself had to acknowledge as the great explorer of the path on which his own thought had unfolded.

1. Evolution of an Approach

The first thing to note about Voegelin's reading of Hegel is that it occurred later in his scholarly career.[4] There is no analysis in the *History of Political Ideas* that was largely written in the 1940s. Only Comte, Marx, and Ba-

---

3 This is the understanding I have set forth in *The Modern Philosophical Revolution: The Luminosity of Existence* (Cambridge: Cambridge University Press, 2008). See especially chap. 2, "Hegel's Inauguration of the Language of Existence."

4 He explains in his "Response to Professor Altizer's 'A New History and a New but Ancient God?'" "For a long time I studiously avoided any serious criticism of Hegel in my published work, because I simply could not understand him." *Published Essays, 1966–1985*, 296.

kunin get an extended treatment there.⁵ Nietzsche receives a passing glance, and there is the very admiring chapter on Schelling that, on Voegelin's own admission, opened his eyes to the flawed conception of a history of ideas approach. The odd aspect of this famous "turn" away from the notion of a history of ideas is that Voegelin was already on his way toward it before the realization dawned. Most readers are struck by the extent to which *The History of Political Ideas* departs from a conventional narrative of ideas to pursue the motivating sentiments that drive them. Long before Voegelin proclaimed that there are no such things as ideas but only the experiences and symbols from which they are derived, he had already exemplified that insight. The Sacrum Imperium, for example, was the evocative aspiration that organized the medieval period, even though it was never a concretely realized idea.⁶ What is significant is that it was contact with German Idealism, specifically Schelling, that brought this insight into full awareness. To the extent that the Idealists were engaged in a common project, that of locating reason within reality rather than outside of it, completing the Kantian self-limitation of reason, it is arguable that this was the most fertile philosophical ground for Voegelin's own inquiry. The impact that the abbreviated exposure to Schelling had is sufficient evidence of the potential. But for some reason Voegelin did not linger any further in material he thought he had sufficiently grasped in order to determine its irrelevance. No doubt a big part of the explanation is that his interest was really in the nineteenth-century messianic activists who drove the modern revolutionary movement. The ideological convulsions that gripped the twentieth century were the main target. In light of that upheaval, the Idealist predecessors appeared as a less consequential prelude. Very far in the past lay Voegelin's insightful reading of Kant that might have provided a bridge into the philosophical richness of the Idealists.⁷ For the moment, the narrative of history pointed toward the ideological madness that had come to dominate the world in Voegelin's own time.

---

5 Eric Voegelin, *Collected Works*, Vol. 8: *Crisis and the Apocalypse of Man*, ed. David Walsh (Columbia: University of Missouri Press, 1999).

6 Voegelin, *Collected Works*, Vol. 21: *The Later Middle Ages*, ed. David Walsh (Columbia: University of Missouri Press, 1998).

7 Voegelin, "Ought in Kant's System," *Collected Works*, Vol. 8: *Published Essays, 1929–1933*, eds. Thomas Heilke and John von Heyking (Columbia: University of Missouri Press, 2003), chap. 8.

That was the lens through which Voegelin later returned to Hegel, whom he eventually came to see as the great exemplar of the project the secular messiahs sought to accomplish. The apocalypse of man ran through the murder of God. From Hegel to Nietzsche, as Karl Löwith had conceived in his parallel study, would henceforth color the reading of Hegel.[8] In other words, the return to Hegel, when it did occur, would be within a context that looked forward to the great aberrations of his thought rather than to its significance within his own intellectual setting. The pattern is not unique to Voegelin, as the allusion to Löwith indicates. Hans Urs von Balthasar had reached a similar judgment, as had Henri de Lubac, to cite only two of the best-informed contemporary readers.[9] As always, Voegelin did not go out on a limb but sought confirmation in the scholarly literature of the day. Certainly there were few authorities that defended the validity of the Hegelian construction or, for that matter, of any of the Idealists. In that respect we are in a very different situation today when, finally, something like a consensus—and indeed a highly appreciative consensus—has formed around their interpretation. The study of German Idealism is now one of the liveliest and most consequential fields of investigation, with attenuations that reach as far as analytic language philosophy and Catholic theology. Seen in their own terms, the Idealists emerge as the greatest philosophical explosion of the modern period, an achievement so singular and significant that the very self-understanding of modernity turns upon it.[10] The expansive attention now lavished on the Idealists is driven in large part by the realization that they possess a unique relevance for the mode in which philosophy must proceed in an age defined by empirical science and the reign of technology. Many of the subsequent philosophical developments draw upon it and are

---

8 Karl Löwith, *From Hegel to Nietzsche*, trans. David Green (New York: Doubleday, 1967; original 1941).

9 Hans Urs von Balthasar, *Die Apokalypse der deutschen Seele: Studien zu einer Lehre von letzten Haltungen*, 3 vols. (Salzburg: Verlag Anton Pustet, 1937–39); Henri de Lubac, *La posterité spirituelle de Joachim de Fiore*, 2 vols. (Paris: Lethielleux, 1979–82).

10 See Robert Pippin, *Hegel's Idealism: The Satisfaction of Self-Consciousness* (Cambridge: Cambridge University Press, 1989), and Terry Pinkard, *German Philosophy 1760–1860: The Legacy of Idealism* (Cambridge: Cambridge University Press, 2002), and, earlier, Charles Taylor, *Hegel* (Cambridge: Cambridge University Press, 1975).

properly seen as a resumption of the impulse that lay within it rather than a rejection of it. Today it would be hard to see Voegelin resisting the scholarly preponderance that has emerged over the thirty years since he stopped writing. Instead he would be more likely to appreciate the extent of his own convergence with Hegel, an apprehension that was not entirely absent from his later assessments, even if they do not arise within his most famous blast against Hegel as a sorcerer.

The assimilation of Hegel to his activist successors is not, of course, the only handicap under which Voegelin labored. A deeper and closer reading of Hegel was simply not afforded by the direction in which Voegelin's scholarly investigations drew him. When I first met him he was already five to ten millennia back in his historical focus on the Neolithic passage graves. The first three volumes of *Order and History* are devoted to the cosmological world of myth, the Israelite revelation, and the Greek discovery of reason. The subsequent enlargement of the empirical horizon in volume 4's *Ecumenic Age* broadens the inquiry but retains only a tangential reference to the modern materials. The theoretical deepening of the final volume does nothing to lessen the summative character of the treatments. Yet even then there is evidence of a reconsideration of Hegel. All we can say is that his account of Hegel remained underway and that the first great denunciation was not his final word. Yet it was his first word, for Voegelin conceded that he had long avoided Hegel as a result of insufficiently understanding him. Clearly, he had bided his time before tackling his most daunting predecessor. Early glimpses of the angle he would take had already emerged in *Science, Politics, and Gnosticism,* essays that were themselves intentionally polemical.[11] Significantly, none of it appeared in the major intervening volume, *Anamnesis,* assembled with the kind of care that marked the volumes of *Order and History*. It was outside of the settled body of work that Voegelin continued to investigate Hegel in a more exploratory manner. Somewhere toward the end of the 1960s the assessment had crystallized sufficiently to be presented in the essay published in 1971. For better or worse, Hegel had become the quintessential modern gnostic. Further reading on the Renaissance magus phenomenon, the Corpus Hermeticum, and Jacob Boehme, which were very

---

11 Voegelin, *Science, Politics, and Gnosticism, Collected Works,* Vol. 5: *Modernity Without Restraint,* ed. Manfred Henningsen (Columbia: University of Missouri Press, 2000; original 1959).

much at the center of Voegelin's interest at the time, served only to confirm that the characterization of Hegel as a conjuror was on the right track. Notably absent is any reference to current Hegel scholarship, with the exception of the idiosyncratic Kojève, or any clear evidence of a rereading of the Hegelian texts. Reliance on a wider scholarly context had reassured Voegelin that he could neglect commentators more closely tied to the Hegelian enterprise. Indeed, by this stage Voegelin had even come to disdain and distrust scholars who were too conventionally close to their material. They would never be able to delineate the full apocalyptic proportions of the enterprise they were investigating. Once he had seized on the most dramatic aspect of a thinker, Voegelin was often loath to revisit and reconsider it. In this regard we recall his treatment of such conventionally acceptable figures as Isaiah and Husserl.[12]

2. Misgivings

It is to Voegelin's credit, however, that this initial characterization of Hegel as the supreme manipulator of the God-man relationship did not remain without qualifications. The need to return to the gnostic apocalypse the great sorcerer had accomplished necessitated a review of it in other perspectives. Even the notion of the gnostic apocalypse begins to modulate, as Voegelin gains a greater appreciation of the project in which Hegel had been engaged. In the final volume, *In Search of Order*, we are very close to the admission that Hegel had resumed the challenge arising from the breakthrough to transcendence that marked the great turning points of history. How was it possible for the symbolization of the transcendent, of Being, to be contained within time? Gnosticism in either its ancient or modern forms, as liberation from the cosmos or absorption within it, could never be regarded as a satisfactory response. In the end, Hegel would come to occupy the same position as St. Augustine in recognizing the dead end of any movement that left nothing further to do within time. Just as the Manicheans had reached the perfection that made spiritual growth impossible,

---

12 See the treatment of Isaiah in *Collected Works*, Vol. 14: *Israel and Revelation*, ed. Maurice P. Hogan (Columbia: University of Missouri Press, 2001), and Husserl, in *Collected Works*, Vol. 6: *Anamnesis*, ed. David Walsh (Columbia: University of Missouri Press, 2002), chap. 2.

an end of history would abolish all that made history meaningful.[13] Kojève had reached that insight in regard to Hegel, but he seemed to assume that the same realization never occurred to Hegel.[14] At any rate, neither Voegelin nor Kojève gave full weight to the attention that Hegel lavished on history itself, especially in the great lecture courses on history, art, religion, and philosophy. No one with that intensity of empirical interest could possibly wish to see it concluded in some putative consummation. Instead, he would be much more likely to realize that the fulfillment of history within time robs history of all meaning. The eschatological end of history is quite different, as Augustine understood, for it is the perspective from which history can be surveyed as a whole. It is therefore a great mistake to read Hegel's remarks about an end as pointing only to an immanent conclusion. He may have left open that suggestion, but his own wide-ranging historical inquiry works forcefully against it. Far from effecting a speculative culmination, Hegel had immersed himself in the unending diversity of materials.

The only thinker who combines the same theoretical penetration with equivalent empirical mastery is probably Voegelin himself. It is a rare combination in the history of thought, dominated as it is by thinkers for whom the philosophical challenges take precedence. The type inaugurated by Aristotle, for whom involvement with the manifold details is just as important, is far less frequent. Even Voegelin's objections to the occasional smoothing of historical untidiness by Hegel cannot quite disguise the realization that the same tendency was present in his own work. It was the acknowledgment of just such a strain that had persuaded Voegelin to abandon the chronological framework he had first imposed on *Order and History*.[15] The irreducible complexity of reality could not be contained in a single overarching narrative. But was that not the problem that first surfaces in the Hegelian enlargement of philosophy into a philosophy of history? The problem of the point of view from which the construction of history is undertaken is first seriously broached there. Augustine had intuited his way toward an escha-

---

13 Peter Brown, *Augustine of Hippo* (Berkeley: University of California Press, 1967), chap. 5.

14 Alexandre Kojève, *Introduction to the Reading of Hegel*, trans. James H. Nichols (New York: Basic Books, 1969).

15 Voegelin, *Collected Works*, Vol. 17: *The Ecumenic Age*, ed. Michael Franz (Columbia: University of Missouri Press, 2000), Introduction.

tological viewpoint, but he had not made the theoretical requirement sufficiently clear. It was Hegel and the Idealists who worked explicitly toward it. They had seen that history could not be regarded as a field of phenomena an observer must investigate from the outside. Rather, history consisted of lines of meaning that include the investigator as well. The only definitive standpoint from which it can be apprehended is the turning point that transcends it, the beginning, or end, or intersection, of the timeless and time. The irruption of the transcendent is the privileged moment from which history can be viewed as history. That is what Hegel named the advent of the absolute or absolute knowledge. Whatever the infelicities of that term, it is clear that both he and Voegelin regarded this as a possibility that turned on the appearance of Christ. It was the arrival of Christ that opened the condition of the possibility of God and man knowing one another. That was always a possibility from the beginning of history, but its recognition takes a long historical unfolding. The assertion that "history is Christ written large" now occurs within a global horizon that is open to multiple breakthroughs to transcendence.[16] Whatever the shortcomings of his elaboration of this insight, it would be hard to deny that Hegel had inaugurated the realization that "the order of history emerges from the history of order."[17]

It is no wonder that the bluntness of Voegelin's dismissal of Hegel in the sorcerer essay should sit so uneasily. At the back of his mind there was surely more than a hint of awareness of his own filiation with the Hegelian project. It is regrettable that a deeper reading of the Idealists did not begin to dislodge the paradigm of the secular messiah, to which Hegel, too, had been assimilated at this point, as the defining pattern of the nineteenth century. Even Schelling, the Idealist for whom Voegelin had expressed the most unqualified admiration, did not merit a return visit after the initial treatment. This is all the more striking in view not only of the impact that the reading of Schelling had on Voegelin's own development, but also in light of the enormous convergence that exists between Voegelin's work and the later Schelling's massive project of a *Philosophy of Mythology* and a *Philosophy*

---

16 Voegelin, "Immortality: Experience and Symbol," *Collected Works*, Vol. 12: *Published Essays, 1966–1985*, 78.

17 This is the opening sentence of *Order and History*, Vol. I, *Israel and Revelation*, 19.

of Revelation.[18] Continual allusions back to these illustrious predecessors can never quite dispel the sense that Voegelin might have overlooked something indispensable for his own work. They had attempted to define a spiritual framework that would be adequate to a world dominated by rational science, and open to a multiplicity of centers of order, while at the same time retaining the full sweep of the classical and Christian tradition. Their attenuated connection with the Promethean strand of the modern impulse is far from defining them, for they are at root Voegelin's collaborators rather than his rivals. This is what explains the peculiar strategy he employs in this most condemnatory treatment.

3. Hegel's End of History

Voegelin announces this strategy early in the essay when he declares that he is going to follow the programmatic statements of Hegel's intentions rather than the more laborious route of a careful reading of the texts.[19] This is to dramatize the audacious character of Hegel's project of self-divinization, an impossibility that the actual texts are designed to obscure. The sorcery turns on Hegel's claim to the self-knowledge of God without having to assert that he has become God. If that is indeed Hegel's project, then there is no doubt that Voegelin has hit upon a secret that might not readily be discerned in the esoteric texts. But what basis do we have for this assertion other than Voegelin's insistence that the programmatic statements do yield this unambiguous interpretation? When we read such infamous suggestions as that the love of wisdom will be replaced by its actual possession, we might be inclined to suspect, with Voegelin, that something quite radical is underway, although we might still hesitate to convict on the basis of what in the end may be only a rhetorical flourish.[20] The evidence, even as it is marshalled by an able prosecutor, complete with the dramatic moment of Napoleon

---

18 For a convenient selection, see *Schelling's Philosophy of Mythology and Revelation*, trans. and reduced by Victory C. Hayes (Armidale: Australian Association for the Study of Religions, 1995), and *Historical-Critical Introduction to the Philosophy of Mythology*, trans. Mason Richey and Markus Zisselsberger (Albany: State University of New York Press, 2007).

19 Voegelin, "On Hegel: A Study in Sorcery," 232.

20 Hegel, *Phenomenology of Spirit*, trans. A.V. Miller (Oxford: Oxford University Press, 1977), Preface, par. 5, 3.

parading outside Jena, may give us pause, but we cannot quite shake the impression that it remains largely circumstantial. One must have already decided that Hegel is guilty of wicked intentions. But that is precisely what is at issue. Statements that amount to little more than flashes of ambition, even overweening ambition, are hardly enough to justify the charge of sorcery. What is at issue is how such declamations are to be taken. For that, the statements themselves are not sufficient evidence. We must probe the actual performance. Even if Voegelin is right that the discursive unfolding is little more than an elaborate second reality to conceal the enormity of the travesty Hegel intends, then it is precisely the exposure of that ambiguity that must be demonstrated. Admittedly that is a more arduous task, yet it cannot be avoided. Voegelin's own justification for avoiding it—namely, that the programmatic assertions are starker than any attempt to achieve them—cannot be sustained. It may well be that the goals clarify what remains obscure in the muddiness of their implementation, but we cannot even be sure of what the goals are before we have gained a clear appreciation of what they are intended to bring about. Ends and means form a unity that must be interpreted as a whole.

It is almost as if Voegelin is departing from his customary hermeneutic of a close reading of the texts. Here we have only a selective reading where even the selections lack an adequate basis to judge their meaning. Are thinkers to be condemned for the rhetorical flights of fancy that festoon their writings rather than for the contents themselves? Can we even be sure that the claims are excessive if we are not sure how they are to be taken? What in the end can the claim to absolute knowledge mean if we have not weighed the different constructions that can be placed upon it? If there is ambiguity, then it must be exposed unambiguously. Ambiguity cannot even be determined apart from the attempt to clarify it. But that means that we begin with a suspension of judgment regarding motivations and intentions. The philosophical construction must reveal the goal behind them rather than the other way around. Statements of purpose must be taken in light of what is accomplished rather than on the first impression with which they may strike us. Results and intentions are a dialectic, and while reading a text we are continually in search of the heart from which it emerges. The shortcoming in Voegelin's account in this essay is that he allowed himself to be captured by the first brilliant suggestion that Hegel was a sorcerer. That became the key to unlocking the texts, and increasing confidence in the diagnosis meant that interpretation became a quest for confirmation. In the end it is a ringing denunciation, but it is a far cry from an actual understanding of Hegel. This explains why Voegelin's essay is rarely cited in the Hegel literature and is a poor place to begin if one wants to understand Hegel. That was my experience when I began, for I was struck by the absence of any detailed reading of what Hegel actually said and was prepared to overlook it in my admiration for Voegelin. I was under his spell.

When I persevered in reading Hegel, it became apparent that one could only make progress if one began with a more generous spirit. Where the texts are ambiguous, it is a better hermeneutic principle to put the best possible construction on them, rather than the worst. If one eventually agreed with Voegelin's harsh judgment, then one would be on firmer interpretive ground and could not simply be accused of misjudgment of intentions. When this is done, one finds it is possible to place an orthodox construction on the claim of absolute knowledge. It does not mean that Hegel has become God, but that he has reached the divine viewpoint as the highest of all things. The wisdom he now possesses does not abolish the love of wisdom. It is simply an alternative formulation of the Delphic judgment of the wisdom of Socrates. He knew that he knew nothing and in that was wiser than all others. Absolute knowledge was the measure that he did not possess and in knowing that, he thereby possessed it in part. There is no doubt that Hegel courts the misconstructions Voegelin and others attribute, but there is no necessity to impose them. Talk of absolute knowledge can suggest one has grasped what is unavailable to all others, but it need not. It can just as easily mean one has glimpsed what can be glimpsed by all, even if most do not. The absolute is not possessed but is the condition of the possibility of all knowledge. Kant had inaugurated this reflection of knowledge on itself, and Hegel had merely carried it a little further. The language of consciousness and *Geist* could have been a subterfuge to cover the ambiguity of the operation, but it could just as easily have been a consequence of the internal unfolding of the meditation. When Hegel asks about that within which consciousness lives, then it can only be known from within. There is neither man nor God but only the poles within which the relationship unfolds. We are remarkably close to Voegelin's own highlighting of the Metaxy as the horizon within which all our thinking occurs. Rather than accusing Hegel of mishandling Aristotle's famous formulation of "thought thinking itself," we are perhaps on safer ground in seeing it as an effort to delineate its meaning more precisely. In

Hegel's account, thought thinks itself more clearly in light of that which is beyond it. Standing in relation to the absolute is inexorable.

There is thus no need to accuse Hegel of abolishing the depth beyond consciousness or of absorbing everything within the dynamics of consciousness.[21] None of what he says makes any sense on the basis of that premise. Voegelin admires the extent to which Hegel recognizes the impossibility of human life and reflection sustaining itself on the basis of its own autonomy. Kant had come dangerously close to that suggestion before pulling back from it. Hegel and the Idealist successors worked strenuously to avoid the implication of a self-contained reason. The contemporary admirers of Hegel place considerable emphasis on the notion of reason as embedded in its historical unfolding. Even if that is the closest they dare go to acknowledging the full metaphysical depth of Hegel, it is still a step up on a path that can eventually accept the full weight of Hegel's profession of faith. At the same time, full disclosure requires us to acknowledge that even Hegel's contemporaries had difficulty affirming his orthodoxy.[22] Hermeneutical procedure, however, requires readers to withhold judgment until all the evidence is in. We should at least consider the possibility that the misunderstanding had already occurred in the earliest reception. After all, access to the Hegelian texts was extremely limited. First impressions and subsequent distortions have a way of hanging around. But our responsibility is to give the widest latitude to the possibility that Hegel might be the one who most thoroughly grounds the metaphysics of philosophy and Christianity in the modern era. When objective science has usurped the claim to knowledge, on what ground can the knowledge of what transcends space and time base itself? It can only be on that which provides the condition of possibility of science that can itself never be included with it. Science rests on the absolute that itself has no basis other than the absolute itself. That is the dialectic on which

---

21 "The principle of construction in the *Phänomenologie*, however, is so simple that it will not be unfair to call it a sleight of hand. As it would prove impossible even for the constructive genius of a Hegel to grind the real God and real man through the machinery of dialectics and come out with a man-god, he roundly does not concede the status of reality to either God or man. The *Phänomenologie* admits no reality but consciousness" (Voegelin, "On Hegel," 223).

22 Schelling was recalled to Berlin in order to "stamp out the dragon's teeth of Hegelianism." See Schelling, *Philosophie der Offenbarung*, 1841/42, ed. Manfred Frank (Frankfurt: Suhrkamp, 1977), "Introduction."

Hegel launches us. It leads inexorably to the recognition that even scientific mastery cannot dispense with that which grounds its own possibility.[23] It is in relation to the absolute that all unfolds. That is the story of history.

This means, contrary to the common misperception to which Voegelin here subscribes, that Hegel does not claim that history has reached its end. As Kojève acknowledged, an end of history would deprive history of all meaning. Why would Hegel have supported such an outcome? This is particularly remarkable given that there was no necessity for him to do so. Hegel surely understood what was apparent to Augustine, that history could only be perceived from its end point, but that the end point could never be included within it. The viewpoint that renders history meaningful is strictly eschatological. Whenever Hegel talks about the end of history, it should be taken in this sense. There is a meaningful movement to history, by which it heads toward the fuller revelation of what is present from the beginning but never fully unfolded within time. Despite the modern emphasis on historical progress toward an immanent fulfillment, it is far more plausible that Hegel understood the dialectical overturning that constitutes its eschatological horizon. Indeed, the unfolding discovery of history is that there is nothing in history that accounts for the possibility of history. The blind link in the chain of necessity, to which Hegel alludes in an early document that Voegelin quotes, is, in the process of contemplating history, already transcending it.[24] There is no necessity to conclude that this signifies a determination to bring history to its conclusion within the system imposed upon it. It may even be that Hegel did not have a system at all. Even his references to an end of history can be seen as an identification of the absolute viewpoint from which alone it can be perceived.[25] Invocation of an end is thus not an apocalyptic pronouncement but a methodological necessity. Without the

---

23 I have amplified this theme in "Science Is Not Scientific," in *Faith and the Marvelous Progress of Science*, ed. Brendan Leahy (Hyde Park, NY: New City Press, 2014), 107–20.

24 Voegelin, "On Hegel," 221.

25 For instance, Voegelin writes: "*Time* is the *concept* itself in its existence, as it presents itself to consciousness as an empty intuition; that is the reason the *Geist* appears of necessity in time, and will appear in time as long as it has not abolished time" ("On Hegel," 227). Viewing history from the perspective of eternity is not the same as evincing a will to abolish it.

end, history would scarcely even be visible. It is only from the perspective outside of it that history can be perceived. The outcome of history is thus the progressive advance in awareness of what constitutes history as the now that is not yet and can never be fully realized within it. The fact of revelation is its content, as Voegelin remarked, an observation that could equally well have originated with Hegel.[26]

It is therefore not surprising that there are virtually no unambiguous pronouncements of the end of history in Hegel, despite its widespread attribution to him. The passages Voegelin quotes are the main proof texts, but they certainly do not admit of a univocal interpretation. Instead we must concede that they can equally be rendered interpretively in eschatological terms. For this reason, we must have recourse to Voegelin's own hermeneutical method, which is to find the core of a thinker's perspective and interpret the writings in relation to it. In this case, however, Voegelin rushed to judgment once he concluded that Hegel was at his core a self-divinizer who sought to make all of reality revolve around himself. The Great Man of history had succumbed to the temptation of abolishing the reality that made him great. A more considered examination of Hegel's actual practice, especially in the extensive historical courses on history, philosophy, art, and religion, would make it clear that there is scarcely a whiff of a consummation. It is the movement of history rather than the conclusion at which it arrives that draws his attention. How else could he lavish such attention on the vast field of historical materials, or meditate so persistently on the rich complexity of forms in the history of art, philosophy, or religion? Far from concluding that the later unfoldings had rendered the predecessors obsolete, Hegel should more properly be seen as arguing for the indispensability and irreplaceability of every stage. Just as there is no such thing as progress in the history of art, there is scarcely more validity to the notion within the history of philosophy or religion. Even politics is a historical whole in which the present cannot be understood except in reference to what it has left behind and which is, for that reason, never simply left behind. Hegel is, in other words, stunningly close to Voegelin's own eventual admission of the simultaneity of all of the phases of history that now stand in relation to one

---

26 Voegelin, *The New Science of Politics* (Chicago: University of Chicago Press, 1952), 78, a remark he repeated in *In Search of Order, Collected Works*, Vol. 18, ed. Ellis Sandoz (Columbia: University of Missouri Press, 2000), 87.

another as the only adequate disclosure of their meaning.[27] Voegelin's own abandonment of the chronological framework is tantamount to the admission that he, too, had been guilty of suggesting that what came before only had the purpose of serving what succeeds it. An immanent end had been built into this conventional narrative. But it is arguable that the insight that overturns it was already present in the Hegelian profession that history was transacted, not in relation to the present, but in light of the absolute. To the extent that Hegel is a philosopher of the absolute, he is the ultimate bulwark against the historically relative. Kojève's reduction of the end of history to its absurdity is only the negative transmission of this insight.[28] Its positive presentation that all that we do, and thus all that constitutes history, is undertaken in relation to the eternal, is the insight of Kierkegaard.[29]

4. The Displacement of God

The big question is whether Hegel meant anything substantive by the term "absolute." Did it have the same theological reference as Kierkegaard gave it? Is the absolute God? This is the great charge Voegelin lodges against Hegel. He is accused of invoking the absolute only as a thinly veiled disguise for the removal of God. Within the dynamics of consciousness, history reduces to its diurnal unfolding and makes no reference to anything beyond it. History is itself the highest framework, and the depth has been abolished. It is curious that this is exactly the position evinced by one of the dominant schools of contemporary Hegel scholarship. While rejecting the charge of imposing a culmination on history, they are at pains to demonstrate Hegel's commitment to history as the indispensable medium of philosophical development, while adamantly rejecting any intrusion from beyond the horizon

---

27 In explaining why the new form that philosophy of history had to take was "definitely not a story of meaningful events to be arranged on a time line," Voegelin went on to sketch what it is. "In this new form, the analysis had to move backward and forward and sideways, in order to follow empirically the patterns of meaning as they revealed themselves in the self-interpretation of persons and societies in history" (*Ecumenic Age*, 106).

28 Barry Cooper, *The End of History: An Essay on Modern Hegelianism* (Toronto: University of Toronto Press, 1984).

29 Søren Kierkegaard, *Concluding Unscientific Postscript to Philosophical Fragments*, 2 vols., trans. Howard V. Hong and Edna H. Hong (Princeton, NJ: Princeton University Press, 1992).

of history.[30] History stands on its own bottom in this uncompromisingly secularist view. Where Voegelin complains about Hegel's abolition of any depth beyond the historical dialectic, the "historicality of reason" school embraces the unrelievedly immanentist horizon it generates. Voegelin bemoans the disappearance of metaphysics while Pippin applauds it. The resulting characterization of Hegel, however, is the same, and equally questionable. Not only does it rest on a studied avoidance of Hegel's invocations of the absolute and God, but it makes it impossible to understand what it was that made Hegel's project possible. It may indeed be that Hegel admitted the impossibility of "metaphysics," as Voegelin also asserted, and it may be that history remained the unsurpassable horizon of thought, as Pippin and others insist. But that did not obliterate Hegel's consciousness of the impossibility of reducing everything to the immanence of history. It may be that Hegel did not find the most perspicuous formulation of what he had in mind and thereby left himself open to such misconstructions. Nevertheless, he did hold firm to the intuitions that guided him as he set philosophy on the path of a movement rather than a stasis. This was what accounted for the often-tortured language of the absolute and of consciousness as the unfolding of *Geist*. The immanent dialectic Voegelin criticizes and Pippin accepts is the very means by which he keeps alive the awareness that history cannot include what makes it possible. It is in the nature of the condition that it cannot enter what it conditions. How, then, can they be held together if they can neither be united nor divorced? Hegel's answer is that they remain in unending relationship to one another, within the dialectic that will not permit them to rest in endless identity. If Hegel's project, as both the theological and secularizing critics admit, is the transformation of truth into a movement rather than a possession, it is the dialectic of movement that is its most appropriate characterization. What cannot be included in history is thereby rendered present but always in the mode of what is not present, because it sustains the movement itself. Without abolishing God, Hegel acknowledges God in the only way that the transcendent can be acknowledged, namely, as the movement toward transcendence that can never be absorbed within immanence. To say that "the state is the march of God in the world"[31] is

---

30 Pippin, *Hegel's Idealism*, and Pinkard, *German Philosophy 1760–1860*.

31 Hegel, *Elements of the Philosophy of Right*, trans. T.M. Knox (Oxford: Oxford University Press, 1967), a lecture addition to par. 258.

not to say anything either about God or the state that would substantively identify them. But it is to intimate the relationship between them that is all that really matters. Neither the state nor God is what it is, but only in the relationship to one another. Just as history can only be known from the viewpoint of the eschaton and the eschaton cannot be included within history, they can, however, be apprehended within this realization. The elevation of that realization to self-consciousness is the signal achievement of Hegel and the aspect in which he advances beyond Augustine. It is certainly the case that the latter had reached the same realization, for he wrote the *City of God* in full awareness of the eschatological status of the two cities. Yet he did not raise his awareness to methodological consciousness. It is for this reason that it had to be continually lost and recovered over the succeeding centuries. With Hegel's elevation of it to a methodological principle, there is at least the possibility of retaining it within our intellectual framework. Even the mischaracterization of Hegel as engaged in the consummation of history that abolishes it has had the merit of rendering his insight less mistakable. We now have at least the possibility of holding the transcendent as transcendent, because it is represented not as a resting place but as its continual supersession. This was an acknowledgment of Hegel's contribution that Voegelin later came to make in a far more ungrudging fashion.[32] One suspects there is a similar dynamic at work in the more secularizing admirers of Hegel who find, in his relentless overturning of all finite manifestations of the divine, a means of nevertheless holding onto it. The mystery remains within the dialectic as its inaccessible underpinning.

If it is thus possible to redeem many of Hegel's formulations without prejudicing them and to concede, as Voegelin later does, that they converge with his own, one wonders what it was that prevented this more capacious reading at the beginning. The need to find an ultimate bearer of responsibility for the later modern disaster was surely strong. But Voegelin, even in the Sorcerer essay, never simply reached an outright condemnation of his great predecessor. Instead it was generously leavened with admiration for

---

32 "Hence, the preceding enumeration should not be read as a critique of Hegel but, on the contrary, as an attempt to clarify and stress his achievement. His rediscovery of the experiential source of symbolization, as well as his identification of the fundamental problems in the structure of consciousness is irreversible" (Voegelin, *In Search of Order*, 85).

Hegel's achievement of an account of truth that no philosopher could afford to neglect.[33] However, the accusatory rhetoric of sorcery, Gnosticism, and apocalypse would for most readers eclipse the more muted expressions of appreciation. Yet both elements were inescapably present. The challenge of reconciling them was not one to which Voegelin was attracted, intrigued as he was by the discovery of ever-new aspects of the magical operation. We may conclude that Voegelin was no more interested in presenting a balanced account of Hegel than he was of any other thinker. He was fascinated by the contribution Hegel could make to the problem of sorcery, rather than the other way around. The excitement of discovery always captured Voegelin's attention. But this tendency meant that he did not always see the instability embedded in his own assessments. In the case of Hegel, it is surely the conception of him as a mystic manqué that seems to give fixity to what is not really a definitive judgment. Voegelin may continually overturn it in his assessment of Hegel as still a mystic, one who gives voice to the in-between status of existence, just as it emerges in all the great symbolizations of order back to Plato's coinage of the notion. The problem, however, is that once the manqué has been pronounced, it blocks the way to its own overcoming. All that most readers remember of Voegelin's account of modernity is the jeremiad, not the reassessment that would lead modernity into its own fuller realization. The revolt against God is still an affirmation of God.

Voegelin knew this well, but he did not manage to find his way to a satisfactory articulation of the extent to which the modernity that seemed to carry theophanic revolt remained tied to theophany. It is arguable that the treatment of Hegel was the most promising opportunity for reaching that more comprehensive assessment. There is no doubt that Voegelin approaches it repeatedly, especially in his remarks about the equivalences that unite both the acceptance and the rejection of the transcendent. We are tantalizingly close to the admission that the mystic manqué remains a mystic. He still lives in relation to the hidden, which, for all the claims of disclosure, is finally never disclosed.[34] The decisive element is thus not the distortion that

---

33 "As a genus of philosophical literature, the *Phänomenologie* is a treatise on *aletheia*, on truth and reality, and a very important one indeed; no philosopher can afford to ignore it" (Voegelin, "On Hegel," 222).

34 We recall the derivation of "mystic" from the hidden or the mysteries into which the initiates entered.

seeks to abolish the tension of existence, but the acknowledgment that it has not been so superseded. Even if Hegel sought to effect the apocalypse of history, it is not the apocalypse but his standing within it as what cannot be surpassed that is of most significance. The end of history bears witness to the eschaton that is beyond history. Voegelin is right that it is the constancy of structure that is most notable.[35] Distortion is premised on what cannot be distorted. The lie can never obliterate the truth, for it depends too intimately upon it. The terminology of first and second reality, to which Voegelin returned over and over again, seemed to suggest something of his own dissatisfaction with its conceptual power.[36] Each time he came back, it seemed as if it was to discover something that had eluded him. Could it be that it was the dialectical character of truth, adduced most penetratingly by Hegel, that was the overlooked aspect? The division into first and second realities has the unfortunate consequence of suggesting that there are competing alternatives. It obscures the extent to which there is only one reality on which the distorting impulse is highly parasitic. None of this is to concede that Hegel is guilty of engaging in a lie or inserting deliberate ambiguity. Indeed, I have strongly argued the contrary. It is simply to suggest that, even if he was guilty, he provides the means of his own remediation. Hegel himself can always be invoked in the redemption of Hegel.

That is the greatness of his thought that Voegelin intuits strongly. Hegel unleashes the fluidity of thinking that can overcome the fixities of which he might be charged. There may still be considerable debate and disagreement about the heterodoxy of one or another formulation of Hegel, but what cannot be doubted is that orthodoxy is the horizon for that examination. Truth is what makes falsity possible. Hegel thoroughly grasped this; it accounts for the penetrating power of his thought. We cannot think outside of the horizon of truth, for we move within its dialectic before we have even begun. At a time when the Kantian revolution seemed to terminate in the irresolvability of the antinomies, Hegel and others grasped the bridge that was tentatively constructed in the Third Critique.[37] Truth is not something

---

35 See the long discussion of this in Voegelin, *The Ecumenic Age*, chap. 5, sec. 2.

36 A lengthy exploration is contained in Voegelin, "Wisdom and the Magic of the Extreme," *Published Essays 1966–1985*, chap. 13.

37 Immanuel Kant, *Critique of the Power of Judgment*, trans. Paul Guyer and Eric Matthews (Cambridge: Cambridge University Press, 2000).

at which we have to arrive but the possibility of any arrival at all. We are already one with truth before we ever set out. It is this realization that was at the core of Hegel's philosophical project as he shifted speculation from thinking about being to thinking within being. It is not so much that logic is the apparatus through which we approach reality as that it is the apparatus through which reality discloses itself to us. All of that reversal accounts for the linguistic strangeness of his thought, with its emphases on consciousness, spirit, notion, idea, and concept arriving at their own truth. Such terms do not function as hypostases but as indices, to use Voegelin's own usage, of the boundary within which thinking is carried on. As the internal dimensions of experience, they do not eliminate the substantive realities of God and man but enable their inner relationship to be explored more adequately. Just like the poles of Voegelin's Metaxy, which can never be included within it, they are nevertheless real as the indispensable condition of anything being between. The further we go with such reflections, the more we realize the convergence of Voegelin and Hegel in their respective thought worlds. There is even the vulnerability of each to the charge of drawing reality into the dynamics of consciousness or experience.

Once the shift has been made from the objectifying account of reality to the prior relationship that makes that possible, from intentionality to luminosity, then the danger of immanentism arises. We may be charged with absorbing all within the dynamics of consciousness. In many respects Hegel may be better placed for a rebuttal of the charge than Voegelin. The latter relies so heavily on the language of experience that it is difficult to defend it in non-experiential terms. Hegel seemed to be aware that no defense was possible except by going through the logic of disclosure itself—that is, that what emerges or appears is itself testament to the wherefrom that cannot emerge or appear, a line of reflection that was later fruitfully pursued by Heidegger. The crucial realization, in any case, is that consciousness is always consciousness of something. There may be debate about the reality status of what it intends, but there cannot be any doubt that it is not identical with consciousness. This was the vein that Hegel mined so successfully that we must regard his work as indispensable to rebutting all charges of solipsism. He even went as far as an examination of his own exercise in phenomenology. If phenomenology drives beyond the phenomenon, how do we characterize the exercise itself? Is it part of phenomenology, or is it more properly regarded as a science of reality? This tension was well reflected in Hegel's two "systems," where the *Phenomenology* was first conceived as a ladder to the *Logic*, and later became an integral part of the *System of Science* within the *Philosophy of Spirit*. Science itself rests on what is not science and yet for that reason must be included within it. The sophistication and depth of the Hegelian analysis is, in other words, breathtaking, and it must be viewed as regrettable that Voegelin made so little use of it as he painfully moved toward an almost identical position. They are virtually united in the insistence that consciousness not only knows reality but is also a part of it, for its most pivotal disclosure is not what it intends but what it renders luminous from within. In light of that massive convergence, we must be inclined to regard all talk of Hegelian sorcery as largely beside the point. In Voegelin's defense, we can only say that he was far from alone in the misreading, for this more positive appreciation of the position of Hegel is only of very recent vintage, apart from the occasional schools of idealism that flourished without themselves being well recognized by the philosophical mainstream.[38]

5. The Impossibility of Dispensing with Hegel

In the end we are inclined to attribute the misreading of Hegel to the power of metaphor itself. Once the epithet of sorcery had been hurled in Hegel's direction, it became difficult to find any alternative account of its fundamental structure. Voegelin's essay itself partakes of some of the mesmerizing effects of sorcery as a rhetorical device. Even today it is difficult to avoid being swept up in its powerful thrust, as we are launched upon a condemnation against which there is no defense. Any imputed defense would itself be further confirmation of the conjuring power of the speculator who is prepared to stir up the depths if he cannot storm heaven. Countervailing arguments serve only to solidify the charge. There is, in other words, something dangerous about invoking sorcery, for it has embedded within it some of the fascinating power it seeks to abhor. We ourselves experience something of its irresistible effect, for rhetorically this essay evinces considerable impact. In my own case it has taken decades to break free of its overwhelming force.

---

[38] One thinks, for example, of British Idealism as carried forth by F.H. Bradley, Bernard Bosanquet, as well as R.G. Collingwood and Michael Oakeshott. A parallel Idealist stream continued in America. Neither connected well with the dominant analytic schools or even with the existentialist approaches on the Continent.

Could it be that, if Hegel is the sorcerer, Voegelin is the sorcerer's apprentice? The suggestion is not as outlandish as it appears, for it does seem that in many respects Voegelin is as much the victim of the rhetorical powers he seeks to control. This is evident in the abandonment of his customary scientific coolness, dispensing with the actual texts for an esoteric reading of the motives behind them, and the rush to judgment on the basis of a rather slim marshalling of evidence. Sorcery is a dangerous game for both the practitioner and the target. Like metaphor, it has its own entrapments built in where the possibility of overturning is endemic. Perhaps it is better to avoid its incendiary potential altogether and proceed with a more pedestrian if less exciting reading of the texts.

In this regard we may draw a second lesson from the shortcomings of Voegelin's reading—that is, that Hegel can only be properly understood if he is placed in the context of his philosophical predecessors and successors. He is, after all, engaged in an extended conversation with Kant and a widening collaboration with the other Idealists, who sought to enlarge the revolutionary opening Kant had made.[39] No longer concerned about whether we know reality or can ground our moral convictions, we now realize that all of our endeavors are compelled to presuppose as much. There could be no thinking outside of the possibility of thought, just as there could be no morality apart from the admission of responsibility. We are already within an intelligible reality and a moral universe before we begin. Hegel and the Idealists made explicit what was only implied by Kant's more cautious delineation of the transcendental. There is a horizon of being within which we move. Human beings cannot hold reality at a distance as if they were outside of it, for they are thoroughly embedded within it. They are the point at which the self-disclosure of reality occurs. The history of philosophy after Hegel is not the story of the collapse of his great systematic ambitions, but the progressive deepening of the actual meaning of the system as a system of life. What Hegel had called his system was never completed, but an ever-living invitation to actualize the impulse of thought from which it had always

---

39 Some sense of the remarkable convergence on problems and questions can be seen in the manifesto that is so representative that its authorship remains in dispute. "The Oldest Systematic Programme of German Idealism," in Frederick Beiser, ed. and trans., *The Early Political Writings of the German Romantics* (Cambridge: Cambridge University Press, 1996), 3–5.

drawn its vitality. The lecture additions every year came to overwhelm the margins of the "system," which—it turns out—was only a syllabus for a viva voce performance.[40] In the hands of Kierkegaard and Nietzsche and, to a lesser extent, Marx, this existential character of philosophy became more abundantly clear. Philosophy became more and more what it had always been: a way of life rather than a speculative result. Contrary to the conventional perception that this was all a reaction against the Hegelian system, we are now more inclined to see it as a continuity and fulfillment. Far from arresting the movement of philosophy and bringing it to a dead end, Hegel had launched it on a new dynamic form that more faithfully reflects the dynamism of life itself. One of the things that makes his formulations both impenetrable and elusive is that he understood that stasis is the death of thought. Only thinking that is continually going beyond itself is true to what it is. To convey that movement through the fixity of words is a considerable challenge, but it is arguable that Hegel presented a tolerable demonstration of it. Voegelin knew this, but he did not recognize his own path from the fixity of ideas to the underlying dynamic of experiences and symbolizations as an almost identical transition.

It was only later that he began to acknowledge that his own enlargement of intentionality to the horizon of luminosity contained much of the Hegelian insight.[41] Then he was prepared to admit his filiation with the sorcerer he had previously excoriated. In light of that later reconsideration, we are naturally inclined to view the earlier essay in a different perspective. Once the convergence with Voegelin's own thought becomes apparent, we must revisit the essay with the suspicion that something more is at work than univocal condemnation. Could it be that Hegel is Voegelin's double?

---

40 The famous *Encyclopedia of Philosophical Sciences*, which comprised *The Logic*, *The Philosophy of Nature*, and the *Philosophy of Spirit*, expanded with the lecture additions that were supplied each year.

41 Even the title of the second chapter of *In Search of Order*, "Reflective Distance vs. Reflective Identity," bears the mark of Hegel's influence, as Voegelin fully acknowledged. Perhaps the most poignant passage is where he sees the connection between Hegel and Hesiod, both of whom must symbolize the gods who are absent, albeit in divergent fashions: "But how does a Beginning begin if there is no acting Beyond and nothing to be acted upon? Hesiod, it appears, has to cope with the same problem as Hegel, with the problem of telling a story that presupposes the experience of the Beyond without symbolizing it" (*In Search of Order*, 90–91).

Or, more accurately, that Voegelin is Hegel's double? It is surely the latter suggestion that accounts for the peculiar vehemence of the essay as Voegelin seeks to distance himself from the great predecessor to whom he senses he is so eerily close. A hint of parricide may even waft through the air. But that, as Voegelin knew, is impossible. Killing the father is tantamount to killing the self, once the identity of their projects is apprehended. If Hegel is the true echo of Voegelin's meditative exploration of the materials of history, then he can no more be denounced than Voegelin can renounce his own work. Instead, Hegel must be viewed as a collaborator who, even with his flaws, was embarked on the same course and therefore an indispensable resource who could not simply be tossed aside. Voegelin's later, more appreciative return to Hegel is an indication of his own growing awareness of the relationship. If it had occurred and included a wider appreciation of Idealist and post-Idealist philosophy, it might well have expanded Voegelin's theoretical apparatus as well as prompted a revision of the wider modernity narrative. The thread of continuity goes all the way back to the Parmenidean statement that thinking and being are the same, for the whole of Western philosophy can be read as a meditation upon it. In Voegelin's terms it is the realization that intentionality, the object relationship, is contained within luminosity, the embracing reality relationship. To the extent that we recognize this as the Hegelian core, we must conclude that the denunciatory tone of the Sorcery essay is something of an outlier within the gamut of reflections on his great predecessor. As usual, it is the later reconsiderations that reveal the relationship more fully, even when they remain in a state of incompleteness.

CHAPTER SEVEN

Christian Theology after Heidegger

Andrew Prevot

In this brief reflection, I do not pretend to be able to offer a comprehensive overview of Cyril O'Regan's works or a conclusive statement about his contributions to theology and philosophy, which are numerous and complex. Nonetheless, I do draw on a range of his published texts in order to uncover and understand something that seems essential to them. In short, I am interested in his carefully worked-out assessment of the possibility of doing Christian theology after Heidegger. An adequate appreciation of this aspect of O'Regan's thought may not unlock all the enticing passageways that are hidden in it, but it does open up many of them and reveals a great deal about the destination to which they lead—in a word, doxology. In a few more words: a type of doxology that is resistant to the dangers of philosophical modernity. Before considering the details of O'Regan's prolonged confrontation with Heidegger, which will occupy the second part of the paper, I shall in the first part discuss the role of philosophical contestation in O'Regan's thought and Christian theology more generally. Heidegger is not the only challenging opponent to face. Moreover, the very idea of doing theology in a way that goes beyond the mere exposition of revelation could use some explanation. To this end, O'Regan finds a helpful ally in Hans Urs von Balthasar.

The Role of Philosophical Contestation in Christian Theology

In *The Anatomy of Misremembering*, O'Regan praises Balthasar for contesting both Hegel and Heidegger.[1] O'Regan shows that this contestation does not take the form of a shallow polemic. Rather, it proceeds by means of a substantive critical engagement with the arguments, genealogies, stylistic forms, and genuine intellectual strengths of these distinct yet related modes of modern thought. If there is a canon of theologians and saints that Christians must remember well (along with, and as interpreters of, sacred scripture) in order to survive and thrive today—including figures such as Irenaeus of Lyon, Augustine of Hippo, Dionysius the Areopagite, Thomas Aquinas, Catherine of Siena, and Ignatius of Loyola, to name only a few—there is also a counter-canon of figures that must be both respected and rigorously resisted. For Balthasar and O'Regan, this counter-canon seems to feature Hegel above all the rest, with Heidegger a close second.

In certain respects, however, Heidegger may be the more demanding of these two philosophical rivals, because he is the more duplicitous and tempting. His later thought especially seems to exhibit something like a doxological reverence for the mystery of being, which may justly attract Christian attention. Moreover, to some extent, the contestation of Hegel can be read as just one massive battlefront in the fight with Heidegger. This is so because Christian theological engagement with Hegel seemingly cannot avoid Heidegger's interpretation of Hegel as the plenary instance of ontotheology. One might even suggest that the obligatory Christian ambivalence toward Heidegger starts at this Hegelian juncture. Not only does Heidegger's thesis about Hegel seem to hold some weight. It also reveals to Christians—perhaps as never before—the gravest consequences of the Hegelian danger: one cannot pray before such a god.[2] In short, Heidegger is attractive in the first instance insofar as he seems to help Christians see why they need to resist Hegel and how they might move beyond him doxologically. But the challenge then becomes this: how do we grant Heidegger the space to read

---

1   See Cyril O'Regan, *The Anatomy of Misremembering: Von Balthasar's Response to Philosophical Modernity*, Vol. 1: *Hegel* (New York: Crossroad, 2014), esp. 2–47 and 519–28.

2   See Heidegger, "The Onto-Theo-Logical Constitution of Metaphysics," in *Identity and Difference*, trans. Joan Stambaugh (Chicago: University of Chicago Press, 2002), 42–74, at 72.

Hegel as ontotheological without relinquishing western philosophical and Christian theological wisdom to the dissatisfying and dangerous fate that they will suffer in Heideggerian and post-Heideggerian hands? I shall return to this question in the second section below.

Balthasar is O'Regan's oft-preferred champion in this contest—not a solitary witness, to be sure, but a theologian of "thick retrieval" who is supported by the tremendous supplementary power of the numerous philosophers, theologians, artists, and saints whose insights he strives to preserve.[3] O'Regan suggests that such *ressourcement* alone, without contestation of Hegel and Heidegger, would not only be a weaker position for Christian theology to take, but may not even be entirely possible for readers in the present post-Enlightenment milieu. Restored access to the best that Christianity has to offer is dependent on memory, and memory is precisely what has been badly damaged in this "modern" age, whose very name associates it with the new casting off the old.

It is true that Hegel and Heidegger seem to promise memory as an antidote to modern forgetting—and this is one of Balthasar's main reasons for turning to them as part of an escape route from an anemic and amnesic neoscholasticism, which in its own way mimics the rationalism of the Enlightenment. Balthasar recognizes, however, that neither Hegel nor Heidegger provides the memory of Christianity or the Christian practice of memory in any unadulterated or fully acceptable forms. O'Regan suggests that one viable path forward thus may be, with Balthasar's assistance, to work our way through these two philosophical misrememberings of Christianity and the western tradition in order to reactivate our capacity for more salutary

---

3 See O'Regan, "Von Balthasar and Thick Retrieval: Post-Chalcedonian Symphonic Theology," *Gregorianum* 77, no. 2 (1996): 227–60. An important one of these supplementary figures is Erich Przywara, whom John Betz shows can also play the role of champion of the fight. See Betz's substantive "Translator's Introduction" in Przywara, *Analogia Entis: Metaphysics: Original Structure and Universal Rhythm*, trans. Betz and David Bentley Hart (Grand Rapids, MI: Eerdmans, 2014), 1–115. That Karl Rahner is also a viable theological representative in this struggle has been demonstrated by Peter Fritz in his *Karl Rahner's Theological Aesthetics* (Washington, DC: Catholic University of America Press, 2014). See also Doug Finn's compelling Augustinian approach in his *Life in the Spirit: Trinitarian Grammar and Pneumatic Community in Augustine and Hegel* (Notre Dame, IN: University of Notre Dame Press, 2015).

forms of cultural and spiritual recollection and guard them against further distortion.

O'Regan's search for a better practice of memory certainly does not imply that he construes the past as pure and the present as impure. On the contrary, he recognizes that contestation was constitutive of the best forms of Christianity in the past and, therefore, must remain operative in the present. His is not a message of nostalgia but rather of ongoing struggle. The intelligent, playful, and yet serious fight with Valentinianism and Marcionism that occupied the attention of the patristic era prefigures the sort of sparring that is necessary for the Christian community to think and develop today in the wake of Hegel the neo-Valentinian (who re-narrates Christianity in opposition to certain of its most fundamental commitments) and Heidegger the neo-Marcionite (whose aversion to Jewish thought and life and exclusive attachment to Greco-German patrimony must be vigorously combatted).

The stakes in these fights are quite high. Nihilistic outcomes of one sort or another seem to wait on all sides. To suggest that these struggles locate us in an apocalyptic battle where definitive events and decisions are made does not, however, isolate the modern age from the rest in a capitulation to its progressive view of time but rather emphasizes, not unlike the Nietzschean doctrine of the eternal return, the extraordinary gravity of each moment, including the present one. For O'Regan, however, unlike Nietzsche—another key member of theology's counter-canon, who intensifies Hegelian perils and feeds Heideggerian prejudices—the apocalyptic character of time has a Trinitarian and Christological meaning.[4] In the final analysis, getting clear about how to praise the Trinity and live in Christ is what is at stake in the hard-fought debates with Hegel, Heidegger, and (we might add) Nietzsche. This hope of finding a way already in history to participate in that doxology which remains eternally the vocation of the blessed is the much-more-than-merely-apologetic motivation of O'Regan's practices of philosophical contestation. We need

---

4 This Trinitarian and Christological meaning is clear in O'Regan, *Theology and the Spaces of Apocalyptic* (Milwaukee, WI: Marquette University Press, 2009). For a classic Christian engagement with Nietzsche and the doctrine of eternal return, see Henri de Lubac, *The Drama of Atheist Humanism*, trans. Edith Riley, Anne Englund Nash, and Mark Sebanc (San Francisco: Ignatius Press, 1995), 17–129 and 469–510. See also Patrick Gardner, "Modern Pentecost: Henri de Lubac on Atheism and the Spiritual Posterity of Joachim of Fiore" (Ph.D. diss., University of Notre Dame, 2015).

to remember well in order to have a future in which "God" will name more than the inevitable demise of the human spirit's strivings—the nihilistic threat that is resisted yet nurtured in different ways by Hegelian, Heideggerian, and Nietzschean renderings of the divine.

O'Regan gives Balthasar a great deal of credit for recognizing the Christian need to contest Hegel and Heidegger and for carrying out this contest in exemplary fashion by maximizing both Christian *ressourcement* and serious confrontation with modern misrememberings. Although Balthasar's work has received some perhaps well-warranted criticism from scholars of Aquinas, Karl Barth, post-Vatican II ecclesiology, Latin American liberation theology, and feminist theology, to name a few,[5] its generative power and creativity have also been appreciated by many theologians with varied interests and commitments.[6] Among sympathetic interpreters of Balthasar, O'Regan makes one of the strongest cases to date for the value of a continued, in-depth study. He helps one understand the Balthasar of *The Glory of the Lord*, Volume 5 (GL5) and shows how the complex evaluation of modern metaphysics that Balthasar makes in this text is prepared, expressed, and elaborated throughout the trilogy and his many other works, from the early *Apokalypse* volumes to the concluding *Epilogue*.

O'Regan has persuaded me that Balthasar deserves the credit that he gives him for this important theological work of contestation. At the same

---

5 See James J. Buckley, "Balthasar's Use of the Theology of Aquinas," *The Thomist* 59, no. 4 (1995): 517–45; Bruce L. McCormack, *Karl Barth's Critically Realistic Dialectical Theology: Its Genesis and Development 1909–1936* (New York: Oxford University Press, 1995); Gerard Mannion, *Ecclesiology and Postmodernity: Questions for the Church in Our Time* (Collegeville, MN: Liturgical, 2007), 59–60; and Karen Kilby, *Balthasar: A (Very) Critical Introduction* (Grand Rapids, MI: Eerdmans, 2012).

6 Among the increasing wealth of interpretations, consider Jennifer Newsome Martin, *Hans Urs von Balthasar and the Critical Appropriation of Russian Religious Thought* (Notre Dame, IN: University of Notre Dame Press, 2015); Kevin Mongrain, *The Systematic Thought of Hans Urs von Balthasar: An Irenaean Retrieval* (New York: Crossroad, 2002); Roberto Goizueta, *Christ Our Companion: Toward a Theological Aesthetics of Liberation* (Maryknoll, NY: Orbis, 2009); Mark A. McIntosh, *Christology from Within: Spirituality and the Incarnation in Hans Urs von Balthasar* (Notre Dame, IN: University of Notre Dame Press, 1996); and Todd Walatka, *Von Balthasar and the Option for the Poor: Theodramatics in the Light of Liberation Theology* (Washington, D.C.: Catholic University of America Press, 2017).

time, I must say that I would not have grasped this Balthasarian achievement with nearly the same precision without O'Regan's painstaking readings. In short, therefore, O'Regan deserves a great deal of credit too! Balthasar's theology needs not merely careful exposition (of the sort provided by Aidan Nichols, which has its own value),[7] but also a conceptually tightening and focusing interpretation that can sort through the thicket of allusions, images, and themes and place the lasting contributions into sharp relief. O'Regan provides this sort of interpretation and more. His detailed knowledge of Hegel and Heidegger, together with their antecedents, contemporaries, and inheritors—not to mention the extensive research on early, medieval, and modern theology; Gnosticism, mysticism, and apocalypticism; phenomenology, deconstruction, and post-structuralism, to list but a few areas—allows him to take stock of the debate from multiple sides and angles, in a sense to "magnify" it and thereby to conserve its gains for future generations.

O'Regan thinks about crucial issues in ways that are distinctly his own.[8] His Balthasarian overcoming of Hegel and Heidegger is productive and unique. We can weigh it against several comparable efforts by Jean-Luc Marion, Jean-Yves Lacoste, Jean-Louis Chrétien, John Milbank, David Bentley Hart, and (in a less overtly Balthasarian register) William Desmond.[9]

---

7 See, among the many helpful expositions by Aidan Nichols, his *Scattering the Seed: A Guide through Balthasar's Early Writings on Philosophy and the Arts* (New York: T&T Clark, 2006), which sheds particular light not only on Balthasar's earliest essays on music and art but also upon a text that is crucial for O'Regan's constructive analysis, namely Balthasar's three-volume *Apokalypse der Deutschen Seele: Studien zu einer Lehre von Letzten Haltungen* (Freiburg: Johannes Verlag Einsiedeln, 1998).

8 One could conclude nothing else after reading his *Gnostic Return in Modernity* (Albany: State University of New York Press, 2001).

9 Key texts would include Jean-Luc Marion, *The Idol and Distance: Five Studies*, trans. Thomas A. Carlson (New York: Fordham University Press, 2001); Jean-Yves Lacoste, *Experience and the Absolute: Disputed Questions on the Humanity of Man*, trans. Mark Raftery-Skehan (New York: Fordham University Press, 2004); Jean-Louis Chrétien, *The Unforgettable and the Unhoped For*, trans. Jeffrey Bloechl (New York: Fordham University Press, 2002); John Milbank, *Theology and Social Theory: Beyond Secular Reason* (Malden, MA: Blackwell, 2008); David Bentley Hart, *The Beauty of the Infinite: The Aesthetics of Christian Truth* (Grand Rapids, MI: Eerdmans, 2003); and William Desmond, *God and the Between* (Malden, MA: Blackwell, 2008). To be sure, other contemporary theological thinkers more sympa-

I do not wish to attempt such a full comparative analysis here, but it would be an interesting and worthwhile project, all the more so with O'Regan's thought in the mix. This analysis would demonstrate that a Christian theology that emerges victorious after contestation with Hegel and Heidegger could be configured in different ways and that these differences could be quite significant. What are the relative strengths and tradeoffs in various iterations of the collective search for a credible post-, non-, or anti-Hegelian/Heideggerian Christian theology? This could continue to be an energizing research question going forward.

Where Do We Stand on Heidegger?

As a first step in this direction, I want to consider somewhat more closely where O'Regan leaves us thus far on the question of Heidegger. Admittedly, we are still awaiting the second volume of *The Anatomy of Misremembering*, which will offer a thorough treatment of the Heidegger-Balthasar relationship, but already there are several indications in other works. Moreover, thanks to Jennifer Newsome Martin, I have had a chance to read manuscript drafts of several of the chapters of this highly anticipated second volume; these inform my perspective, but I will not cite them directly since they are not yet published. In addition to treating articles that O'Regan has written explicitly about Heidegger, I shall also consider certain ways in which Heidegger becomes a pivotal concern in texts about Hegel, Eckhart, Marion, and Desmond.

There is perhaps no better place to begin than with O'Regan's review of Laurence Hemming's *Heidegger's Atheism: The Refusal of a Theological Voice*.[10] O'Regan contends that Hemming's argument has three interlock-

---

thetic to Heidegger and post-Heideggerian thought than the figures on this list could also be worthy conversation partners: for example, Merold Westphal, *Overcoming Onto-theology: Toward a Postmodern Christian Faith* (New York: Fordham University Press, 2001); John Caputo, *Demythologizing Heidegger* (Bloomington: Indiana University Press, 1993); Richard Kearney, *Anatheism: Returning to God after God* (New York: Columbia University Press, 2010); and Thomas Carlson, *Indiscretion: Finitude and the Naming of God* (Chicago: University of Chicago Press, 1999).

10   See O'Regan, "Heidegger's Atheism (book review)," *Modern Theology* 20, no. 4 (Oct. 2004): 625–28, and Laurence Paul Hemming, *Heidegger's Atheism: The Refusal of a Theological Voice* (Notre Dame, IN: University of Notre Dame Press, 2001).

ing theses which, although stimulating and instructive, ultimately do not persuade, at least not in their strongest formulations: first, that Heidegger's thought is continuous (despite all talk of a poetic and neo-pagan *Kehre*) and thus permanently rooted in its ostensibly Christian (Pauline, Lutheran, Kierkegaardian) beginnings; second, that Heidegger's understanding of the death of God is consistent with Christian theology's need to rid itself of metaphysical idolatry; and third, *pace* Marion, that Heidegger himself therefore provides a respectable form of post-metaphysical Christian theology. O'Regan counters these claims by arguing that Heidegger's readings of Hölderlin and the idiosyncratic *Contributions to Philosophy* merit at least some recognition of significant discontinuity, that Heidegger's ties to Nietzsche strongly suggest that his atheism cannot be merely methodological, and that a one-sided theological affirmation of Heidegger is too selective and ignores the legitimate worries of Christian critics such as Balthasar and Marion. In short, O'Regan is not convinced. Nevertheless, he refuses to dismiss Hemming's argument precisely because Hemming refuses to dismiss Heidegger's. By recognizing the Christian roots of certain (even later) Heideggerian themes and the possibility of distinguishing Christian experience from apodictic philosophical reasoning, Hemming manages to be, by O'Regan's lights, at least half right. Hemming welcomes what really must be welcomed from Heidegger. What Hemming misses, or perhaps merely does not concede, is the need for an equally robust unwelcoming of Heidegger.

O'Regan specifies his preferred Balthasarian balance of welcoming and unwelcoming, or "valorization" and "critique," in two essays devoted specifically to the subject.[11] Some of the key areas of contention are as follows. First, there is the consideration of "phainesthetics"—that is, the blending of a phenomenological ontology and epistemology with a transcendental aesthetics that honors beauty as the way of access to truth. On this point, O'Regan finds considerable agreement between Balthasar and Heidegger. Nevertheless, he notes that Balthasar prioritizes a theological contempla-

---

11 See O'Regan, "Von Balthasar's Valorization and Critique of Heidegger's Genealogy of Modernity," in *Christian Spirituality and the Culture of Modernity: The Thought of Louis Dupré*, eds. Peter J. Casarella and George P. Schner, S.J. (Grand Rapids, MI: Eerdmans, 1998), and "Hans Urs von Balthasar and the Unwelcoming of Heidegger," in *The Grandeur of Reason: Religion, Tradition, and Universalism*, eds. Peter M. Candler, Jr., and Connor Cunningham (London: SCM, 2010), 264–98.

tion of glory, which (and this is just one among many of the perceived advantages of Balthasar over Heidegger) demands a stronger connection with the good, particularly as disclosed in divine revelation. Second, there is the challenge of defining nihilism and more precisely what sort of thought overcomes it. On this issue, O'Regan argues that Balthasar acknowledges some value in Heidegger's lament about the forgetting of being and the proposal of ontological difference. At the same time, however, Balthasar contends that a more successfully anti-nihilistic respect for ontological difference demands a properly theological doctrine of *analogia entis*, in the style of Erich Przywara, which respects divine transcendence over creaturely being. Third, there is the question of theodicy—the "why?" that appears in enormously different ways in Gottfried Leibniz and Angelus Silesius—and how to respond to it. O'Regan shows that Balthasar opposes Heidegger's purely contingent, Heraclitean interpretation of whylessness with a Christological and Trinitarian doctrine of grace, more consistent with Silesius's Christian context and commitments that get covered over, to use a Heideggerian locution, in Heidegger's rendition of the same.

Fourth, there is the matter of genealogy—including the questions of which sources are more problematic, which more helpful; the size of each of these sets; and the criteria of evaluation. Heidegger's interpretation of metaphysics as ontotheological seems, by his estimation, to undermine virtually the entire western tradition, with the exception of a few Greek and German poetic, mystical, or philosophical luminaries (e.g., Heraclitus, Eckhart, and especially Hölderlin), who must themselves be read in a particular way to meet Heideggerian requirements. O'Regan emphasizes that Balthasar's symphonic thought is much more hospitable to the broader Western canon of artists and intellectuals (including but not limited to Heidegger's favorites, whom Balthasar reinterprets as more nearly reflective of Christian glory). Moreover, Balthasar allows sources from sacred scripture and various doctrinal, theological, spiritual, and sacramental traditions to speak in ways that resist Heideggerian condemnation. Fifth, there is a question of the style of apocalyptic. O'Regan maintains that Heidegger's *Ereignis*, which at least provides some resistance to modern technocracy, is countered and surpassed by Balthasar's Johannine hermeneutics of scripture and salvation history, which are centered in Trinitarian love. Sixth, there is a debate to be had about forms of life. Against Heidegger's prescribed poetic dwelling, which is characterized by a secularized *Gelassenheit* to the event of being, O'Regan shows that Balthasar seeks to retrieve distinctively Christian modes of mission, kenosis, sanctity, prayer, liturgy, and loving action, carried out in Christ and the Holy Spirit.

The second volume of *Anatomy* will certainly develop these contrasts in more detail and add more contact sites to the list. This summary does, however, provide a reliable sense of some of the main lines of O'Regan's complex assessment of Heidegger. Another text to consider in this regard is his essay "Answering Back,"[12] which defends Augustine against early Heideggerian suspicions of an insufficiently ecstatic doctrine of time, later Heideggerian charges of ontotheological commitments, and post-Heideggerian depictions of a "post-modern Augustine," such as the one found in Derrida and Caputo, who seems mainly to have passions and questions.[13] A crucial part of O'Regan's argument is a rescuing of Plato from any simplistic accusations of rationalism suggested by Heidegger's controversial reading of the allegory of the cave in *Platons Lehre*. More importantly, though, O'Regan emphasizes—not unlike Marion in *Au lieu de soi*—the doxological character of Augustine's approach to questions of God, being, the self, time, creation, and so on.[14] If a telltale sign of ontotheology is the impossibility of prayer, then the author of the *Confessions* and the *Enarrationes* does not turn out to be a very plausible representative.

These direct treatments clarify O'Regan's positions. If we were to focus solely on them, though, we might underestimate the extent to which critically engaging Heidegger is a fundamental motif of O'Regan's work. I suggest that these essays are not occasional pieces or side projects but rather clues about what is most deeply at stake in his thought. To test this claim, let us consider *The Heterodox Hegel*. Is this in any meaningful sense a book belonging to the pursuit of a Christian theology after Heidegger? I want to assert provocatively that it is. In the introduction, after clarifying the nature of the act of interpretation attempted in the text, O'Regan writes: "Where

---

12 See O'Regan, "Answering Back: Augustine's Critique of Heidegger," in *Human Destinies: Philosophical Essays in Memory of Gerald Hanratty*, ed. Fran O'Rourke (Notre Dame, IN: University of Notre Dame Press, 2013), 134–84.

13 See Caputo and Michael J. Scanlon, eds., *Augustine and Postmodernism: Confessions and Circumfession* (Bloomington: Indiana University Press, 2005).

14 See Marion, *In the Self's Place: The Approach of Saint Augustine*, trans. Jeffrey L. Kosky (Stanford, CA: Stanford University Press, 2012).

the intimacy between theology and philosophy is such as to point to an intrinsic unity, modern philosophers and philosophically minded theologians have not been shy in speaking of 'ontotheology.' While the term is ugly, it can be justified on the pragmatic grounds that it is current in the modern critical assessment of Hegel." The endnote appended to this sentence cites Karl Löwith and Heidegger without much comment. But the following endnote demonstrates the greater seriousness of the Heideggerian position: "Löwith uses the term *ontotheological* to point to the de facto connection between religion, i.e., Christianity, and philosophy in Hegel's work. By contrast, Heidegger is pointing to an intrinsic connection that occurs at the infrastructural level of Hegelian thought wherein Being is identified with 'the ground of Being' and consequently hypostatized."[15] Like Heidegger, O'Regan seeks an understanding of an intrinsic connection between theology and philosophy in Hegel. The remainder of the book can, therefore, be read as a sustained reply and counterproposal to Heidegger's thesis about "the ontotheological Hegel." O'Regan's rival interpretation of "the heterodox Hegel" accepts this basic Heideggerian insight but greatly overpowers it in terms of hermeneutical precision.

O'Regan is far from satisfied with Heidegger's heuristic sketch of the ontotheological constitution of Hegelian metaphysics. He agrees that there is a problem and, more precisely, a grave threat to doxology that has something to do with conceptual overreaching and the turning of "God" into the ground of a system of knowledge or being. But he offers contemporary philosophers and theologians a more detailed and convincing discussion of this problem, which exposes Hegel's narrative techniques; his relations with Luther, Boehme, mysticism, and Gnosticism; and the various "swerves" involved in his nontraditional reconfiguring of Christian Trinitarian theology. What O'Regan gives us here is a way to oppose Hegel, as Heidegger powerfully suggests that Christian theologians must, but without any need to pay the exorbitant price that comes with strict fidelity to Heidegger's approach—namely the obligation to countersign his sweeping indictment of tradition as ontotheological, the consequence of which is an inability to remember well. O'Regan's contestation of Hegel not only does the work that Heidegger's seems to do without as high a cost. It is also stronger than

---

15   O'Regan, *The Heterodox Hegel* (Albany: State University of New York Press, 1994), 3 and 372, n7.

Heidegger's because it is more textual (versed in both primary and secondary literature) and more responsible to Christian sources. In this way, it provides a valuable model for critical engagement with other philosophers before or beyond Hegel that might also be implicated in something like an ontotheological distortion of Christianity. Although Balthasar would likely support this strategy of resistance, it is clearly an original contribution by O'Regan and arguably proceeds at a greater level of philosophical sophistication than Balthasar's comparable anti-Hegelian critique in GL5 and elsewhere (certainly with more focus and depth).

O'Regan's article on Balthasar's treatment of Eckhart in *The Thomist* performs a similar service.[16] It shows how the Eckhartian tradition of *Gelassenheit* might be recovered, as Heidegger would recommend under certain dubitable conditions of finite ontological transposition, but without any need to accept such conditions or to jeopardize continued Catholic reception of the wisdom of Aquinas—or, for that matter, Maximus the Confessor. In this article, O'Regan's careful reading of a key Heideggerian source gives us, once again, a better alternative to Heidegger, while explicitly taking seriously the challenge that he poses. O'Regan retains the revitalizing possibilities for thought and life about which Heidegger begins to remind us but avoids his unhelpful imprecisions and excessive genealogical restrictions. In short, *The Heterodox Hegel* and the *Thomist* article exemplify an effective way to contest Heidegger in the Christian theological consideration of both counter-canonical opponents (such as Hegel) and canonical representatives (such as Aquinas, Maximus, and conceivably Eckhart, who occupies an intriguing place of double inclusion in Heideggerian and Christian canons).

Dialogues with Contemporaries

To appreciate the extent of O'Regan's forays with Heidegger, one must also take into account his interpretations of contemporary Christian thinkers who have been greatly influenced by Heidegger. His review of Hemming's book provides some indication of this interest, as, of course, do his writings on Balthasar, but two other interlocutors worth considering more closely are Marion and Desmond. In "Jean Luc Marion: Crossing Hegel," O'Regan argues that it is not enough to contest Heidegger, as Marion does masterful-

---

16 See O'Regan, "Balthasar and Eckhart: Theological Principles and Catholicity," *The Thomist* 60, no. 2 (1996): 203–39, especially 207, n7.

ly in both his more nearly theological and more nearly phenomenological works. One must also explicitly take on the heavy burden (a cross, to be sure) of contesting Hegel. This contestation is necessary because any stipulated borders between theology and phenomenology (or "Revelation" and "revelation") that might be enforced for the apparent protection of both domains are always already vulnerable to haunting by a Hegelian spirit, which gives itself the right to cross such borders with impunity. As O'Regan puts it: "Borders, nexuses, betweens—this is where Hegelian discourse is to be found; indeed, this is what Hegelian discourse founds."[17]

Marion's first strategy for resisting Heidegger involves impressive re-readings of Nietzsche, Hölderlin, Levinas, Derrida, and Heidegger as imperfect witnesses to a Pauline and Dionysian adoration of divine distance. O'Regan applauds this approach elsewhere as consistent with Przywara and Balthasar, while suggesting that he favors Balthasar's thicker and more phainesthetic execution.[18] Marion's second strategy (spanning the period from *Reduction and Givenness* to *In Excess*) involves a rethinking of the Heideggerian "*es gibt*" through possibilities of saturated givenness intimated but not thoroughly elaborated in Husserl's first philosophy and thoroughly unanticipated by the categorical constraints of Kant's first *Critique*. It is this second strategy that seems to insist most on disciplinary borders. Yet already, by granting phenomenology the power to interpret Christian themes (despite the apparent proscription of Husserl and the objections of Dominique Janicaud and Paul Ricoeur),[19] this approach provides considerable evidence of these borders' permeability and, therefore, a certain susceptibility to Hegelian-style border crossing. O'Regan does not accuse Marion of "being" Hegelian; rather, he merely urges Marion to resist this danger of haunting more vigilantly.

---

17 O'Regan, "Jean-Luc Marion: Crossing Hegel," in *Counter-Experiences: Reading Jean-Luc Marion*, ed. Kevin Hart (Notre Dame, IN: University of Notre Dame Press, 2007), 95–150, at 132.

18 See O'Regan, "Unwelcoming of Heidegger," 267–70, and Marion, *Idol and Distance*.

19 See Dominique Janicaud, "The Theological Turn in French Phenomenology," trans. Bernard Prusak, in *Phenomenology and the "Theological Turn": The French Debate* (New York: Fordham University Press, 2000), 16–103, and Paul Ricoeur, "Experience and Language in Religious Discourse," in *Phenomenology and the "Theological Turn,"* 127–46.

O'Regan gives us reason to believe that Desmond's "metaxological" trilogy—which thinks being, ethics, and God in relation to "the between"—fares better on this precise issue.[20] Desmond confronts Hegel's dialectical appropriations of borders and conjunctions directly and offers a clear theoretical alternative in the form of the "metaxological." But what interests me most here is a different question, more pertinent to the discussion of Christian theology after Heidegger, namely the question of whether such a Christian theology should interpret itself as "metaphysical" or "postmetaphysical," whether this choice of affiliation matters, and what exactly is at stake in it.

There are a number of interpretive possibilities here. Perhaps few thinkers would be audacious enough to claim "ontotheology" as a badge of honor, in hopes of reversing the meaning of this typically negative epithet. But there is also the possibility of completely refusing Heidegger's description of metaphysics as ontotheological, whether through argumentative refutation, preemptive dismissal, or simply by ignoring it. If, however, one is willing to concede some legitimacy to Heidegger's concerns, one may nonetheless distinguish metaphysics into ontotheological and non-ontotheological types, perhaps corresponding to premodern and modern epochs or to categories of analogy and univocity, respectively. This seems to be Milbank's approach, and for the most part Balthasar's as well, on whom Milbank depends.[21] A similar, yet perhaps significantly different, possibility would be to treat ontotheology as a pervasive danger of erotic overemphasis that must be, but also can successfully be, resisted in the practice of metaphysics. This appears to be Desmond's view.[22] Finally, one can accept the Heideggerian

---

20 For O'Regan's interpretations of Desmond's trilogy, see his "Metaphysics and the Metaxological Space of the Tradition," *Tijdschrift voor Filosofie* 59, no. 3 (1997): 531–49; "The Poetics of Ethos: William Desmond's Poetic Refiguration of Plato," *Ethical Perspectives* 8, no. 4 (2001): 272–306; "What Theology Can Learn from a Philosophy Daring to Speak the Unspeakable," *Irish Theological Quarterly* 73 (2008): 243–62; and "Naming God in *God and the Between*," *Louvain Studies* 36 (2012): 282–301.

21 See Milbank, *The Word Made Strange: Theology, Language, Culture* (Cambridge, MA: Blackwell, 1997), 45, and Balthasar, *The Glory of the Lord: A Theological Aesthetics*, Vol. 5: *The Realm of Metaphysics in the Modern Age*, trans. Oliver Davies et al. (San Francisco: Ignatius, 1991), 9–47 and 646–56.

22 See O'Regan, "Metaxological Space," 534, and "What Theology Can Learn,"

claim that metaphysics is structurally ontotheological and yet attempt to rethink Christian sources and perhaps classical and modern philosophers as well in post-metaphysical terms, perhaps by reading them phenomenologically (here we find Marion's position) or deconstructively (here we find the Derridean Caputo).[23] The choice in this case depends on whether one thinks phenomenology is sufficient to avoid metaphysics or, on the contrary, that unremitting deconstruction is the last resort.

O'Regan appears too worried about the distorting tendencies of both phenomenology and deconstruction (and especially the latter) to embrace this last option. Such varieties of post-modern hermeneutics seem to him likely to be complicit in new sorts of misremembering, even if they succeed in placing us after modernity. And yet he appreciates the formidability of Heidegger's critique. This judgment leaves O'Regan in the company of Milbank, Balthasar, and Desmond—an intermediate space in which metaphysics (not unlike the Heideggerian thought that opposes it) occasions a response of ambivalence, involving both welcoming and unwelcoming. Although O'Regan, like Milbank, tends to be more sympathetic to the ancients and accepts the validating criterion of analogy, he seems reluctant to draw the dividing lines as sharply as Milbank often does. O'Regan is attracted to the interpretive flexibility displayed by Balthasar and perhaps especially by Desmond, through which they discern various impediments (whether "ontotheological" or otherwise) and true breakthroughs of metaphysical wonder in particular cases. O'Regan offers these two thinkers as representatives of theology and philosophy at their best, and yet he does not fiercely police the borders between them. In the effort to take what is needed from Hegel and Heidegger and stand guard against what is threatening, O'Regan recommends no figures more highly than Balthasar and Desmond, and perhaps what he wants above all is a combined reception of the two.

If I have any response to add here, it would be perhaps only to propose (as I have elsewhere) that Chrétien makes a significant contribution to the

---

249; Desmond, *Being and the Between* (Albany: State University of New York Press, 1995), 13–19, and *God and the Between*, 242–52.

23 For a good treatment of both options, see Caputo, "The Hyperbolization of Phenomenology: Two Possibilities for Religion in Recent Continental Philosophy," in *Counter-Experiences*, 67–94.

discussion of Christian theology after Heidegger.[24] In short, he reveals the possibility of an approach to doxological thinking that is flexible about the nature of phenomenology and therefore open to the disclosures that take place in theological, philosophical, spiritual, and poetic sources. He is more aptly classified as a phenomenologist than as a metaphysician, especially if one considers the manner of his argumentation: it is descriptive rather than deductive, transcendental, or speculative, and the question of being is not at the fore. And yet one would be hard pressed to find any signs of pervasive misremembering in his work. Phenomenology does not set up borders or restrictions for him the way it does for Marion. The question on my mind is what O'Regan thinks of this other possibility, alongside Balthasar and Desmond or as supplement to them. O'Regan notes that Desmond has certain phenomenological tendencies of his own: he seems to correct what is problematic in this tradition (a latent Cartesianism) and to capitalize on what is promising (descriptive finesse).[25] But what, precisely, is the relation of metaphysics and phenomenology in his work, and how does this differ from what one finds in the perhaps more rhetorically post-metaphysical Chrétien? Might we hope for a characteristically erudite and illuminating treatment of this matter from O'Regan in the near future?

---

24 See my *Thinking Prayer: Theology and Spirituality amid the Crises of Modernity* (Notre Dame, IN: University of Notre Dame Press, 2015), 140–59.

25 See O'Regan, "Metaxological Space," 541–43.

CHAPTER EIGHT

Delighting in the Truth

St. Augustine and Theological Pedagogy Today

TODD WALATKA

COMMUNICATING THE RICHNESS OF the Christian tradition in a world that is often hostile, whether openly or more subtly, to Christian faith and to students—even Catholic ones—who see the world perhaps only weakly through a full Christian vision, presents deep theological, pastoral, and pedagogical challenges. Leading students into an even relatively adequate understanding of the truth of God in modern classrooms, therefore, seems to demand not only a profound understanding of the Christian tradition but also a pedagogical expertise and deftness that is supremely sensitive to one's audience, its assumptions, and its particular needs. We have many models in the Christian tradition of remarkable teachers who met similar challenges with a simultaneity of faithfulness to the past and responsiveness to the present: Benedict of Nursia, Maximus the Confessor, Teresa of Avila, John Henry Newman, Martin Luther King, Jr., and many others come to mind. In this brief essay, I will think through the challenges of teaching theology today by focusing my attention on two such teachers: Augustine of Hippo and, if I may be so bold as to place him in such esteemed company, Cyril J. O'Regan. Cyril, of course, would most certainly decline placement at such a table of honor, particularly if one stubbornly demands that today's master-teacher be an expert in the latest educational technologies and pedagogical tricks of the trade. Indeed, he once joked that providing a handout to undergraduates was "about as much pedagogical sensitivity that [he] is capable of."[1] Cyril's pedagogical toolbox is probably not filled with what one might find in many educational programs across the country; indeed, this fact is part of what makes his masterfulness as a teacher so difficult to capture and to imitate. This challenge of naming what is so captivating in Cyril's teaching can be met, in part, by starting with someone else—Augustine, and, in particular, book 4 of his *De Doctrina Christiana*.

Book 4 of Augustine's classic on interpreting and teaching sacred scripture turns its attention more directly to the question of teaching that which has been discovered in one's engagement with Christian truth.[2] I will suggest a number of fundamental themes from Augustine in this brief essay, but I would like to start with a thread that runs through the book as a whole: namely, a call to delight in the truth and in one's audience's embrace of the truth. Augustine's text maintains a remarkable balance on the function of rhetoric with regard to "delight." On the one hand, even when lacking a certain eloquence, "the matter itself is pleasing when it is revealed simply because it is true."[3] Accordingly, the teacher of Christian faith "should prefer to please more with the things said than with the words used to speak them; nor should he think that anything may be said better than that which

---

1 In Cyril O'Regan, "Forgetting and Misremembering: Modernity and the Double Catastrophe Faced by Contemporary Theology," at St. Thomas University on October 5, 2015 (https://www.youtube.com/watch?v=a8AcuiWh94w), at the 12:20 mark in the video. I am grateful to Peter Fritz for this reference. I am grateful to a number of Cyril's former students for their input on Cyril's strengths as a teacher and mentor. In addition to Peter Fritz, comments from Andrew Prevot, Troy Stefano, Danielle Nussberger, Leonard DeLorenzo, Brian Hamilton, and Jennifer Newsome Martin contributed to this essay.

2 Augustine of Hippo, *De Doctrina Christiana*, 4.1.1 [henceforth *DDC*]. All quotations from *De Doctrina Christiana* are from Saint Augustine, *On Christian Doctrine*, trans. D.W. Robertson, Jr. (Englewood Cliffs, NJ: Prentice Hall, 1997). Although it is important to note that the distinction between "discovering" the truth (books 1–3) and "teaching" the truth (book 4) should not be overdrawn—there is much to learn about teaching the truth in the opening three books, for example—the basic distinction does indicate a shift in the work, a shift announced by Augustine himself (1.1.1; 4.1.1).

3 Augustine, *DDC*, 4.12.28.

is said truthfully."[4] On the other hand, in the face of opponents whose rhetorical skills exhilarate and move their audiences to falsehood, the Christian teacher must present the truth and use whatever rhetorical devices are necessary in order to arouse and move others to the truth. For "while the faculty of eloquence, which is of great value in urging either evil or justice, is in itself indifferent, why should it not be obtained for the uses of the good in service of truth?"[5] Indeed, one could rightly argue that *because* one is speaking the truth, "a need for greater powers of speaking" is even more urgent.[6] The balance to be maintained in these matters has to do with the orientation of the teacher to truth itself. It is important for Augustine that the Christian teacher has an eloquence that "teaches, delights, and moves" one's audience,[7] but, given that rhetorical delights can just as easily serve what is to be detested as what is to be loved, what is more foundational is the teacher's own delight in the truth and the willingness and even joy in undertaking the task of guiding others. Ultimately, the great teacher seeks to lead students to "feast delightedly" on the truth itself.[8]

I would be hard-pressed to find a better description of Cyril's approach to teaching than "delighting in the truth." He is certainly a masterful and cheerful rhetorician who delights in a skillful display of eloquence or finding the precise image or word that is right for the occasion. Nevertheless, it is the pressing need to communicate to others the fullness of Christian truth that one observes so powerfully in his classroom and writings. Augustine's vision of the teacher who delights in the truth could be unpacked in various ways. As embodied by Cyril in particular, an unrelenting commitment to the Gospel is unmistakably seen in his perceptive and sensitive diagnosis of error and his generous patience in accompanying others on their own journey to truth.

---

4   Augustine, *DDC*, 4.28.61.

5   Augustine, *DDC*, 4.2.3.

6   Augustine, DDC, 4.4.6. See John C. Cavadini, "The Sweetness of the Word: Salvation and Rhetoric in Augustine's *De doctrina christiana*," in *De doctrina christiana: A Classic of Western Culture*, ed. Duane W.H. Arnold and Pamela Bright (Notre Dame, IN: University of Notre Dame Press, 1995), 164.

7   Augustine, *DDC*, 4.12.27. Augustine makes explicit that this triad is drawn from Cicero.

8   Augustine, *DDC*, 4.11.26.

Part I. "The expositor and teacher of the Divine Scripture, the defender of right faith and the enemy of error, should both teach the good and extirpate the evil."[9]

The Christian faith is not taught in a context that stands neutral to the proclamation of the Gospel. Preachers and teachers do not encounter in their audiences *tabulae rasae* ready and simply awaiting the truth. Nor is this reality simply a matter of encountering a world that is eager but only partially able to receive the fullness of God's gift of life (the perennial "not yet" of Christian eschatology). Instead, history is marked by an antagonism that Jon Sobrino calls the "certainly not" to the Kingdom: what Augustine describes as the enduring presence of the darkness of the "city of man."[10] Augustine's own career as a Christian teacher in opposition to various corruptions of the Gospel testifies to this reality. His service to the truth throughout his sermons, theological treatises, controversial works, and biblical commentaries includes an energetic engagement with movements and figures that he judges to lead away from the truth. Augustine's insistence on opposing error in service to truth is certainly no less urgent for the contemporary Christian teacher. Delighting in the truth demands a naming and repudiation of error. Yet what is the proper way to take up this task as a teacher? How does one seek the truth and denounce falsehood without falling into the temptation of partisan polemics and unfair caricatures of opponents? How does one teach in such a way that both truth and error can be heard and recognized for what they are? It is on this need in particular that Cyril is an extraordinary guide and teacher. He manages to be a *masterful diagnostician of error* and yet at the same time is *capaciously generous* in engaging others.

Perceptive diagnosis is exactly what is needed in the contemporary world, as it is not always clear *what* the problem is or even that there *is* a problem. There is a particularly pernicious—because so utterly pervasive—form of error in modernity that makes it nearly impossible to see the error itself because it has shaped the very way we see the world: our very assumptions about what could be truth or how to adjudicate truth already lead

---

[9] Augustine, *DDC*, 4.4.6.

[10] For Augustine, see books 15–18 of *The City of God*. For Sobrino, see Jon Sobrino, *Jesus the Liberator: A Historical-Theological Reading of Jesus of Nazareth*, trans. Paul Burns and Francis McDonagh (Maryknoll, NY: Orbis, 1994), 125.

us astray. As Cyril writes in his recent *Anatomy of Misremembering*, "the Enlightenment becomes nothing less than the air that people breathe in the modern world," and its defenses are impregnable as long as the Enlightenment itself provides the criteria for judging truth and forming critique.¹¹ A key task of the Christian teacher today, therefore, is to help students perceive what hidden assumptions about the world, truth-claims, and values are veiled under the category of commonsense. What is needed is the revelation, akin to John Henry Newman's masterful engagement with liberalism, that "what once could be identified with the views explicitly espoused by a particular party [has] now become ethos; what once had been argument now [has] become presupposition."¹² What is needed, therefore, is *narrative* and *contextualization* to indicate that ideas often taken as natural and obvious—for instance, reason apart from faith must adjudicate truth claims; or it is more important to be ethical and nice than pious and religious—have a decisive whence in human history and thus need to be interrogated.

Cyril is an absolute master of such narrative and contextualization. The experience of many of his students—and the readers of his books on modernity—is that a veil has been lifted, and they are able to see the world and themselves in a new and transformative way. As he submits ideas and thinkers to "genealogical trial,"¹³ he opens a plentitude of avenues of thought and of living in the world for his students. Such experiences are the hallmark of distinguished teaching. In his near-classic work on college teaching, Ken Bain describes the most successful teachers as having a "sustained, sub-

---

11   Cyril O'Regan, *Anatomy of Misremembering: Von Balthasar's Response to Philosophical Modernity,* Vol. 1, *Hegel* (New York: Crossroad, 2014), 2. For two other examples of such diagnosis see David Bentley Hart, *The Experience of God: Being, Consciousness, Bliss* (New Haven, CT: Yale University Press, 2013), 50–64, on how modern scientific presuppositions unconsciously but dramatically impact our conception of God, and Willie James Jennings, *The Christian Imagination: Theology and the Origins of Race* (New Haven, CT: Yale University Press, 2010), on how modern theology functions within an examined and unseen "diseased social imagination" (7).

12   Cyril O'Regan, "Newman's Anti-Liberalism," *Sacred Heart University Review* 12, no. 1–2 (Fall 1991/Spring 1992): 87. This general point is made by Newman in John Henry Newman, *Apologia Pro Vita Sua,* ed. David J. DeLaura (New York: Norton & Company, 1968), 200.

13   O'Regan, *Anatomy of Misremembering,* 50.

stantial, and positive influence on how ... students think, act, and feel."[14] Of course, many studies of higher education point to significant failure in regard to such lofty goals.[15] How often do students leave a course seeing the world or approaching the world in a new way? How often does an introductory physics course lead to students actually *thinking* and *seeing* the world with a Newtonian perspective? How often does a survey of modern theology amount to more than an encyclopedic collection of thinkers and facts? Yet it is precisely this "more" that students of Cyril experience so profoundly. His historical narratives and contextualizations unveil hidden presuppositions and crucial historical, theological, and philosophical connections so clearly and evocatively that students are empowered to engage the past and their present in new and fruitful ways.

What I have always found particularly striking and compelling in Cyril's work is the unmatched combination of *precision* and *generosity* of his diagnoses. The most dangerous temptation of modernity is not the outright abandonment of religion; thus, it is not enough simply to present a broadside rejection of modernity. Modernity is so alluring because there is much good—even Christian good—within it and because its assumptions govern much of the world in which we live. If we are to reject, it is incumbent upon us to reject *correctly*. Appearances of error are often really reappearances of earlier thought forms under a new guise.[16] To take just one example, Hegel's ideas are so dangerous and enticing because of their intimate relation to traditional Christian thought, but they are ultimately a "misremembering" of the tradition, a "haunting" of ancient gnostic discourses, a "counterfeit" and "simulacrum."[17] A key part of this precision, however, is the generous way that Cyril presents the figures he engages. *Because truth is at stake*, the

---

14 Ken Bain, *What the Best College Teachers Do* (Cambridge, MA: Harvard University Press, 2004), 5.

15 See, in addition to Bain's *What the Best College Teachers Do*, Derek Bok, *Our Underachieving Colleges: A Candid Look at How Much Students Learn and Why They Should Be Learning More* (Princeton, NJ: Princeton University Press, 2006) and Erik Mazur, *Peer Instruction: A User's Manual* (Upper Saddle River, NJ: Prentice Hall, 1997).

16 See Cyril O'Regan, *Gnostic Return in Modernity* (Albany: State University of New York Press, 2001).

17 O'Regan, *Anatomy of Misremembering*, 110–11.

views of another must be presented in their strongest and most compelling forms possible. His small book *Theology and the Spaces of Apocalyptic* is exemplary in this respect.[18] At the conclusion of the book Cyril makes clear his preference for Balthasar and the "pleromatic" form of apocalyptic, yet I still remember Catherine Keller remarking at a panel on the book that it was the best presentation of her thought that she had ever read. I found the same thing in his presentation of Johann Baptist Metz in *Spaces of Apocalyptic*. Thinkers are understood deeply and rendered powerfully by Cyril, presented in a way that they would certainly recognize themselves.[19] This generosity toward intellectual friends and foes alike offers manifold gifts to students of Christian theology. It models authentic Christian love;[20] it enables students to be moved by what moved others;[21] and it displays a confidence that

---

18   Cyril O'Regan, *Theology and the Spaces of Apocalyptic* (Milwaukee, WI: Marquette University Press, 2009).

19   As one of Cyril's students remarked regarding his strengths: "[Cyril has] incredible generosity in reading figures and reconstructing their arguments in as powerful a way as possible. Cyril never beats up straw figures; if anything, he raises up the strength of counter-arguments beyond themselves(!) before addressing them" (Troy Stefano).

20   As Hans Urs von Balthasar says, "What could be more Christian than to hear out what one's fellow Christian has to say? This readiness is an integral part and an important sign of a living faith. Just as true love of God is shown in love of neighbor and cannot be divorced from it, so too a willingness in faith to accept God's truth cannot be separated from an openness to the word and truth of one's neighbor ... in a dialogue, a willingness to hear out the other is more important than talking. Such an eagerness to listen is in fact a dimension of our very faith" (Hans Urs von Balthasar, *The Theology of Karl Barth: Exposition and Interpretation*, trans. Edward T. Oakes, S.J. [San Francisco: Ignatius, 1992], 16).

21   In this way, Cyril embodies Barth's famous remark more than anyone I have met: "For me it would be a canon of all research in theological history, and perhaps in all history, that one should try to present what has engaged another person, whether in a good way or in a way less good, as something *living*, as something that has *moved* him in some way and that can and indeed does move *oneself* too; to *unfold* it in such a way that, even if one finally takes some other route, the path of this other has an enticing, or, if you like, a tempting attraction for oneself. Disregard of this canon, I think, can only avenge itself by rendering the attempted historical research unprofitable and tedious" (Karl Barth, *Letters 1961–1968*, ed. Jürgen Fangmeier, Hinrich Stoevesandt, and Geoffrey W. Bromiley, trans. Geoffrey Bromiley [Edinburgh: T&T Clark, 1987], 234 [letter 239]). I first came across this quote

Christian theology and truth can withstand its strongest adversaries.

Ultimately, the generosity of the Christian teacher is grounded in delighting in the truth, wherever it is to be found. As Augustine notes, "Every good and true Christian should understand that wherever he may find truth, it is his Lord's."[22] Joseph Ratzinger once remarked that Vatican II was a turning point in the Catholic Church because it represented the Church's overcoming its "anti-modernistic neurosis";[23] it represented the Church turning to the world with *confidence* in the truth it proclaimed. It is this confidence that the Christian teacher must embody in the context of the contemporary world. This requisite confidence is that which does not sustain itself by destroying caricatures or denying truth outside of theology or the Church, but instead diagnoses error clearly and precisely while simultaneously presenting a powerful vision of Christian truth. Cyril is clearly a teacher who is sustained by such delight and confidence in the truth and who is able to communicate the richness of the Christian tradition in such a way as to foster a sustained and substantial impact on how students see and live in the world.

Part II. "And the best method is that in accordance with which he who hears, hears the truth, and understands what he hears."[24]

Even a cursory reading of book 4 of *De Doctrina Christiana* will note the emphasis Augustine places on addressing the precise needs of one's audience. If one thinks of the teaching moment at its most basic level as an interplay among teacher, content, and student(s), it is the intellectual, spiritual, ethical, and/or affective transformation *of the student(s)* that is the sign of great teaching. A wonderfully clear and energetic oratorical performance fails at the most basic level if one's audience is unable to follow it or if it simply reinforces problematic biases or intellectual laziness. Augustine urges the teacher to take great care in how the truth is presented, taking into ac-

---

in a syllabus on the Christian Tradition from my colleague Randall Zachman; it captures in a powerful way what it looks like to learn the thought of Luther, Calvin, Voltaire, or whomever else from a great teacher such as Cyril.

22 Augustine, *DDC*, 2.18.28.

23 Joseph Ratzinger, *Theological Highlights of Vatican II*, trans. The Missionary Society of St. Paul the Apostle (New York: Paulist, 2009), 27.

24 Augustine, *DDC*, 4.10.25.

count the needs of one's audience and the teacher's desired end for students. He notes that at times a grand rhetorical style is necessary to move one's audience; other times a subdued presentation is what the situation calls for; and some subject matter may be entirely inappropriate to certain audiences. What makes one's pedagogical choices successful is the impact on the students. One must aim to speak "in a manner suitable to persuasion, but if he does not persuade, he has not attained the end of eloquence."[25] Leading others to the truth and, even more, to delight in the truth, is the exact challenge of teaching. Defending truth and combatting error in the abstract is one thing; *teaching* is another.

This aspect of Augustine's Christian teacher reminds me a great deal of St. Benedict's depiction of the required qualities of an effective abbot. The abbot must recognize the immense importance of his task and, therefore, never deviate from the truth in service of selfish ends; he must be a living example of the life of discipleship; he should not show favoritism except that which comes from praise of the accomplishment of the good; he must be deeply sensitive to the needs of monks, offering firm arguments, stern demands, tender patience, or cheerful encouragement depending upon the situation; and, ultimately, he must not "[treat] lightly the welfare of those entrusted to him. Rather, he should keep in mind that he has undertaken the care of souls for whom he must give an account."[26] Even if the roles of abbot and teacher are not interchangeable, Benedict's demands on the abbot are quite similar to Augustine's vision of the great teacher. If the teacher is to move others forward in accepting and living out the truth, he or she must attend carefully to those in his or her care.

It is important to note the obvious from the start: such demands raise the bar immensely for the teacher. It is clear in Augustine's text that the Christian teacher is expected to know a great deal and know it deeply—thus the first three books on how to discover the truth of Scripture. Such knowledge is a great asset, but it also presents its own challenges since, as we all know, experts are often poor teachers of novices. Novices and experts tend to organize and access information differently, and experts are always in danger of teaching as if their audience were like themselves—akin

---

25 Augustine, *DDC*, 4.25.55.

26 Saint Benedict and Timothy Fry, O.S.B. (ed.), *The Rule of St. Benedict in English* (Collegeville, MN: Liturgical, 1982), ch. 2.

to an expert chef instructing a novice to "cook until the sauce is at a good consistency," forgetting that the novice may not know what "a good consistency" is.[27] In one sense, I cannot imagine a person in greater danger of falling victim to the weaknesses presented by expertise than Cyril. If ever there were an expert! Yet he manages to succeed precisely in leading those new to theology into its richness and depths. For many students, it may appear that Cyril more or less just walks into class and speaks off the cuff, but, in reality, his work ethic in preparation for teaching is astounding. He has what one of his students aptly calls a "blue-collar approach to teaching."[28] One of his most beloved courses is his seminar on post-modernism. Even with material he knows inside out and on which he has published a great deal, he will spend hours shaping and reshaping his remarks, figuring out the most effective way to present the material in light of the intellectual and even spiritual challenges his students might face. Another temptation of expertise is to see the classroom as simply a place to perform—and be admired for—one's intellectual ability. Teaching is a performance of sorts, but one with an end beyond the performance itself, namely, with the purpose of bringing students closer to the truth. Eloquence and mastery are too often displayed out of vanity or a desire to be recognized, or out of a desire to perform one's intellectual and rhetorical superiority. But, as Augustine notes, "he who speaks eloquently is heard with pleasure; he who speaks wisely is heard with profit."[29] Of course, Augustine will also note that a combination of eloquence and wisdom is best, and such a combination is precisely what is experienced by students of Cyril. His teaching is no less eloquent for his attention to the needs of his students, but instead of a performance for the sake of praise, his immense rhetorical skills are put to the service of his students. As one of his students noted, such attention is on great display when he responds to students' questions and comments: "[Cyril] has an ability to make even poorly conceived questions or comments seem brilliant in the way that he finds the germ of truth or insight in it and transforms it, giving it dignity but never colonizing the question so that it becomes his. It still

---

27 For one clear account of this phenomenon, see Susan A. Ambrose, et al., *How Learning Works: 7 Research-Based Principles for Smart Teaching* (San Francisco, CA: Jossey-Bass, 2010), 46–58, 95–102. The example of the chef is from p. 99.

28 Peter Fritz.

29 Augustine, *DDC*, 4.5.8.

remains the student's question or insight, but the truest or most compelling version of it."[30]

This comment on Cyril's response to student questions is worth pausing over. Of the many characteristics of Cyril as a teacher that his former students highlighted, his *depth of attention and responsiveness* was most frequently and enthusiastically recommended. The generosity remarked upon above with regard to fellow theologians is—if it were possible—even more powerfully demonstrated in Cyril's guidance of students. As one student describes it, Cyril "exhibits the very charity so rare and so necessary in the academy in the attentiveness and dare I say admiration he lends to his students' own work."[31] Cyril understands deeply—usually more than students themselves—the strengths and weaknesses of his students and what precisely they need at a particular moment. Such understanding flows in part from a profound grasp of the modern world, but even more important is a willingness and desire truly to understand the other. Parallel again to his ability to present the views and arguments of others with great clarity and vigor, perhaps Cyril's greatest gift to his students—applicable to undergraduates but even more so to the graduate students under his guidance—is his incredible and unceasing commitment to help them fine-tune *their* arguments and broaden *their* theological and philosophical imaginations.[32] The sheer diversity of dissertations directed by Cyril—on Balthasar, Augustine, Hegel, Russian Orthodoxy, Rahner, post-colonialism, Newman, the Tübingen School, liberation theology, Henri de Lubac, Simone Weil, Franz Staudenmaier, and others—is simply amazing. But more important than an ability and willingness to work with such diverse student interests is *the manner in which he does it*. My own experience working with Cyril—and this is an

---

30   Jennifer Newsome Martin.

31   Leonard DeLorenzo.

32   As another student describes working on a dissertation with Cyril: "Throughout the time that I worked on the dissertation, I began to feel increasingly less like a student in need of some basic affirmation that Cyril was graciously prepared to give me and more like a junior colleague, with whom he was willing to engage in a genuinely critical and intellectual conversation. It was not as though he ever wanted to spar with me, pitting his point of view against my own. Rather, his allegiance was always to the best conceivable version of my argument. He would push back against me, for me—that is, with my argumentative aspirations in mind" (Andrew Prevot).

experience shared by many others—is that of him helping me find my own voice, not repeating his. Cyril's teaching and mentorship is a wonderful example of bell hooks's call for teachers to "approach students with the will and desire to respond to [their] unique beings."[33] It is a living out of Hans Urs von Balthasar's account of a love that helps the other overcome timidity through "inviting kindness ... at love's bidding, the object ventures to be what it could have been but would never have dared to be by itself alone."[34]

Conclusion: "Let [the teacher] so order his life ... that he offers an example to others, and his way of living may be, as it were, an eloquent speech."[35]

Although most of the fourth book of *De Doctrina Christiana* focuses on the act of teaching, a key thread of the text highlights the witness of the teacher's life. The teacher's *life* is to proclaim the truth as much as any speech, and indeed, Augustine argues, "the life of the speaker has greater weight in determining whether he is obediently heard than any grandness of eloquence."[36] Students of Cyril are likely to see the world and the Christian tradition in a new way; part of this phenomenon is the cogency and power of his arguments, but it is also the presence and witness of the person of Cyril himself. They are given an enduring example of delighting in the truth and an incredible devotion to the progress of others. Particularly in the present age and among young adults who seem to value "authenticity" above all else, Augustine's exhortation regarding the coherence of person and message is crucial. The Christian teacher must proclaim in word and deed that there is truth, that this truth can be found, and that the truth brings great joy.

Much of Augustine's vision of the masterful teacher comes down to basic orientation. Why does one pursue knowledge? Why does one desire to stand before a room of students or serve as their mentor? A mixture of vanity, pride, and need for power can easily infect even the best teacher, and Augustine warns against all of these temptations. Accordingly, he demands

---

33 bell hooks, *Teaching to Transgress: Education as the Practice of Freedom* (New York: Routledge, 1994), 13.

34 Hans Urs von Balthasar, *Theo-Logic I: Truth of the World*, trans. Adrian Walker (San Francisco, CA: Ignatius, 2000), 114–15.

35 Augustine, *DDC*, 4.29.61.

36 Augustine, *DDC*, 4.27.59.

that Christian wisdom must be patiently and passionately sought out for its own delights and for the betterment of others. It is with the latter that I would like to conclude. Cyril's graduate students have often remarked on how generous he is with his time. Even though he is a prolific writer with multiple deadlines almost every month, he cheerfully and generously gives of his time and does so with patience and full attention. I hope my experience can speak for scores of others in this regard. As I worked through magisterial figures during my graduate coursework, Cyril delighted as I came to a glimmer of understanding. As I progressed in my dissertation, he pressed, questioned, and encouraged me in order to help me find my voice and argument. In the last six years as his colleague, his encouragement and confidence in my work has been an incredible gift. In all of these various phases, Cyril has embodied the concluding exhortation for the Christian teacher in *De Doctrina Christiana:* he "labor[s] in sound doctrine, which is Christian doctrine, not only for himself, but also for others."[37]

---

37 Augustine, *DDC*, 4.31.64.

CHAPTER NINE

Philosophical and Theological Historiography in *The Red Wheel*[1]

Brendan Purcell

It is perhaps the case that we can locate three intertwining facets of Cyril's intellectual trajectory in his early foundation at University College Dublin (UCD). Of course, no one could have predicted this would be the case, but it looks to be at least plausible upon reflection. Cyril began the explicitly philosophical aspect of his lifetime's search for truth and transcendence in UCD's three philosophy departments: Metaphysics, Ethics & Politics, and Logic & Psychology. I began full-time teaching of undergraduate students there in the early 1970s. The freedom of faculty there to advance courses that draw on a multitude of discourses (philosophical, religious, theological, historical, and ideological), the breadth of the philosophy department that refused to exclude either analytical or continental forms of thought, and the implied—and sometimes explicit—respect for the insights of human tradition as they come to us in the present all find echoes in Cyril's considerable opus. His astounding ability somehow to integrate philosophy, theology, history of religion, and literature into a unifying cohesive viewpoint may have begun as early as his UCD years.

---

1 An earlier version of this article was published in *Claritas: Journal of Dialogue and Culture* 3, no. 1 (March 2014): 40–51. © 2014, Purdue University Press. Used with permission.

The contest to remember correctly in the context of massive cultural amnesia, especially with respect to Christian beliefs, practices, and forms of life have been at the center of Cyril's work from his first major publication, *The Heterodox Hegel*, through his *Gnostic Return in Modernity* volumes, his magisterial work on Hans Urs von Balthasar entitled *Anatomy of Misremembering*, his articles on Saint Augustine, and his recent spate of essays on Blessed John Henry Newman. And, of course, UCD lays claim to have been founded by Newman. Finally, his broad familiarity with Russian literature and theology would not implausibly have its roots at UCD; certainly, its germination would have been encouraged there. So the following is offered as a reflection on the kinds of courses I was allowed to teach and Cyril was permitted to take at UCD in view of these three areas of concern—interdisciplinary thought in search of truth, remembering against the backdrop of cultural amnesia, and the significance of Russian religious thought—that Cyril has brought to fruition in his own work. While I will not directly advert to Cyril's work in each case, it should be clear how these significant strands of his work are interwoven through the considerations of philosophical anthropology that I seek to teach.

Aleksandr Solzhenitsyn's *The Red Wheel*—Overcoming Historical Amnesia

To convey how his approach to the Nazi experience differed from current historiography, Eric Voegelin referred to Nietzsche's *On the Advantage and Disadvantage of History for Life*. Nietzsche had classified history as monumental, antiquarian, or critical. Monumental history aimed at inspiration from the past, antiquarian history at restoring it. But for Nietzsche, "only one who in a present emergency is in imminent danger of being crushed, and who seeks relief at any cost, has the need for critical, that is, evaluative and judgmental history." For Voegelin, what Nietzsche meant by critical history has to do with "the judgment of a past epoch that arises from a new spirit. In order to pursue critical history, therefore, it is not enough to *speak* differently—one must *be* differently. *Being* differently, however, is not something that is brought about by foraging in the horrors of the past; rather, on the contrary, it is the revolution of the spirit that is the precondition for being able to judge the past critically."[2]

---

2 Eric Voegelin, "The German University and the Order of German Society," in *The Collected Works of Eric Voegelin*, Vol. 12: *Published Essays, 1966–1985*, ed. Ellis Sandoz (Baton Rouge: Louisiana State University Press, 1990), 3–4.

Voegelin understood the major historiographies of ancient Israel, classical Greece, and ancient China as emerging from such a revolution of the spirit, in answer to the cultural destruction wreaked by world empires.³ He lists a series of those he called spiritual realists whose fate was not even to be *mis*understood in their own time—figures like Plato, Dante, Dostoevsky, and Nietzsche.⁴ *The Red Wheel* is Solzhenitsyn's immense historiographic response to the Soviet ideological empire. Surely the most extraordinarily unequal contest was that between the "calf" and the "oak"—an empire whose top party ideologist, Vadim Medvedev, successor to Mikhail Suslov, as late as 1988 could say: "to publish Solzhenitsyn's work is to undermine the foundation on which our present life rests."⁵

Since, as we've said, it's not the first time a historiographic work has tried to make sense of a civilizational catastrophe, we'll recall here an earlier historiographic quest for the meaning of a historical epoch in some sense equivalent to Solzhenitsyn's. This might not add anything to *The Red Wheel* but may enrich our appreciation of its implicit philosophical and theological density. So, from the Greek classical experience I'll suggest an equivalent to *The Red Wheel* in Homer. Then, as a theological profile for Solzhenitsyn's work, I'll draw on the central Christian insight into the meaning of history in the forsakenness of Jesus on the Cross as agonized expression in space and time of the inner life of the Trinity.

1. Homer's epic aetiology of the suicide of a civilization and *The Red Wheel*⁶
Since both Achaeans and Trojans spoke the same language and invoked the same gods, Voegelin reads the Homeric work as an aetiology of the civilizational disaster of a common Greek-speaking world at war with itself.

---

3 Eric Voegelin, "World Empire and the Unity of Mankind," in *The Collected Works of Eric Voegelin,* Vol. 11: *Published Essays 1953–1965,* ed. Ellis Sandoz (Columbia: University of Missouri Press, 2000), 134–55.

4 See Eric Voegelin, *History of Political Ideas,* Vol. 3: *The Later Middle Ages,* ed. David Walsh (Columbia: University of Missouri Press, 1998), 71.

5 John Dunlop notes how "Medvedev singled out *The Gulag Archipelago* and *Lenin in Zurich* for particularly scathing comments," in "The Solzhenitsyn Canon Returns Home," *Stanford Slavic Studies* 4, no. 2 (1992), 429.

6 Georges Nivat is one of several Solzhenitsyn interpreters who notes the Homeric element in *The Red Wheel,* where its dramatis personae, and perhaps Russia her-

He shows how Homer diagnosed the source of the disaster in the vices of its aristocratic anti-heroes. In terms of later Platonic categories, we can see these heroes as radically disordered through, for example, Achilles's anger, Paris's lust, and the stupidity of the Achaean King Agamemnon and the Trojan King Priam. The point of the diagnosis is that these failings are not merely occasional, but express deep-rooted refusals to engage with reality.

Anger: The *Iliad* opens with the phrase "The Wrath of Achilles," as if to underline just how Achilles's vice is central to the near-destruction of the Achaean army. He has been insulted by King Agamemnon and, although he heads the Achaean army's most powerful fighting force, no apology by the king will satisfy him. Only when his best friend Patroclus is killed because of his inaction does he admit how much he has *enjoyed* being angry (*Iliad*, XVIII, 108–09). The obvious equivalent for Achilles's anger is Lenin's massively self-indulgent and self-righteous hatred—not only of the Tsarist regime, but of anyone who in any way stands in the way of his own will. Even Sukhanov/Himmer, with only a short spell in jail to complain of for signing the Vyborg Manifesto, allows himself to be overtaken by this hatred—and let's presume that Lenin enjoyed his anger-fueled hatred just as much as Himmer did.[7] And there is always the mind-numbing and unremitting hatred of the educated classes for the Tsarist government.[8]

---

self, achieve the "wisdom through suffering" of epic heroes. See his "Restituer à la Russie son histoire: *La Roue rouge,*" in *Alexandre Soljenitsyne: Le courage d'écrire,* ed. Georges Nivat (Paris: Éditions des Syrtes, 2011), 184, 186. While Cyril's work on Gnostic discourses strives for a kind of taxonomic precision such that those for and against can accept the description, he nevertheless outs his own position clearly at the end of *Gnostic Return in Modernity*: "I see this modern line of discourse as a fabulous catastrophe in a double sense" (236).

7 Amazed at finding himself sitting at a massive desk, deciding on the freedom or imprisonment of high-ranking members of the Tsarist regime, Himmer, recalling his three months in prison, muses: "Revolution, that is revenge too! Revenge above all! The feeling of omnipotence filled him with revolutionary pride: how everything has changed!" *März Siebzehn, Zweiter Teil,* trans. Heddy Pross-Weerth (Munich: Piper Verlag, 1990), ch. 225, 257. [Due to my inability to read Russian, I've had to depend on the vicissitudes of *The Red Wheel*'s translations into English, French, and German, while the final volume of *The Red Wheel* is still being translated into French.]

8 Briefly, in Alexandre Soljénitsyne, *Réflexions sur la revolution de Février* (Paris: Fayard, 2007), 109.

Lust: Another profoundly destabilizing vice is conveyed by Paris's lust for Helen. As with Achilles, Paris refuses to consider that this lust will lead to the continuance of the civil war: nothing can stand between him and his desire for sexual fulfilment (*Iliad*, III, 437–47). Especially in *November 16* we can see how Zina's love affair symbolizes an infidelity at the heart of Russia, as does Vorotyntsev's with Olda. But perhaps here, too, we can group the disastrous priority the Tsar gave to family relationships over his responsibility both to the seven million soldiers at war and to all the Russian people. Included here can also be the Tsarina's indulgence of Rasputin, and Crown Prince Michael's preference to be with his wife rather than resolve the abdication crisis. All of these, while surely not falling under the category of lust, can be seen as irresponsible preferences for one's intimate sphere over and against the fate of Russia, both in 1917 and for the next seventy-five years.[9]

Stupidity: Stupidity in an ordinary citizen or soldier is not too serious a matter, but, as Solzhenitsyn has remarked in *August 14*, it can destroy a society when it occurs at the level of leadership.[10] It is this suicide of an entire society due to the stupidity of its rulers that Homer wants to highlight in his depiction of Kings Agamemnon and Priam. Agamemnon allows a "false dream" (what a psychoanalyst would call "wish fulfilment") to seduce him into thinking he can overcome the Trojan army without Achilles and his men, which earns him the cautious rebuke of Nestor, one of his advisers (*Iliad*, II, 76–83). Only later does he rue this willfulness, but blames the gods for it (*Iliad*, XIX, 78–144). And King Priam of Troy, too, instead of urging Helen to end the conflict, "addresses her as his 'dear child,' nowise to be blamed for the war; it is all the fault of the gods" (III, 146–70).[11] Perhaps no vice is focused on more in *The Red Wheel* than stupidity, a stupidity that is lethal when again and again it shields from reality the leading personalities in the

---

9   See Soljénitsyne, *Réflexions sur la révolution de Février*, 56.

10 "We may feel pity for the novice soldier when, caught in the evil toils of war, he first faces bullets and shellfire; but the novice general, however dazed and nauseated he may have been by the fighting, we can neither pity nor excuse." *August 1914*, trans. H.T. Willetts (London: Bodley Head, 1989), ch. 40, 302.

11 Eric Voegelin, *The World of the Polis* (Baton Rouge: Louisiana State University Press, 1956), 95. All my Homeric analogies are drawn from Voegelin's perceptive reading of Homer in the light of a philosophy of politics.

Court, in the Duma, and in public life.[12]

Irresponsibility as underlying all the disorders: In the first pages of the *Odyssey*, Homer focuses on the disordering belief that underlies all of these vices: the characters invariably blame the gods for their misdeeds. This is so common that Homer has Zeus "reflecting that men, through their own folly, create sorrow for themselves 'beyond their share'" (*Odyssey*, I, 34).[13] A modern version of blaming the gods would be Tolstoy's fatalism, strategically expressed in his conclusion to *War and Peace*, and opposed by the author of *The Red Wheel*.[14] On the other hand, there's the ideological determinism most clearly expressed by Himmer or the meaning imposed on the events by Marxists who realized that the revolutionary events didn't fit into their categories.[15] (Whether any ideologists, progressivist or Marxist, actually believe in historical determinism is, of course, another issue.)

Precisely through its diagnosis of the Greek disaster, Homer's epic leads beyond itself to make way for a universal philosophy for the whole of humanity. Similarly, *The Red Wheel* is not only the great epic of the twentieth-century catastrophe of the Russian people. Through the contrasting light, shadow, and darkness of its immense cast of characters—good, flawed, mediocre, and downright evil—there can be discerned the moral and spiritual foundations not

---

12   Almost any chapter of *The Red Wheel* will provide examples of what Voegelin calls "criminal stupidity," occurring whenever a political leader's stupid orders or instructions lead to the deaths of millions of human beings, "even if he himself does not understand this at all." See his *Hitler and the Germans*, eds. & trans. Detlev Clemens and Brendan Purcell (Columbia: University of Missouri Press, 1999), 106. Just one example would be the Provisional Government's non-arrest of Lenin and its do-nothing response to the armed workers' murder of three soldiers; see *Avril dix-sept I*, trans. Anne Coldefy-Faucard, and Geneviève and José Johannet (Paris: Fayard, 2009), ch. 89, 586.

13   Voegelin, *The World of the Polis*, 109.

14   Briefly in the famous declaration against Tolstoyan determinism in *August 1914* (1989, ch. 40, 302), a rejection expanded in the long discussion between Sanya and Varsonofiev in ch. 5 of *November 1916*, tr. H.T. Willetts (New York: Farrar, Straus & Giroux, 1999).

15   "Himmer explained to him that power had to be bourgeois at first because without preparation the proletariat was incapable of creating state power." *March 1917/Node III, Book 1*, tr. Marian Schwartz (Notre Dame, IN: University of Notre Dame Press, 2017), ch. 127, 478.

only for Russia but for every twenty-first-century society faced with the same ideologies, progressivist or ideological, still exercising powerful appeal today.

2. Voegelin's philosophical understanding of history

As with his *Gulag Archipelago*, Solzhenitsyn's approach to history has always been at the level of critical history in Nietzsche's sense. But there's more to critical history than even Nietzsche saw. In *Hitler and the Germans*, Voegelin applied Plato's and Aristotle's insights in philosophical anthropology, where they understood human existence as occurring within the space-time universe yet intrinsically oriented beyond it. This transcendent orientation is due to our participation in the divine ground of our existence. Our principal task, then, as Aristotle put it, is "to immortalize as much as possible," to live our earthly existence simultaneously in and toward eternity.[16]

History, then, is the flow of this mortal/immortal existence, what Voegelin calls the flow of our existence in the eternal presence of the divine. Quoting T.S. Eliot's phrase from his *Four Quartets*, "the intersection of the timeless with time," Voegelin affirms history as "a pattern of timeless moments."[17] In fact, Solzhenitsyn comes very near to this formulation in *The Red Wheel*, where Peter Struve is aware of the need to live simultaneously in the past, present, and future, a temporality grounded in the trans-temporality of divine being—represented symbolically in the text by the image of the noonday sun: "The people live simultaneously in the present, the past and the future. And we are obligated to our great past ... Otherwise this won't be freedom but the Huns-invasion of Russian culture ... Generously, the holiday had been granted a triumphant sun."[18]

---

16 In his *Nicomachean Ethics*, Book X, vii, 8.

17 In *Hitler and the Germans*, 71, Voegelin speaks of the "presence" of human existence lived in openness to God's judgment, where "the meaning of the past and the future will become generally interpretable only when starting out from this presence. For otherwise everything would proceed irrelevantly in an external stream of time."

18 *March Seventeen, Book 1*, ch. 44, 206–7.

3. A theological profile for *The Red Wheel*—Piero Coda[19] on Sergei Bulgakov's kenotic theology

Christ's Descent into Hell

In his study of Sergei Bulgakov, Piero Coda discusses how in his *The Lamb of God* Bulgakov speaks of what St. Paul in his Letter to the Philippians, 2:7, describes in terms of Christ's self-emptying or kenosis on the Cross. In that self-emptying, "Christ undergoes the punishment for our sins. Such a punishment, as was his taking on of sin, was equivalent to what awaited humanity, that is, the suffering of hell." Coda quotes Bulgakov as seeing this to be "the greatest kenotic concealment of the divinity."[20]

The Trinitarian Meaning of Kenosis

For Bulgakov, "the divine mystery ... is that the Father receives the Son in the emptying of his death and keeps him until the resurrection." Nor does this self-emptying occur only in the Son: "This forsakenness of the Son is an act of the Father, which means that he both accepts the death of the Son and participates in it. Because to allow the Son to suffer on the cross is certainly not death for the Father, yet it is a kind of spiritual co-dying in the sacrifice of love."

> And the Holy Spirit is deeply involved in the event of the Son's forsakenness and death: the Son's devastation and death mean that he is also forsaken by the Spirit.... The Holy Spirit returns, so to say, to the Father when the Son's death is accomplished in the intensity of the divine forsakenness.... So this aspect of the Holy Spirit's participation in the Son's kenosis ... in some way extends the Son's kenosis to the third Person. Because this is the kenosis of Love in Person (the Holy Spirit): not to be manifested to the Well-Beloved (the Son).[21]

---

19   Cyril O'Regan, in *The Heterodox Hegel* (Albany: State University of New York Press, 1994), several times refers to Italian philosopher-theologian Coda's *Il negativo e la trinità: Ipotesi su Hegel* (Rome: Città Nuova, 1987). See *Heterodox Hegel*, 5, 8, 63.

20   Piero Coda, *L'altro di Dio: Rivelazione e kenosi in Sergei Bulgakov* (Rome: Città Nuova, 1998), 140.

21   Coda, *L'altro di Dio*, 139–41.

This means for Bulgakov that "The sacrifice of the Son presupposes the reciprocal sacrifice of the entire Holy Trinity...."[22]

The Red Wheel's Implicit Theology of History

I am not saying that Solzhenitsyn is consciously drawing on Bulgakov's understanding of the relationship between the forsakenness of Jesus on the Cross and the Blessed Trinity, but Bulgakov's approach will, I think, illuminate various moments in *The Red Wheel*. Coda shows how, for all his limits, Hegel was perhaps the first of the moderns to assert the centrality of Christ's death out of self-sacrificing love and the Trinity for an adequate comprehension of history.[23] And Solzhenitsyn's implicit Christianity has led him to an understanding of the Russian tragedy as in some way a participation in the forsakenness, death, and resurrection of Christ, where that event is also an irruption of the inner life of the Trinity into history, and indeed into Russian history. *The Red Wheel* is full of hints of a theology of history, many of them already well commented upon. David Walsh has noted that General Samsonov's redemptive significance in the story far outweighs his military incapacity.[24] And Bulgakov's kenotic theology in *The Lamb of God* encourages us to see Samsonov as the sacrificial lamb, representing both the dying Christ and the dying, if not suiciding, Russia. Not only is Christ, the incarnate Son, forsaken; in their losing the Son, the Father and the Holy Spirit are also forsaken. This is what I have been calling the explosion of the unlimited interpersonal Love into our world of space and time. In the Trinity, each of the Persons "loses," "becomes nothing" for the sake of the other, and it is this eternal life of Love that the self-emptying of Jesus brings into our world.

And, of course, the Trinitarian conclusion to *November 1916* could be seen as the therapeutic center of the whole *Red Wheel* cycle.[25] It is enacted by Zina's slow pilgrimage through the church of Our Lady of Tambov, where her soul unites as Trinity her separate iconic encounters of God

---

22   Ibid.

23   Piero Coda, *Il negativo e la trinità: Ipotesi su Hegel* (Rome: Città Nuova, 1987).

24   See David Walsh, *After Ideology: Recovering the Spiritual Foundations of Freedom* (San Francisco: HarperCollins, 1990), 167.

25   I was first alerted to the importance of this passage by David Walsh in his *After Ideology*, 168–69.

the Father, Christ the Savior, until finally, in receiving absolution, "another Breath, the Spirit, hovered over her and stole tremulously into her."[26] In his "Repentance and Self-Limitation in the Life of Nations," and later in *Rebuilding Russia*, Solzhenitsyn has focused on the need for purification and repentance across the whole society if Russia is, like Zina, to be able to free itself from the great rocks weighing its soul down, one by one.[27]

Russia's Descent into Hell

If we move on to chapter 430 of the third volume of *March 1917*, called "The Presentation of the Cross," we get some more theological clues. Vera is attending the church service with her nanny, whose preferred place in the church is beside the icon of Christ's Descent into Hell, again reminding us of Bulgakov's understanding of Christ's Holy Saturday in Hell: this is what St. Paul calls Christ's becoming sin for us (2 Cor. 5:21), his in some way identifying with us in our own willed forsaking of God.

The chapter concludes with a magnificent promise of endurance, an endurance oriented toward the resurrection of Jesus—and, we can say, of Russia as well. The congregation's chant, "we prostrate ourselves before Thy Cross, O Lord," seemed to have "a unifying power which nothing on Earth could shatter." As with the inner life of the Trinity, where there is both the utter oneness of perfect Communion and the utter freedom of Persons in Love, there is "a fraternal rushing together where each one yields to the other ... a space was left which allowed one to fall face down on the ground, then to kiss the great silver cross surrounded by flowers without thorns. By Thy Cross the power of death will be destroyed."[28]

Throughout *The Red Wheel*, dreams are taken as prophetic messages,[29]

---

26 Solzhenitsyn, *November 1916*, 988–99.

27 Alexander Solzhenitsyn, *From Under the Ruins* (Harmondsworth: Penguin, 1974), 105–43; *Rebuilding Russia: Reflections and Tentative Proposals* (London: Harvill, 1991), 45ff.; *November 1916* (ch. 75), 997.

28 *Mars Dix-Sept*, III (Paris: Fayard, 1997), ch. 430, 276, 280.

29 Other prophetic or dream messages are Kuzma's dream of the old man weeping uncontrollably—for Kuzma, but he realizes, perhaps also for Russia, in *März Siebzehn: Erster Teil*, ch. 69. Or the prophecy of the old man of Uglitch, in *März Siebzehn: Zweiter Teil*, ch. 236, where Vsevolod hears of the terrible times awaiting Russia, which will last until seven generations from the present.

perhaps none more so than Varsonofiev's dream in chapter 641 of *March 1917*, which might be an answering dream to Raskolnikov's frightening vision of a horde of terrorists tearing themselves apart, itself an anticipation of the unleashing of Dostoevsky's *Devils* on Western civilization. Varsonofiev dreams he is in a Stock Exchange, with a huge crowd all looking in different directions, quite unlike the united congregation Vera had been part of. "A young boy whose face glowed with a wonderful light" came before the crowd, and "Varsonofiev understood that the boy was Christ and that he held a bomb!—to blow up the entire planet!" Unable to bear the tension, Varsonofiev woke up, but "The horror of that cosmic explosion still gripped him."[30]

Varsonofiev's reflections continue on what is one of his central themes, "that all the events of our own life and also those of others, are connected to us and between them, not only by the clear connections of cause and effect seen by the whole world, but also by secret connections ... which we do not even suspect—not only their existence but that they have a determining effect, they form souls and their destinies." Returning to the contents of the dream, he wonders which Stock Exchange it was—not Petersburg, not Moscow, maybe not even in Russia, or at any rate, "not only Russia. The meaning was universal."[31]

Now his thoughts move indistinctly in the direction of the redemptive effect of the cosmic explosion: "it wasn't only annihilation, it was Light too, the boy's face shone with too great a radiance." And "these unknown forces are at work! In a dimension we're unaware of something great is coming about—and perhaps the whirlwinds that have passed through the streets of Russian towns these last few weeks are only a dim reflection of this."[32]

Another dream of Varsonofiev is about a mysterious ceremony where a small group of twelve—priests and laypeople—are sealing up a church, aware they'll be imprisoned when they've done this. Again, he thinks that "the explosion at the hands of the luminous young boy has even wider dimensions" than this symbol of imminent and dire persecution, and he concludes with an apocalyptic insight into the revolutionary upheaval that in some way matches the paradoxical resurrection through destruction being brought about by the

---

30   *Mars Dix-Sept*, IV (Paris: Fayard, 2001), ch. 641, 563–66.

31   Ibid.

32   Ibid.

young Christ. Speaking of the empty celebrating of the crowds in the streets, he notes that "The people didn't see that their rejoicing only concealed the great Disaster.... Everyone was amazed at the colossal upheaval which occurred without any force whatever. Yes, without any earthly force."[33]

The battle for Russia's soul between utter hatred and utter love

Solzhenitsyn has nothing of the Tsarina's pietistic religiosity, which—not unlike the Homeric anti-heroes—conveniently ascribes all causation to God. Rather, for Solzhenitsyn, "God doesn't intervene so simply in human affairs. He acts through us and means us to find a way out for ourselves."[34] Voegelin warns against a demonizing of Hitler, which would avoid the real mystery of human evil[35]—that famous line between good and evil we're told about in *The Gulag Archipelago* that every human heart can wander across. Instead of portraying Lenin as a satanic figure, *The Red Wheel* allows him to speak and think for himself in such a way as to approach Voegelin's preferred characterization of Hitler, drawing on the words of English historian Alan Bullock—eerily accurate for Lenin:

> To achieve what he did Hitler needed talents out of the ordinary which in sum amounted to political genius, however evil its fruits ... mastery of the irrational factors in politics ... insight into the weakness of his opponents ... gift for simplification ... sense of timing ... willingness to take risks ... considerable consistency and an astonishing power of will in pursuing his aims.... [But] these remarkable powers were combined with an ugly and strident egotism, a moral and intellectual cretinism.[36]

Still, behind and beyond as well as in and through Lenin, it is possible to envisage a cosmic battle between Jesus Forsaken on the Cross and the Evil One, enacted on the battlefield of Russian humanity. The implications

---

33   *Mars Dix-Sept*, IV (Paris: Fayard, 2001), ch. 641, 563–66.

34   *Times Literary Supplement*, Interview with Solzhenitsyn, May 23, 1975, 562.

35   See his *Hitler and the Germans*, where he criticizes historians who employ Goethe's term "demonic" to characterize Hitler, 147ff.

36   Ibid., 151.

of that battle have scarred humankind since it was fought out in Russia from the second decade of the twentieth century. Solzhenitsyn quotes Sergei Bulgakov, writing at Constantinople in 1922 after his expulsion from the USSR: "Why has Russia been rejected by God, condemned to putrefy and die? Our sins are grave, but not sufficient to explain this historically unique destiny. Russia has not deserved this destiny, it's like the lamb that bears the sins of Europe. It's a mystery we have to accept in faith."[37]

Partly answering Bulgakov's anguished question, *April 1917* gives at least an echo to Vera's experience that "By Thy Cross the power of death will be destroyed." In chapter 91, Xenia meets Sanya at a Moscow students' party, noticing his cross of St George. In her brilliant performance of the czardas, "she came to see, with clarity, how he would be in the future. Towards the meeting with the Future! Ours!" Later, "He was orthodox, and not for a joke. (We'll definitely get married in church)." It's not surprising she dreams of a kind of love that mirrors the Love of the Trinity: "With all her being, Xenia felt another love, where, while you loved, you didn't make war. Where, however, to abdicate your freedom didn't mean to give up freedom completely!"[38]

A Candle in the Wind

In an illuminating essay, Andrey Nemzer focuses on how this young couple bears within them a hope for the future of Russia.[39] In Апрель 17, the couple strolls in the Alexander garden, and she is telling him how, during the days of revolution while walking there, she saw children playing and dreamed of having a son. "But this is just what Sanya desired: exactly! Exactly a son! They were able to open up to each other, to speak of him as if he were already born." After praying at the Iverskaïa chapel, they "set off and again passed by the Alexander garden. Again, they speak about him—our son. How they would live—for him. How they would bring him up. And how they would give him all the best."[40]

---

37 Soljénitsyne, *Réflexions sur la revolution de Février*, 117.

38 Soljénitsyne, *Avril dix-sept, I* (ch. 91), 594, 596, 597.

39 André Nemzer, "Comment se termine La Roue rouge," in *Le phénomène Soljénitsyne: Écrivain, stratège, prophète* (Paris: François-Xavier de Guibert, 2009), 147–69. All references here to the still-untranslated second volume of *April 17* (using its Russian title) are taken from Nemzer's essay.

40 Апрель 17, II, 367, 369.

Nemzer remarks: "A son will be born—he will become that writer whose word will make his parents live again, their love, their Russia, which, plunged into darkness, will remain for him unique and forever beloved." He sees this occurring through a book (*The Red Wheel*) that will help to bring Russia back to life, and continues: "We can understand why it is indispensable that the future author should appear here."[41] He quotes Varsonofiev in *Апрель 17*: "Does anything in the world exist stronger than the line of life, exactly life, which binds the descendants to their ancestors?"[42]

We remember Solzhenitsyn's remark that "If we wait for history to present us with freedom and other precious gifts, we risk waiting in vain. History is us—and there is no alternative but to shoulder the burden of what we so passionately desire and bear it out of the depths."[43] Like King Pelasgus in Aeschylus's *Suppliants*, faced with the life-imperiling decision "to act or not to act," he has indeed performed his own *De Profundis*—where at times it seems as if he alone expressed Russia's "One Word of Truth." He exemplified in himself the same revolution of the spirit he asked of his fellow Russians: "'deliberate, voluntary sacrifice.... We shall have to 'rediscover our cultural treasures and values' not by erudition, not by scientific accomplishment, but by our form of spiritual conduct, by laying aside our material well-being and, if the worst comes to the worst, our lives.'"[44]

In *The Red Wheel*, "the true protagonist is Russia herself."[45] We can suggest

---

41 Nemzer, "Comment se termine *La Roue rouge*," 164.

42 *Апрель 17*, II, 369. Nemzer continues in a footnote: "It goes without saying that Varsonofiev doesn't know what will become of his visitors. And even less that he could suppose a son would be born to them who would write about the Russian revolution as he would probably have done. But it's just after this unexpected visit to the hermit—with good reason misunderstanding the restless political affairs, and (rightly) convinced that 'history isn't made in meetings'—that he admits to himself: 'it's only through earthly events that we can carry out cosmic battles.' He thinks about leaving his familiar house to go somewhere to seek his path, to act. 'This young couple, happy to be alive, had come to Varsonofiev for a purpose. It restored faith and compassion to him. And the spirit of decision'" (*Апрель 17*, II, 555–56). In: "Comment se termine *La Roue rouge*," 165, n46.

43 *From under the Rubble*, 1974, x. See Walsh, *After Ideology*, ch. 4, "Ascent from the Depths."

44 Ibid., 271ff.

45 "Interview with Nikita Struve," in John B. Dunlop, Richard Haugh, and Mi-

that for Russia—and for all of humanity in this new century—few more than Solzhenitsyn have fulfilled Alex's hope in *Candle in the Wind*: "I'd like to help pass on to the next century one particular baton—the flickering candle of our soul."[46] Daniel Mahoney remarks that Solzhenitsyn believes Providence plays a special role in the individual life of human beings, but also in the collective life of nations and peoples. This affirmation of Providence is *the* key to understanding Solzhenitsyn's religiosity."[47] It's out of that conviction that Solzhenitsyn "recited every day in the final period of his life"[48] his 1997 "Prayer for Russia":

> Our Father, All-Merciful!
> Don't abandon your own long-suffering Russia...
> In her woundedness...
> And confusion of spirit....
> Don't let, don't let her be cut short,
> To no longer be.
> So many forthright hearts
> And so many talents
> You have lodged among Russians.
> Do not let them perish or sink into darkness
> Without having served in Your name.
> Out of the depths of Calamity
> Save your disordered people.[49]

Not unlike Homer's *Iliad*, Solzhenitsyn's Providence-centered historiography and spiritual conviction invites us to recover the spiritual foundations of Western civilization. In the different key of a lifetime of dedicated and courageous scholarship, Cyril O'Regan's immense œuvre surely is another massive recovery of the transcendent sources of Judeo-Christian culture at a time, indeed, of mortal danger.

---

chael Nicholson, eds., *Solzhenitsyn in Exile: Critical Essays and Documentary Materials* (Stanford, CA: Hoover Institution Press, 1985), 312.

46   Aleksandr Solzhenitsyn, *Candle in the Wind*, tr. Keith Armes (London: Bodley Head, 1973), 134.

47   Daniel J. Mahoney, *The Other Solzhenitsyn: Telling the Truth about a Misunderstood Writer and Thinker* (South Bend, IN: St. Augustine's Press, 2014), 188.

48   Ibid., 190.

49   In *The Solzhenitsyn Reader: New and Essential Writings 1947–2005*, eds. Edward E. Ericson, Jr., and Daniel J. Mahoney (Wilmington, DE: ISI Books, 2006), 634.

CHAPTER TEN

O'Regan as Origen in Alexandria

ANN W. ASTELL

There are two men in every one of us.
—Origen Adamantius

The self is an idiot—there is something other in it, more intimate to it than it knows with complete determinacy.... It is its own voice and the voices of others.
—William Desmond

IN AN UNUSUALLY SELF-REVEALING memoir, Cyril O'Regan writes about a childhood experience dating from the days when his family lived in public housing in a poor district on the outskirts of Limerick City, Ireland. A neighbor, whom O'Regan names "Mike," regularly came home soused on Saturday nights, after the pubs had closed, and played Mozart loud enough for young Cyril to hear. "The music," O'Regan reflects, was "a small act of heroism, Mike's declaration of hope that beauty could and maybe ultimately would win out over the ugliness that enveloped a person and seeped into the soul."[1] Unlike "the Catholicism that saturated our public lives," he observes, "Mike's Mozart made the darkness luminous."[2]

---

1   Cyril O'Regan, "Ambassadors of Divine Glory," *Reflections: A Magazine of Theological and Ethical Inquiry from Yale Divinity School* (2015). See http://reflections.yale.edu/article/divine-radiance-keeping-faith-beauty/ambassadors-divine-glory. Accessed June 4, 2017.

2   Ibid.

In O'Regan's recollection, hearing Mike's Mozart was a prelude that tuned his ear to poetry: "In high school I began to learn that literature, poetry in particular, could serve the same purpose. The poets came and went—Blake and Shelley, Yeats and Eliot, Mandelstam and Akmatora, Milosz, Hölderlin, Rilke, Benn, Baudelaire, Rimbaud, Char, Neruda and Paz, Hughes and Heaney. All of them provided a music of here, the music of what passes and ties together the scattering of time and the implosion of space."³ In their poetry, O'Regan discovered again and again the "signature of that divine music [he] shared with Mike,"⁴ the signature of the Incarnate Word, crucified on Calvary.

From the time of his school days, O'Regan confesses, "An appreciation of the grace-like features of literature never left me."⁵ This is so despite his keen awareness of artistic beauty's historical propensity to offer itself, especially in modernity, as a rival to grace, an idolatrous substitute for religion.⁶ In this regard, O'Regan would defend poetry against itself, not only against philosophy and history, literature's usual contenders in the academy.⁷ Echoing Dostoevsky's Prince Myshkin, O'Regan avers: "The beauty that [truly] saves comes in the night and may not be recognized when it comes, because it has not forgotten the traces of the ugliness overcome."⁸ Indeed, precisely in its fleshly woundedness and vulnerability, the hard-won beauty of music and poetry points to the cross of Christ, thus overcoming the conflict that has "made it difficult [since the Reformation] to think of theology and beauty as anything other than bitter rivals."⁹

---

3   Ibid.

4   Ibid.

5   Ibid.

6   See Cyril O'Regan, "August Rivalries: Post-Romantic Contesting of the Biblical Narrative in Harold Bloom and Philip Pullman," *Religion and Literature* 46, no. 2-3 (2014): 35-51, 219-20.

7   On poetry's excellence over philosophy and history, see especially Philip Sidney, "Defence of Poesy," first published in 1595. On the complementarity of poetry and philosophy, see William Desmond, *Philosophy and Its Others: Ways of Being and Mind* (Albany: State University of New York Press, 1990), 34-39.

8   O'Regan, "Ambassadors of Divine Glory."

9   Ibid.

Readers of O'Regan's academic books and articles are well aware of his abiding interests in the beauty that Hans Urs von Balthasar names "the glory of the Lord,"[10] the theological aesthetics of Hegel,[11] the poetry of William Blake and Friedrich Hölderlin,[12] the hymns of John Henry Cardinal Newman,[13] and the philosophical aesthetic of William Desmond.[14] Some readers may also have noted the beautiful dedicatory poems—to his wife Geraldine, his son Niall, and his brother Tommy—that preface O'Regan's various books. Most would be surprised, however, at the sheer volume of O'Regan's own poetry and at the consistency with which he has practiced it for years as a necessary companion to his academic writing, an incarnational counterbalance to the heady abstraction and acute analysis of his published prose, perhaps even as a life-giving means of personal purification, integration, and illumination. In contrast to O'Regan's philosophical theology, his poetry, like a Shakespearean fool's wisdom, gives a stammering utterance to what cannot be articulated clearly and definitively.

In lyrics entitled "Earth" and "Theologian,"[15] O'Regan contrasts ini-

---

10   See Cyril O'Regan, *The Anatomy of Misremembering: Von Balthasar's Response to Philosophical Modernity* (Chestnut Ridge, NY: Crossroad, 2014). Cf. Hans Urs von Balthasar, *The Glory of the Lord: A Theological Aesthetics*. Vol. 1: *Seeing the Form*, ed. Joseph Fessio, S.J., and John Riches (San Francisco: Ignatius Press, 1982).

11   See Cyril O'Regan, *The Heterodox Hegel* (Albany: State University of New York Press, 1994); *Gnostic Return in Modernity* (Albany: State University of New York Press, 2001); *Gnostic Apocalypse: Jacob Boehme's Haunted Narrative* (Albany: State University of New York Press, 2002).

12   These poets are treated in forthcoming volumes of O'Regan's book series on Gnosticism. On Hölderlin, see Cyril O'Regan, "Aesthetic Idealism and Its Relation to Theological Formation: Reception and Critique," in *The Impact of Idealism: The Legacy of Post-Kantian Thought,* Vol. 4: *Religion,* ed. Nicholas Adams (Cambridge: Cambridge University Press, 2013), 142–66.

13   Cyril O'Regan, "Foreword," in *Heart to Heart: A Cardinal Newman Prayerbook* (Notre Dame, IN: Ave Maria Press, 2011), vii–xx.

14   Cyril O'Regan, "The Poetics of Ethos: William Desmond's Poetic Refiguration of Plato," *Ethical Perspectives* 8, no. 4 (2001): 272–306. Nota bene: I take the epigraph to this essay from William Desmond, *Art, Origins, Otherness: Between Philosophy and Art* (Albany: State University of New York Press, 2003), 177.

15   These two poems by O'Regan belong to a larger set entitled *Poetry Sacred and Profane.*

tially the poet and the theologian not only through images of darkness and light, but also by pronominal gender. "The poet is always she: / Wet womb, water receiving, / Concave waiting on spears of light.... She is clarity's thief" ("Earth," 1–3, 10). The theologian, by contrast, is "he": "He is round as an O / Being's rivet, no / Choice but to be / the purr of fullness"—he whose satisfaction "wipes its hands / On an infinite circumference / leaving no stain," and whose smiling answers, ever orthodox, forestall questions ("Theologian," 1–4, 5–10). Only in his dreams does the theologian acknowledge the power of earthen desires "deep / under his house" and enter there "the labyrinth worshipping / ancient chthonic gods" ("Theologian," 15–16, 19–20), whose very darkness paradoxically protects the mystery of light. There, in the ground beneath his house, perhaps the "he," the theologian, finds himself also to be a "she," a poet, in an encounter with beauty. In a passage familiar to O'Regan, Simone Weil (1909–1943) likens the world's beauty to the "mouth of a labyrinth," at the center of which "God is waiting to eat" the lovers of beauty, but only to transform them: "[They] will have become different, after being eaten and digested by God."[16]

O'Regan's "O"

O'Regan's *Origen in Alexandria*—a large collection of forty mainly unpublished, undated, and still tentatively arranged poems—effectively grounds the well-rounded "O" of the academic theologian who inhabits a two-storied house of flesh and spirit.[17] An irresistible pun associates Origen, the great third-century Father of the Church, with the beginnings, the origin, both of Christian theology per se and of the poetic, multi-layered, biblical exegesis that bridges the Old and New Testaments—for example, in Origen's famous commentary on the Scriptural poem, the Song of Songs. "O'Regan" and "Origen" do not exactly rhyme, nor is the *persona* of the lyrics to be identified straightforwardly with author's "I." Still, a tri-syllabic consonance and the matching letters O, R, G, and N announce an anagrammatic wordplay, marking the collection as a signature piece. ("I don't need to confess," Cyril

---

16 Simone Weil, *Waiting for God,* trans. Emma Craufurd (New York: Putnam, 1951), 164.

17 Subsequent references to individual poems in *Origen in Alexandria* are parenthetical, by title and line number(s).

confides, "that he [Origen] is channeling an alternative me."){[18]}

Through the pun on origin, the "O" of Origen also recalls the Greek letter omega and its counterpart, alpha (at the opposite end of the alphabet), to inscribe a Christological allegory of the Incarnate Word: "I am the Alpha and the Omega, the beginning and the ending" (Rev. 22:13; cf. Rev. 1:8). The first poem of *Origen in Alexandria* intones the quest: "On the delta the questions end / And begin. Who is my father? / My father my father? God? Adam? / My soul returning? The cross / I did not carry?" ("Who Is My Father," 8–12). The questions of origin quickly metamorphosize into questions of location and identity: "Where are you? / Lost in the maze of the delta / Beyond the stars who are you? / Where do you begin?" (12–15).

The questions of place, in turn, transpose the questions of paternity. The speaker is "lost in the maze of the delta" ("Who Is My Father," 13), a place named after the triangular, fourth letter of the Greek alphabet and associated by its shape with feminine fertility. The chthonic "labyrinth" of the closing lines of O'Regan's "Theologian" thus reappears here as a "maze." The speaker of the great theological and philosophical questions wanders in a womblike delta, which is also the site of Alexandria, a city (we are told) named after Alexander the Great, who founded it in answer to an oracle: "The city rises from the clasp of water / And heat and hungers to continue / Beyond any reason the philosopher provides" ("Who Is My Father," 27–29). (Alexander, we may recall, questioned an oracle concerning his own true paternity, legend naming his father not Philip II of Macedon but the god Ammon, rumored to have impregnated Alexander's mother Olympias in the mythic form of a dragon or serpent.)[19]

Like Eliot's *Wasteland* (1922), but lacking that occult poem's accompanying authorial footnotes, O'Regan's *Origen in Alexandria* employs an ancient and distant place, Alexandria, as a figure for the present modern scene. A Hellenistic citadel in an indeterminate time, Alexandria mirrors present-day western pluralism, uprootedness, and syncretism in its own cosmopolitan intermingling of Egyptian, Greek, Hebrew, Roman, and Christian traditions; in its challenges to identity formation; in its iconic wonders of library, lighthouse (*Pharos*), and necropolis. In this prismatic Alexan-

---

18 Personal email correspondence, dated July 6, 2017.

19 See Claude Mossé, *Alexander, Destiny and Myth*, trans. Janet Lloyd (Baltimore, MD: The Johns Hopkins University Press, 2004), esp. 73–93, 179–80.

dria, the sun-worshipping pharaoh Akhenaten and his queen are reduced to "hieroglyphs / Of the story they long to purge," their unforgiven "passion for the simple" ("Akhenaten," 26–27, 21) meeting with rebellion and the revenge of the Sphinx. The confusion of things in the city may benumb the soul, inducing somnolence even in the sentry, but the creative tension in the mix is also, as some of O'Regan's lyrics express, inherently apocalyptic, volatile, monstrous, expectant.[20] In their own way, O'Regan's visionaries thus echo Yeats's repeated sentiment in "The Second Coming" (1919): "Surely some revelation is at hand" (3, 9).

Apocalyptic themes come to the fore in several of O'Regan's poems. In two lyrics from "Waiting for the Barbarians," for example, he pictures Alexandria as its citizens face an imminent invasion. Choking on a bone, some cling to the denial of eschaton: "The world does not grow old" ("Waiting for the Barbarians," 46). Their best hope is that the barbarians will bring more of the same, affirming their own tottering belief in the world's eternity. Understanding the "barbarian" as a speaker of a strange, ungrammatical language, others anticipate the intrusion of divinely foreign speech as a saving means to purify their own, too-tired sophistry and self-deception: "The barbarians are our god, last hope / To dry the marsh we sink in" (2, 15–16). Envisioning the barbarians as Jacob's angels descending "by ladders from a hole in the sky" to offer sacrifice in the city, these Alexandrians find themselves speaking "the unsayable," becoming barbarians themselves: "They are already here / They are our souls turned inside out" (8, 13–14).

In another poem, "Apocalypse," the speaker—a Noah-figure—faces the deluge in the strength of a divine promise: "All I need is the promise of light. / Inundation can be postponed / While I build my ark" (1–3). A new Adam, this Noah dreams of an ark where "words are not slippery," where "all animals find their names" (4, 7). Pledging himself for a new creation, the speaker regrets that the city and its environs are unprepared for conversion: "The delta is snot-green viscous / Refusing the cleansing of the sea" (20–21). Still, he recalls how a thrown stone once skimmed the surface of the water to clear an "opening to the bluest sky" (24). The poem's ambiguous final image refashions the theologian's "O" and answers to Noah's

---

20 For an analysis of apocalyptic themes in contemporary theology, see Cyril O'Regan, *Theology and the Spaces of Apocalyptic* (Milwaukee, WI: Marquette University Press, 2009).

declared need for a "promise of light": "I sense torches dance in a circle / challenging the numb franchise of night" (28–29).

The "I" in *Origen in Alexandria* is often poised on an edge between life and death, rising and falling, sleep and wakefulness, even as the city itself stands between the sea and the desert, banked on the mighty river that flows from Egypt into the Mediterranean. In "On the Nile," imagery, identity, and location are suitably fluid. Twice repeating the conditional clause "If the world is a sketch / in the possible" (1–2, 28–29), the speaker dreamily wonders aloud whether he indeed has ever existed in his own right: "It might / Be I was never there, nor here" (2–3), or whether he has simply served as a conduit of received doctrine, "Only rehearsing instruction / To the soiled and the broken" (4–5), "Catechizing the cabbage plant / and the dirty sunt" (15–16), "fated only to remember / Another's notes and words / In the fog of the never happened" (31–33).

River-like, ferrying "a teacher" who rides "on the river's uncatchable center" (8–9), the words of the poem's speaker identify him both with the teacher who catechizes and, metonymically, with the labyrinthine river that flows and seasonally overflows: "And I am the river plodding / Before the rainy season" (12–13). The contrast between the river's center and its bank effectively transposes in a horizontal plane the vertical contrast in "Theologian" between upper and lower stories of the theologian's house. Even before the rain, the boundaries of the river blur with the marshy land at its sides—a blurring the poet associates with sex and fertility: "I enter the pores of the girl- / Woman who will always find / Her way to the edge" (20–22). Similarly, the borderline between waking and sleeping, between dreaming and waking, proves permeable and potentially fruitful: "the silence is arable / And I can throw my seed" (43–44). The river's name, Nile, obliquely evokes that of the poet's son, Niall, even as the collocation of the teacher's catechizing word and the river's seed recalls events and parables from the Scriptures—Jesus preaching from a boat (Lk. 5:3; Mk. 4:1), baby Moses in the wicker basket among the river's reeds (Ex. 2:3), the sower throwing seed that sometimes lands on good soil (Matt. 13:1–23).

The Nile, in its dreamy, fecund wandering, sometimes resembles another origin for O'Regan—the dark, watery, and formless waste of Genesis 1 over which the wind of the Spirit hovers like a brooding bird. The poet speaks of a yet-unrealized potential in himself, an inchoate waiting to be and to become: "I am not born today, / I puddle, a moist claim / leaking everywhere and nowhere / ... / I am not born. Love / Has not yet crossed my path / And named me" ("I Am Not Born," 1–3, 25–27). A creative, divine, and human naming follows in Genesis—the beauty it awakens soon to be occluded, however, by the serpent's misnaming, human sin, and lost love. Evoking the biblical land of exile "east of Eden" (Gen. 4:16; cf. Gen. 3:24), the speaker of "Loneliness" laments the human unmaking that results from the alienation between fallen man and woman, their "divorce" after "a nuptial union always at the beginning" (22–23): "East of the loneliness you feel / Is the loneliness you are / The birth of the remains / The remains of your birth / What would have been" (1–5).

The poem "Adam" explores the post-lapsarian memory of Adam's own origins through voices he confusedly remembers having heard: the voice of the tree of temptation, of the serpent ("one of the stippled things"), of an unnamed speaker, of a whisperer—all of whom continue to tempt him. The tree pronounces doom: "You / Have put your hope to sleep, / Strangled what you love" (1–3). Speaking truth to mislead, the slant-eyed serpent denies responsibility: "I have not named you. / You swim tadpole / In the fluid of the possible" (16–18). The third voice denies that a paradisiacal beginning ever occurred: "You are always where you are / Fallen to, the animals never / Answered to their names" (20–22). And the whisperer cleverly refashions the misogynistic association of womanly fickleness and betrayal with that of Lady Fortune, blindly spinning her wheel: "Your mother was a weaver of arcs / Nowhere intersecting" (32–33). The latter insinuation leaves Adam speechless in reply, but also wondering plaintively whether he owes his existence purely to a personified Fortune: "Is she the chisel / In the mangle of accident? / ... / Is she everything I am?" (38–39, 42).

By contrast, the speaker in "Vision" identifies perseverant hope itself with the searing memory of a lost paradise: "Whatever it is, it arrives / Exhausted, its origin a far country" (1–2). Tending to this vision, the speaker finds himself stripped naked by it, peeled "to the bone / exposed to the snake's blind look" (5–6). Freshly graced by revelation, but mortal and still vulnerable to the tempter, the visionary's hope for salvation waits for, and rests upon, the fulfillment of another's promise. The new creation for which he waits inevitably recalls the beauty of the first: "I wait and scan the sand / between the reamed grief / of a barren now and the wild / orchards of then" (9–12).

Inhabiting Alexandria

Apart from Origen himself, to whom O'Regan devotes a single poem (discussed in part 3 of this essay) and whose voice (refracted through O'Regan's) may or may not be heard in other, anonymous lyrics, the lyric *personae* of *Origen in Alexandria* may roughly be divided into three types: those named for biblical figures (Moses, Jacob, Job, Hagar, Adam), those impersonating mythic figures (Ulysses, the Cyclops), and those representing philosophers and rhetoricians of the ancient schools. None of these figures speaks, of course, in his own right, but as they are imagined to speak by a poet, draped in Origen's cloak, who identifies a shadowy, possible side of himself with each of them, calling it by their names.

Exposing these shadows to light in fragmentary confessions of first-person speech, O'Regan retools an ancient grammatical assignment—namely, the invention by pupils of speeches such as the young Augustine gave when, following "the paths set by poetic fictions," such as Virgil's *Aeneid*, he "recite[d] the speech of Juno in her anger and grief that she 'could not keep the Trojan king out of Italy.'"[21] Whereas Augustine found such classroom exercises a distraction from true self-knowledge and a prideful incitement, however, O'Regan employs them precisely as a path to a humble self-knowledge; an opening to love, compassionate confession, and praise. The mask of the assumed *persona* is "double-edged," as William Desmond explains: "An outward seeming, the mask is a potentially deceptive show of self that masquerades as something other.... [But] the mask also makes apparent, *brings out* into the open what would otherwise be lost in labyrinthine inwardness."[22]

In the case of the impersonated biblical figures, O'Regan draws inspiration from Jewish midrash, the exegetical practice of inventing phrases and stories to fill in gaps in a given narrative account and thus to tell and to understand the biblical tales somewhat differently.[23] As Daniel Boyarin remarks, "In midrash, emotional and axiological content is released in the process of generating new strings of language out of the beads of the old."[24]

---

21 Augustine, *Confessions*, trans. Henry Chadwick (Oxford: Oxford University Press, 2008), 1.xvii (27), 19.

22 Desmond, *Philosophy and Its Others*, 78.

23 For an introduction to midrash, see Robert Alter, *The Art of Biblical Narrative*, 2nd ed. (New York: Basic Books, 2011).

24 Daniel Boyarin, *Intertextuality and the Reading of Midrash*, 2nd ed. (Bloom-

Boyarin and others note important differences between the allegorical exegesis of Origen and the midrashim of the rabbis,[25] but O'Regan's poetic practice finds in them an overlapping complementarity. Origen's writings evince both a firm, vertical correlation of letter and spirit, on the one hand, and a transformative, horizontal yoking of text with text, on the other—a yoking similarly practiced by Jewish exegetes and inspired by a long Judeo-Christian tradition. A student of the Jewish sages Philo of Alexandria and Paul of Tarsus, Origen learned much from them. Interpellating a complex allegory or "other-saying"—inclusive of historical (typological), moral (tropological), and Christological meaning—into the very letter of Scripture, Origen writes, for example, in his commentary on the Song of Songs:

> **O daughters of Jerusalem** [Sg. 1:5], ... [h]ow have you come to forget what is written in your Law as to what Mary suffered who spoke against Moses because he had taken a black Ethiopian to wife? [See Numbers 12] How do you not recognize the fulfillment of that type in me? I am that Ethiopian. [HISTORY] *I am black* [Sg. 1:5] indeed by reason of my lowly origin [HISTORY]; *but* I am *beautiful* [Sg. 1:5] through penitence and faith [TROPOLOGY]. For I have taken to myself the Son of God, I have received the Word made flesh." [CHRISTOLOGY][26]

The declaration of the commentator, "I am that Ethiopian"—a declaration in which Origen not only impersonates the Bride of the Song, the Church, but also identifies himself with Moses's foreign wife as a historical type of that Bride—provides a model for O'Regan's own multi-layered lyric impersonations.

Given O'Regan's propensity in *Origen in Alexandria* to give voice to figures who are physically vulnerable, passionate, and morally and psychologically flawed, and who speak from the dark side of themselves, another

---

ington: Indiana University Press, 1994), 110.

25 Ibid., 108–10.

26 Origen, *The Song of Songs, Commentary and Homilies,* trans. R.P. Lawson (New York: Newman Press, 1956), 93. I have added italics and bolding to mark the biblical passage and signaled the allegorical levels in the exegetical expansion.

passage in Origen's commentary on the Song deserves quotation: "In the beginning of the words of Moses, where the creation of the world is described, we find reference to the making of two men, the first *in the image and likeness of God* [Gen. 1:26], and the second *formed of the slime of the earth* [Gen. 2:7]... . Paul, who understood what Moses wrote much better than we do, [said] that there are two men in every one of us."[27] While "the inner man is renewed from day to day [2 Cor. 4:16]," the "other, that is, the outer, he [Paul] declares to be corrupted and weakened in all the saints and in such [a way] as he was himself."[28] In Origen's understanding, "there are ... synonymous and analogous expressions [in the Scriptures], applicable both to the inner man and the outer man the fleshly, outer man," so that "you may find the names of the limbs of the body used metaphorically with reference to the soul."[29]

O'Regan's lyrics present speakers with biblical names who tell their stories in a manner that departs from what is recorded of them in the Bible. The effect is not to undermine biblical truth and authority, but rather to defamiliarize the characters, to make the reader aware of alternative possibilities ("what might have been, have happened, had not ..."), and thereby to recognize more deeply the working of grace.

The biblical Hagar, for example, is Sarai's Egyptian maidservant and the mother of Abraham's first-born son Ishmael. In chapters 16 and 21, Genesis records that Hagar, proud in her pregnancy, had treated the still-barren Sarai insolently; that her mistress Sarai had retaliated against her; and that, driven out into the wilderness after Isaac's birth, a thirsting Hagar and Ishmael were saved from death by an angel through the discovery of a well. O'Regan's poem "Hagar's Complaint" tells it otherwise. There Hagar protests Sarah's cruelty, the "legal insolence against flesh" (7), and the injustice done to her son, but she is so traumatized by her exile and the desert's heat that she hears no angel's salutation near the well, but rather "a demon voice ... promising survival" (23); distrusting it, she decides to kill her only son: "I will crush the head of Ishmael / Against the scalding rocks" (23–25). The eerie transformation of the tale imagines Hagar's killing of Ishmael to pre-

---

27 Origen, *The Song of Songs*, 25.

28 Ibid.

29 Ibid., 27.

cede (and perhaps to motivate?) Abraham's (mercifully interrupted) sacrifice of Isaac, related in Genesis 22. At the same time, the exile of Hagar by the well in the wilderness prefigures the later exile of the Israelites in Babylon, weeping at the riverside, unable to sing Zion's songs, but eager for revenge: "Happy shall he be who takes your little ones / and dashes them against the rock" (Ps. 137:9).[30]

Scripture famously narrates the lonely ascents of Moses to the height of Mount Sinai and his descents from there, carrying the Lord's messages and commands to the people assembled below. O'Regan's Moses speaks in first person, detailing his sensations of dizziness, his downward looks, his nervous expectation: "Each step brought me higher / In the ladder of risk" ("Moses on the Mountain," 9–10). This discomfited Moses finds himself followed up the mountain by a dog, "the impossibly thin / Violator of the holy mountain" (18–19)—a creature surely inspired by Matilda, O'Regan's own dog, but also by the biblical injunction that promises death to anyone, "whether man or beast" (Ex. 19:13), who crosses the border set by God. In the poem "Moses on the Mountain," the speaker cannot say what occurred up there, "a happening / ... / Or a non-happening" (22–24), and he is completely unsure of what he did afterward, cataloguing a list of possibilities in the form of questions. He concludes noncommittally (and comically), "Whatever the truth, I am always / Somewhere with the dog ..." (44–45). The intertextual reference is a commonplace: a dog is man's best friend. One is left with the suggestion that Moses, who is said to have spoken with God "face to face, as a man speaks to his friend" (Ex. 33:11), indeed somehow died on the mountain (together with his friend the dog?) in fulfillment of the seemingly contradictory word: "'you cannot see my face; for man shall not see me and live'" (Ex. 33:20).

Next to Moses's dog, O'Regan's Job stands as a fitting companion for his Moses. A comic figure, sorely tried, this Job considers his options after the whirlwind from which God has spoken to him in an overwhelming show of power, wisdom, and cosmic beauty. The biblical Job repents, declines to question God any further, and falls silent before God's majesty (Job 42:1–6). O'Regan's Job admits, "Yes, the first impulse / Is to repent. Asking / Seems a small surrender / In such a whelming" ("After the Whirlwind," 1–4). Inti-

---

30 For biblical quotations here and throughout, I use *The Holy Bible,* Revised Standard Version, Catholic Edition (San Francisco, CA: Ignatius Press, 1994).

mate with the God with whom he has quarreled, Job concedes, "You beat / Me mute ... / ... / And leave me a question forsaken" (30-34). Still, this Job, unlike the Job of the Bible, hazards a final comment: "Some nights even gods / Need the clown's forgiveness" (49-50).

Against this epiphanic lightness in *Origen in Alexandria* recurs the thematic darkness of dreaming. Isaac's son Jacob—his brother's cheat, his father's deceiver—is said to have dreamt a dream at Bethel of a ladder stretching from earth to heaven, upon which the angels of God ascended and descended (Gen. 28:12). Later, about to encounter his estranged twin brother Esau, Jacob wrestles with an angel and obtains from him the blessing and the name Israel (Gen. 32:24-30). O'Regan's Jacob, by contrast, recalls not this first angelic dream but another imagined one, the cause of his anxiety toward death: "Perhaps before time began I climbed / And found an angel whimpering / About not being" ("Jacob's Ladder," 10-12). Clinging to comfortable daytime sensations of smell, sound, and touch, this Jacob fears the falling asleep at night and its dreaming, not unlike Shakespeare's Hamlet after him, whose famous "To be or not to be" speech turns on the thought of dreams in death: "to sleep, to sleep, perhaps to dream" (*Hamlet* III.1). More than life's struggle, symbolized in "the wrestling and the gorge / Of blood," Jacob fears the terror "Of falling interrupted by falling / Down the red rungs of scream" (16-17).

Strange angels seem to inhabit Alexandria—angels in the form of humans, humans in the form of angels. Speaking in chorus, one group of them declares their ability to astonish, but not to teach; to speak, but always to "shatter the legerdemain of speech" ("Winging It," 6). They give us permission to imagine them, if we will, as winged creatures "flying in the ether of our world," but they insist: "what is / IS" (10, 12-13), recalling the theophany granted to Moses at the burning bush (cf. Ex. 3). Another angel (if he, in his ecstasy, may be so called) walks more lightly on air than Peter walked on water, having no fear of falling (cf. Mt. 14:29-31): "I am walking on the air / The seeing blue hold[s] me up" ("I Am Walking on the Air," 1-2).

The denizens of O'Regan's Alexandria include not only figures from the biblical world, driven into a strange diaspora, but also pagan philosophers, rhetoricians, and scholars. Similar to the ancient character sketches of Theophrastus (371-287 B.C.), these tend to go unnamed by any proper name, to be identified only by academic types. The first-person speaker of "Encyclopedist," for example, begins abruptly by declaring his misconceived ambition: "I thought I wanted / To say everything / To spread the library / Of symbols over the desert / And sea, prove the world / Round" (1-6). He has learned in the failed attempt, however, the severe limits of language to designate, to communicate, to suffer translation, to match the fecundity and the particularity of things.

In a poem entitled "Sophist," an unnamed speaker sketches the character so named, while the Sophist himself is appropriately denied the use of first-person utterance, because he has, in fact, nothing of his own to say: "A pundit of many schools, his way / Is word's conspiracy to hide darkness, / Rucked things and emptiness" (1-3). Socrates, by contrast—a great critic of the Sophists, courageous foe of "Shady compromises, assumed truths" ("Socrates," 3)—is addressed by his proper name in the second-person of apostrophe, to mark his absence, exile, death: "Yes, untimely the wound / Making you far from Athens" (14-15). In "What Diotima Really Said," the lady philosopher of Plato's *Symposium* also addresses Socrates by name, in the second person: "After you left, Socrates / I said to the blind / Stones who mutter the wind / We rest under the shadow, / Consumed in the banquet / Of love's furious waiting" (34-39).

Other philosophers in O'Regan's Alexandria inspire less personal attachment and respect. In "Philosopher's Dream," the unnamed speaker paints an unflattering picture of the philosopher obsessed with sameness: "Everywhere he is the same. / Always the same dream / Dreaming same's victory" (1-3). The forceful voice in "Apologist for the Unchanging" distances himself from received doctrines, pre-Socratic, Platonic, Aristotelian: "I deny that I am Parmenides' stooge, / That the circle is eternally tight" (1-2); "I am not Plato's jester" (8); "I offer no explanation for the child / whose body is a lip hanging on nothing" (12-13). Indeed, this learned apologist speaks as a Christian theologian: "I am grateful for a trace, a leaving, / Ready to say amen to the evening red / That will break the coldest heart" (15-17). To this speaker has come a revelation through Incarnation: "I know the circle is broken. / I have heard the whisper / Of the breaker who brings / Fierce time and death / As a gift, the word / Inside the silence" (18-23).

For the Neoplatonists, the Homeric tale of Odysseus's circular return home to Ithaca after a long wandering served as an allegory of the soul's return to the eternal fatherland.[31] Closely examined, however, the myth is at

---

31 See Robert Lamberton, *Homer the Theologian: Neoplatonist Allegorical Read-*

odds with the philosopher's dream of sameness, for neither Ithaca nor Odysseus remain unchanged. Unheard by the philosopher in his dream of sameness, "The figures cry their open secrets / And their cries' emptinesses, / And dream elsewhere" ("Philosopher's Dream," 54-55). Like the words sent out to circumnavigate the sea—words that return to the encyclopedist "speaking a language / That was no language at all" ("Encyclopedist," 13-14), the voyager Odysseus (a.k.a. Ulysses) is transformed by his encounter with the round-eyed Cyclops, his alter ego.

Alluding to Ulysses' blinding of Polyphemus in "Philosopher's Dream," O'Regan devotes an entire poem, "Cyclops," to the topic. Building upon the wordplay in Homer, where Odysseus at first names himself "no man" to the one-eyed monster (not a man) who has imprisoned him and his men in the cave, O'Regan employs the English homonym "eye / I" to signal the strange identification between the man who is "no man" (an "i"), who lies and acts savagely, and the inhuman / subhuman cyclops he blinds: "And then I am victory / And victim, siren, / Scheme and plot" ("Cyclops," 12-13).

In O'Regan's retelling, the exit from the mythic cave of Polyphemus inevitably evokes and refashions the forced exit into light of still-blinded, but gradually seeing (or painfully retreating), prisoners in Plato's famous allegory of the cave (*Republic* 514a-520a). Standing at the exit, the poet's Ulysses—or is it Polyphemus?—holds (via metonymy) not a stake but a tong, such as one might use in tending a fire, and contemplates choices: "At the exit i am / A tong holding who / i was, turning facets / Of who i will be" (15-18).

In a series of paradoxical reversals in the second half of O'Regan's "Cyclops," the already blinded one, standing in light at the cave's exit, "see[s] him leave, watch[es] / The small boat laugh westward" (25-26), while the other looks back at the "retreating hole"—the stake-pierced eye? The cave?—"that will last see / The sky's slight leaning" (33-35). Each may say of himself, mirrored in the other: "I pity the once me" (21). When the poet speaks of a "Glance hanging loose / At both ends" (31-32), he suggests a mutual sighting of Polyphemus and Ulysses, an altered self-perception through the pain of a blinding, and the possibility of a humanizing conversion: "When i say I" (46).

---

ing and the Growth of the Epic Tradition (Berkeley: University of California Press, 1986).

Origen and O'Regan on the Spirit

According to Origen (following Moses and Paul), "there are two men [earthly and spiritual] in every one of us."[32] In the *Commentary on the Song of Songs,* Origen finds a corresponding distinction in the levels of Scriptural signification: "All things in the visible category can be related to the invisible, the corporeal to the incorporeal, and the manifest to those that are hidden.... But this relationship does not only obtain with creatures; the Divine Scripture itself is written with wisdom of a rather similar kind."[33] For Origen, the inspired mode of the Scriptures' composition not only witnesses to Christ as the Word made flesh, but also constitutes an "incarnation" of the Spirit that warrants, and indeed demands, the pneumatic ("spiritual" or "allegorical") interpretation of the biblical letter and its historical referent (cf. 2 Cor. 3:6). "If the Logos in His Incarnation is God-Man," writes R.P. Lawson, "so, too, in the mind of Origen the incarnation of the Pneuma in Holy Scripture is divine-human."[34]

The word "spirit" appears in the title of two of O'Regan's poems. In "Spirit of Renewal," the poet celebrates "spirit" as a "she," whereas in "Origen on the Spirit," O'Regan uses the pronoun "he." The gendered difference in pronouns may be accidental, since the two poems are widely separated in the present arrangement of the manuscript, but it may also mirror Origen's own anthropological distinction (following Plato, but also Paul in 1 Thess. 5:23) between "soul" (*psyche*) and "spirit" (*pneuma*).[35] (The Latin word *anima,* regularly used to translate *psyche,* is feminine in gender, while *spiritus* is masculine.)

The soulful spirit celebrated in "Spirit of Renewal" is closely attuned to the human heart and its psychology, its attunement to sacramental signs. A virtual personification of hope, of life's animating breath, she manifests her

---

32 Origen, *The Song of Songs, Commentary and Homilies,* 25.

33 Ibid., 223.

34 Lawson, "Introduction," in Origen, *The Song of Songs, Commentary and Homilies,* 9.

35 As R.P. Lawson explains, "In the letter, visible to all, it has a body; in the hidden meaning inherent in it, it has a soul; and it has a spirit in the element of heaven of which it offers an image" ("Introduction," in Origen, *The Song of Songs, Commentary and Homilies,* 9). The Greek word *psyche* is feminine in gender, but *pneuma* is neuter, not masculine.

youthful, feminine presence in every season: in the springtime, when "you spring up the promise of the rose / In the impossibly green garden" ("Spirit of Renewal," 7-8); in the summer, when you "find intimations / In the water laughing on the stones" (9-10); through burden's release "in the early Fall evening" (12); in winter's dark, when "the candle flickers / But will not flicker out" (16-17). The poem concludes with a beautiful Eucharistic expression of gift and gratitude: "[She] who gives you back to yourself" (4) is also "the one who thanks you lavishly / For having come with empty hands" (19-20).

The Spirit of "Origen on the Spirit," by contrast, transcends human life and exceeds the body's senses, leaving the poem's speaker initially "voiceless" ("Origen on the Spirit," 2); "eyeless" (4); "left without sensation" of touch (9); his olfaction altered and overpowered: "I drown in sweet" (11); tasting "the innuendo of fire" (15), all his physical senses "scattered ... lost" (16-17).[36] A three-part poem, the first section records this unmaking, this "kill[ing]" of him (15), by the Spirit who suddenly descends at noon in "a dervish of wind [to] give grace" (3). Shaken out by this "ecstasy" (21), "baptized" by this Spirit (13), the speaker is left "empty / Of paths" (21), in a "far country of desolation" (20), in "an unrecognizable city that yet recalls / The one from which [he] came" (18-19).

In the second section, the converted speaker rises *ex nihilo* as a new creation: "From nothing I am raised to nobody. / I am his, the wild God's, the God / Of Nebuchadnezzer, Daniel, Deborah" (23-25). "Anoint[ed] ... with holy / Dissatisfaction," he renounces the "idols" that would keep him "safe from / The sacrament of change" (28-31). Having received the gift of tongues, a glossolalia of sorts, the speaker can now "Say without effort the right thing / In the wrong way" (34-35) and also "Say with effort the wrong thing / In the right way" (38-39), plaguing the pharaohs of the world with divine demands and prophecies: "I whirr / like locust, noise promising / An eating down to the roots" (35-37). Possessed by the Spirit, this prophet lives "outside the gates of Jerusalem / Or any plausible city" (42-43), including Alexandria.

---

36 For a recent treatment of Origen on the spiritual senses, see Mark J. McInroy, "Origen of Alexandria," in *The Spiritual Senses: Perceiving God in Western Christianity*, eds. Paul L. Gavrilyuk and Sarah Coakley (Cambridge: University of Cambridge Press, 2012), 20-35.

Unlike parts 1 and 2 of "Origen on the Spirit," part 3 features not the "I" of the initial speaker, but the "He" of the Spirit and the "I" of the Incarnate Word, who, in a closing speech marked off by quotation marks, points back to the Spirit who has first directed us to Christ. Origen/O'Regan celebrates the hypostasis of the Spirit in the Scriptures as a prophetic incarnation, reminiscent of Elijah's miraculous sustenance (1 Kgs. 19:8): "He is the incognito in reading, / What makes words travel across / The desert and not die of thirst" (44–46). Veiled in the fleshly letter of the text, the Spirit, the "secret" of revelation, transforms and spiritualizes the recipient, "leaves you as your own ghost" (48–49). Most importantly, the Spirit enfleshed in the Scriptures points "to the place where the cross / hangs from the sky" (51–52), witnesses to Christ crucified, and "makes / The Nazarene the uninvited guest of all / Stories" (55–57). This Scriptural inspiration, this gift of the Spirit, is also Christ's dying expiration (Lk. 23:46)—a kenotic breath that infuses the last breath of every mortal: "the scream of the soldier / Set upon by an enemy, the cry / Of hunger, the moan of cold, / The last whisper as breath shoves / Its way into darkness" (64–68).

In the last eleven lines of "Origen on the Spirit," the poet dares to impersonate Christ himself as the Word Incarnate, speaking in praise of the life-giving Spirit: "'It is through him that I give the dead / A face, give them voice, above all give / Them touch'" (72–74). Prodigal in love, incarnate through the Spirit, the Son has journeyed to a far country, identified himself with sinners, in order to return them to his Father (cf. Lk. 15:11–24): "It is through him that I am found / As lost" (79–80). The same Spirit through whom the risen Christ enlivens the members of his mystical body, "Bone of bone in the valley of bones" (63), is also the bond of love joining the Son to the Father, creation with its creator: "'It is through him ... / ... that my cry echoes / Out beyond the galaxies reaching / For my father who cries with me'" (79–82).

The composition of "Origen on the Spirit" post-dates the first beginnings of *Origen in Alexandria,* but that poem—rich in biblical allusion, theological depth, emotive range, and verbal complexity—anchors the collection as a whole, giving a concentrated expression to many of its themes. Its teaching is precisely that which strong poets, as "ambassadors of glory," can and do impart: "that one has been loved and can love, ... that we have been given the impossible power to forgive others and ourselves."[37]

The only poem in *Origen in Alexandria* with a proper dedication, "Origen on the Spirit" appropriately honors Kilian McDonnell, O.S.B. (1921-), a colleague of O'Regan when they were both faculty members at Saint John's University. McDonnell's theological writings during his tenure there (1964-1992) chiefly concerned pneumatology, the gift of the Spirit in Baptism, and the Catholic Charismatic movement in its relation to ecumenism. At age seventy-five, the Benedictine monk and theologian turned his attention to poetry and has published four volumes to date, many of his poems—like O'Regan's own—giving speech to biblical figures.

While McDonnell has effectively counterbalanced his academic theological investigations, at one end of his career, with the lyricism of poetry at the other, the poise O'Regan seeks has involved a constant back-and-forth between the two genres during the very years when he has been most productive as a publishing theologian. One suspects that O'Regan's voluminous prose owes much to his practice of poetry; perhaps it even finds an origin of sorts precisely there: in poetry's short lines, verbal sparseness, ambiguity, breath, and bone. The well-rounded "O" of O'Regan's theologian is never really far, after all, from the "O, O, O, O" of Shakespeare's heartbroken Lear (*King Lear,* 5.iii); the "Oh!" of surprise, awe, and ecstasy; and the "O" of prayer's invocation.[38]

---

37 O'Regan, "Ambassadors of Divine Glory."

38 Writing this essay brings back the happy memory of a day-long Lumen Christi symposium on poetry and theology held on the campus of the University of Chicago. There, in the company of Regina Schwartz, Richard Streier, David Tracy, Thomas Levergood, Donald Platt, and Kevin Hart, I first got to know Cyril O'Regan, now my much-admired colleague and friend.

CHAPTER ELEVEN

"As love, the giver is perfect"[1]

Love at the Limit in the Thought of Cyril O'Regan

Jay Martin

Introduction: Developing the Agapeic Hints

It is incumbent upon me from the beginning to confess the cowardice in what follows. By claiming to retrieve an inchoate theology of love in Cyril's work and attempting to wrest it from its almost exclusively diagnostic register, the question of love of and for Cyril can be secured behind the screen of dispassion, both preserving the dignity of those who love Cyril, as well as deferring the indignity of the one who, in psychoanalytic language, occupies the "position of the beloved." There will likewise be the shameless imposition of a largely foreign discourse—namely, psychoanalysis and its French iterations, the likes of which figure less than magisterially for Cyril—that aids and abets in the sublimation of what a braver tribute might offer, namely, a definitive account of the charity of Cyril O'Regan, a reckoning of what love for Cyril is at its essence, and how it is exemplified by him.

Yet the shape of my training under Cyril, together with the peculiar fiber of my own intellectual and moral character, sets before me the more

---

1 Cyril O'Regan, *Gnostic Apocalypse: Jacob Boehme's Haunted Narrative* (Albany: State University of New York Press, 2002), 119.

proximate and imminently less lofty goal of elaborating a psychoanalytic—or better, a psychotheological—reading of Cyril's writing on love. That is, I intend to bring into the open this inchoate character of his theology of love and its possible motivations, which will remain here by necessity fundamentally undisclosed. Whatever necessity there is in such circumspection that leaves the question of love unanswered—to wit, what love is in general and what it is for Cyril—my unreadiness to answer is in no way exculpated simply on the grounds that the question is itself unanswerable.

Petrine Readiness: Toward Salutary Confrontation

1 Peter 3:15, which has been taken as a sort of *carte blanche* for so many an eager apologist, demands not an answer (ἀπολογίαν) as such but rather a readiness (ἕτοιμοι), a readiness to answer of a heart that sanctifies Christ as God. My contention is that the inchoate character of love in Cyril's thought is a manifestation of this Petrine readiness, a readiness to give, a readiness to answer, even when, in the last instance, the whole of the answer is not totally given. Thus, what will be investigated here will not be the phenomenon or even the meaning of that readiness or in what it consists, but rather in what it signifies. Thus, we must approach it from within the signifying chain, as one signifier in the network of other signifiers, conscious and unconscious, that constitutes the discourse of Cyril's theology. In other words, in his reticence to articulate a positive theology of love, Cyril gives us a sign, but as Jacques Lacan puts it, it is "a sign of an absence";[2] it is a sign of Jonah (Matthew 12:39).

Petrine readiness, moreover, is not the key by which a theology of love is unlocked, for, as Jean Laplanche reminds us, psychoanalysis is not in the business of opening locks but rather of dismantling them.[3] Petrine readiness is what is glimpsed in a moment of what is called *anamorphosis* or visual resistance in Lacanian theory, seen as the spectral presence of a non-answer to the question of love, visible only upon gaining a certain vantage. It is not the answer itself but the sign of the lack of an answer—or better, the sign of the constitutive lack *in* any answer to the question of love. Thus, a theology of love is not merely hidden in Cyril's theology, but is rather a hidden hiddenness,

---

2   Jacques Lacan, *The Psychoses: The Seminar of Jacques Lacan, Book III*, ed. Jacques-Alain Miller, trans. Russell Grigg (New York: W.W. Norton, 1993), 167.

3   Jean Laplanche, "Psychoanalysis as Anti-hermeneutics," *Radical Philosophy* 79 (September/October 1996): 12.

a seafloor rather than the depth that is marked by it. The pressing issue, of course, is the matter of vantage and how to gain it. Yet a preliminary question, and one that is patently fair, is whether such a vantage is worth seeking, if the only promise upon reaching it is to see better what is not there.

Narrative Swerve: Love in Analysis

Despite the absence of an explicit theology of love, I argue that love does retain a perennial importance for Cyril, constituting a central diagnostic criterion of theological assessment in his engagement with Valentinian *gnosis*, Boehme, Hegel, and Heidegger, among others. In each case, the fullness of love, as demonstrated by the biblical and subsequent theological tradition, is diminished, whether in the service of Hegelian Trinitarian speculation, the agonism of Valentinian *gnosis* (or Behemism), or Heidegger's relative subjugation of love to philosophy, on the rare occasion that he speaks of love. Yet doctrinal correctness, too, especially in such cases, must be brought under the mantle of love, such that it becomes a marker and manifestation of that which animates genuine theological inquiry and assessment. Though it would be too daunting a task to provide a thick description of Cyril's hermeneutic, it is enough for present purposes to characterize it as agapeic, if in so doing we follow Pascal: "Truth is so obscured nowadays, and lies are so well established, that unless we love the truth, we shall never recognize it."[4] Granted, Cyril rarely summons Pascal's polemical tone, but he does follow both his correlation of love and truth and his recognition of the demands that love makes on truth.[5]

---

4 Blaise Pascal, *Pensées*, trans. A.J. Krailsheimer (New York: Penguin, 1966), no. 739. A very similar idea is found is William Desmond's agapeically construed hermeneutics of generosity, though Desmond directs it toward charity in interpersonal exchange; see William Desmond, *Perplexity and Ultimacy: Metaphysical Thoughts from the Middle* (Albany: State University of New York Press, 1995), 124–25: "Seek the strength in the other, the point of ripeness, or if not that, seek the promise of ripeness in the other. And if one seeks the good in the other, do not define this good simply in terms of its congruence with oneself; let this promise of the good of the other emerge; welcome and make way for its emergence for itself."

5 Interestingly, the notion of love making demands on truth is a subtle, though constitutive, feature of Benedict XVI's 2009 encyclical *Caritas in Veritate*. See Benedict XVI, *Charity in Truth = Caritas in Veritate* (San Francisco: Ignatius Press, 2009). Benedict insists that "charity demands justice" by giving any and all commit-

For Cyril, the status and relative conceptual health of love within these various systems effectively indexes the ways in which other conceptual topoi, such as doctrines of God and the Trinity, the incarnation and Christology, the cross and passion of the Lord, pneumatology, ecclesiology, and apocalyptic and eschatology, among others, have fared. If love suffers some contraction, it is a safe bet that those other theological concepts have as well. Yet, at the same time, the conditional can be read inversely such that the weakening or deranging of doctrine can be seen as indicative of a weakening or deranging of love.

This directional reversibility in the relationship between love and doctrine pushes the matter of the one's priority over the other into a state of undecidability, the same undecidability at play in the challenging words of 1 John 4:8: "Whoever does not love does not know God, for God is love" (NRSVCE). Loving and knowing are brought into a conditional relationship that is predicated upon the identification of God as love. The surrounding verses only amplify this undecidability. In the midst of John's exhortation to love, we are told in verse 7 that love is *from* God (ἐκ τοῦ θεοῦ ἐστιν), as well as that anyone who loves is born *of* God (τοῦ θεοῦ γεγέννηται) and *knows* God (γινώσκει τὸν θεόν). Thus, there is no knowledge of God without love, yet in loving, both our origin and our end in God is expressed and demonstrated. Moreover, John's mode of address to the faithful as *beloved* (ἀγαπητοί) not only implies his own position as *lover* (that is, as one who loves, as one who situates himself with respect to a beloved), and thus one who knows and is of God, but it is also an invitation to his reader to effect a subjective transformation from the position of the beloved, in which they are addressed, to the position of lover, to which they are called.

Interestingly, the conditions of the possibility of this conversion—and it is in fact true *metanoia*—from beloved to lover more closely resembles the shift in subjective positions in the analytic setting than the transactional

---

ment to justice in the world "theological and salvific value" (14). Moreover, "The demands of love do not contradict those of reason. Human knowledge is insufficient and the conclusions of science cannot indicate by themselves the path towards integral human development. There is always a need to push further ahead: this is what is required by charity in truth. Going beyond, however, never means prescinding from the conclusions of reason, nor contradicting its results. Intelligence and love are not in separate compartments: *love is rich in intelligence and intelligence is full of love*" (59; italics in original).

shifts brought about in standard discursive exchange. The transformation of the beloved into lover is not predicated upon the actualization of a deep potency or the awakening of a deeper self, nor is it simply the natural response to being loved (by God, by others), as it is sufficiently commonplace for a beloved to persist in belovedness without also becoming a lover. It is precisely the preoccupation of maintaining the possibility of this transformation of beloved to lover that is at the heart of both Cyril's critical engagement with the deficient accounts of love in question, as well as what keeps him from articulating a positive theology of love himself. That is, for Cyril, as with John's epistle, only love—that is, the act of loving—is necessary.

Transferences: (Non-) Defensive Posture

In Book VIII of the *Seminar*, Jacques Lacan provides his most sustained treatment of the Freudian notion of transference and its structural relationship to love through an extended commentary on Plato's *Symposium*, a text in which Lacan recognizes "the first psychoanalytic transference."[6] Though he almost certainly coined the term "transference," Freud identifies transferences as phenomena that have characterized human interaction long before the advent of psychoanalysis, as a means of explaining the human tendency to transfer to new situations the sediment of past experiences. Lacan takes up Freud's notion but adjusts it in important ways: "Transference does not fall under any mysterious property of affectivity and, even when it reveals itself in an emotional [*émoi*] guise, this guise has a meaning only as a function of the dialectical moment at which it occurs."[7] In short, Lacan translates the affective frame of Freud's understanding of transference into the idiom of subjectivity, as something that obtains within the structure of subjectivity and intersubjective relations rather than in the emotions. It is also important to note that Lacan adopts the Socratic preference for "*Eros*" as both the proper name for and highest form of love, which not only foregrounds the narrative centrality of the Eros myth to the *Symposium*, but also "classifies love (as a kind of object-directed desire) and proceeds from this to charac-

---

6 Jacques Lacan, *Transference: The Seminar of Jacques Lacan, Book VIII*, ed. Jacques-Alain Miller, trans. Bruce Fink (Malden, MA: Polity, 2015), 16.

7 Jacques Lacan, "Seminar on 'Presentation on Transference,'" in *Écrits: The First Complete Edition in English*, trans. Bruce Fink (New York and London: W.W. Norton, 2006), 184.

terize and relate the objects desired."[8] Thus, Lacan uses "*Eros*" synecdochally, as a part for the whole of the Greek understanding of love.[9]

What is critical to Lacan's notion of transference in Seminar VIII is an extended and rather thick analogy between the analyst-analysand relationship and the relationship between a beloved and a lover, which centers on the possibility, subverting the standard Greek paradigm, of the transformation of the beloved into a lover. For Lacan, both teacher-pupil and the analyst-analysand relation must be oriented toward the efficacious subjective transition from the second term (pupil, analysand) to the former as the ultimate goal of the relationship itself. In the analytic setting, the goal is for the analysand to recognize her transferences and to denature them, such that the analyst becomes effectively redundant. More precisely, the inherent redundancy of the analyst is recognized and formalized.

Granted, the historical particularities of the teacher-pupil/lover-beloved relationship, as well as the Greek notion of love as such, do not necessarily obtain in the modern academic context, yet its structural elements persist. Interestingly, without any sort of nostalgia for pederasty, Lacan wonders why this aspect has disappeared from the teacher-pupil relationship. Lacan's answer is startling. He writes: "One of the reasons, which will perhaps surprise you if I propose it here, is that for us, at the stage we are at, love—and its phenomenon, culture, and dimension—has for some time now been disconnected from beauty."[10] Yet in order to reintegrate love with beauty, we need not restore lascivious behavior to the teacher-pupil relationship, but rather seek a repetition of the coincidence of love and beauty, only this time in the register of comedy.

On this point, Lacan continues, we can see why Aristophanes, Socrates'

---

8   John A. Brentlinger, "The Cycle of Becoming in the Symposium," in *The Symposium of Plato*, trans. Suzy Q. Groden (Amherst: University of Massachusetts Press, 1970), 8.

9   Moreover, it is worth noting that *agape* appears only twice in *Seminar VIII*, and then only in passing. In each case, however, Lacan, like Benedict XVI, expresses some doubt that *agape* and *eros* are necessarily mutually exclusive, and goes on to consider how this exclusionary understanding came to be and to what ends it serves. See Lacan, *Transference*, 128, 162, and for an overview of Lacan's thinking on *agape*, see Bruce Fink, *Lacan on Love: An Exploration of Lacan's Seminar VIII*, Transference (Malden, MA: Polity, 2016), 115–24.

10   Lacan, *Transference*, 33.

quite literal mortal enemy, receives such a pivotal role in the *Symposium*. On the connection between love and comedy, Lacan makes two points. First, that "love is a comical feeling,"[11] and as such, there is an internal and necessary connection between love and comedy, such that, despite Aristophanes' key role in Socrates' death, it must be the comedian *par excellence* who delivers the most profound speech at the symposium. Second, he continues, "love is giving what you don't have,"[12] which is a recurring claim in Lacan's thought. Though the immediate context is his response to Agathon's speech, Socrates' true target is Aristophanes, who exclaims just a few lines earlier, "for whatever we have not or know not we can neither give to another nor teach our neighbor" (196e).[13]

For Lacan, the lover appears as the desiring subject, as a lacking subject with respect to the object of desire: "One cannot love without presenting oneself as if one does not have, even if one does. Love as a response implies the domain of not having."[14] In the *Symposium*, the correlation of love and lack comes in Socrates' recounting of Diotima's discourse on love (201d–212b) in place of his own speech. In Lacan's view, Socrates concedes his opportunity to deliver his own speech not out of fear of offending Agathon, but rather as an exemplification of the very topic of the symposium (love, *eros*)—that is, Socrates' deferral should be understood in some way as a loving gesture in which Socrates enters the domain of not having. Narratively, though, Socrates' deferral to Diotima is peculiar, insofar as Diotima is not herself present. Rather, Socrates rehearses his earlier conversation with her, giving an account of his "lesson from her in love-matters" (201d) and admitting that it was Diotima who had disabused him of his own understanding of love, which had closely resembled Agathon's (201e).

---

11   Ibid.

12   Ibid., 34.

13   Moreover, Lacan's phrase is also an almost certain allusion to Plotinus's claim that the One gives what it does not have in *Ennead* V.3.15 as a gloss on how differentiation can arise from utter ontological simplicity. Additionally, Julia Kristeva, in a post-Lacanian key, provides a fascinating exploration of the notion of love in the *Symposium* and its relationship to Plotinus (and Ovid) in *Tales of Love*; see Julia Kristeva, *Tales of Love*, trans. Leon S. Roudiez (New York: Columbia University Press, 1987), 103–21.

14   Lacan, *Transference*, 357.

Thus, Socrates both narrates and performs the transformation he hopes to elicit from Agathon and the others. Moreover, his reference to Diotima is not a subtle self-valorization in which mere supporting evidence is adduced, but is rather a display of the humility gained by the transformative nature of love into which he was initiated by Diotima. On this point, and perhaps to belabor the matter, we can thus make sense of why Socrates would forfeit the prestige of giving the most oratorically sophisticated instance of "praising love as beautifully as he can" (177d), which was, ostensibly, the purpose of gathering the symposium altogether.

In her discourse, however, Diotima explains that love is neither good or bad nor beautiful or ugly (202b), precisely because love lacks such things and so desires them. The *neither-nor* of her articulation marks the precise point at which dialectic is surpassed and the necessity of myth comes to light, insofar as dialectic "is solely what can be accessed by purely and simply bringing the [binary] law of the signifier into play."[15] Lacan explains that love belongs more properly to belief than knowledge, "lying between *epistéme* and ἀμαθία (*amathía*) [ignorance], just as it lies between the beautiful and the ugly," and as such it eludes the binary logic of the signifier. Thus, love is μεταξύ, "between."[16] "How then," Diotima asks, "can [love] be a god, if [love] is devoid of things beautiful and good?... So you see ... you are a person who does not consider Love to be a god" (202d). Thus, Diotima provided Socrates the very same service he renders to Agathon in the *Symposium*, namely, dispelling the notion that love is a god.

For Diotima, love is a great spirit, a site of mediating exchange between the mortal and immortal (202e), which Socrates seems not to question. Yet his response is jarring. Following Diotima's fairly lengthy, and decidedly non-mythological, explanation of how this spiritual mediation between God and humanity functions, Socrates simply asks, "From what father and mother sprung?" (203a), an ironic allusion to his response to Agathon (in 199d), which prompts Diotima to tell the myth of Eros, the child of Poverty (Πενία) and Resource (Πόρος), who from his birth was an "attendant and minister to Aphrodite" (203c). On Lacan's reading, that love has desire for its birthright registers both love's inherent lack or poverty, which it receives from its mother, as well as the drive for beauty, which is its paternal inher-

---

15 Ibid., 119.

16 Ibid., 122.

itance. Thus, what is lovable "is the truly beautiful, tender, perfect, and heaven-blest, but the lover is of a different type ..." (204c). The lover lacks and, moreover, desires precisely what and because it lacks.

Perhaps more importantly for Lacan, however, is the narrative introduction of the myth of Eros. Though Diotima is able to give a philosophical account of how love mediates between the mortal and immortal, only myth can speak deeply of love's nature and origin. "When one arrives," Lacan continues, "and in plenty of fields other than love, at a certain terminus regarding what can be obtained at the level of *epistéme* or knowledge, myth is necessary in order to go further."[17] This discursive shift from dialectic to myth is critical, as love, for Lacan, is marked by a shift in signification, a giving way of one discursive genre to another. Though it is not identified *as* love, beauty is not excluded from the domain of love; it is what gives it its directionality and orients it toward its object, making it desirable.

Furthermore, though the discursive shift to myth surpasses the binary logic of the signifier, its constitutive relation to beauty both grounds love within the signifier's field of effects, but also maintains the metaphoricity of love as a signifier, if, as Lacan does, one understands metaphor in terms of substitution. Thus, it is in the substitution of the function of lover (as a subject of lack) by the function of the beloved (the object of desire) that the signification of love is produced,[18] or, more simply, when the beloved behaves like a lover. In his summation of the entirety of Greek myth, Lacan comments that the gods regard nothing else as sublime or marvelous as the loving beloved.

Thus, as such, Lacan inadvertently provides a framework for a psycho-theological reading of salvation history in which we can see the moments

---

17 Ibid., 118. Lacan defines myth and its Platonic function in the following way: "Everyone knows that they are speaking in myths, μυ/qouj (*mýthous*). I am not talking about myths in the common meaning of the word, for μυ/qouj le/gein (*mýthous légein*) does not mean that but, rather, 'what people say.' And in all of Plato's work ... myths arise when Plato needs them in order to fill the gap in what can be assured dialectically" (119). As Lacan is well aware, myth has an additional function in the *Phaedo*. If myth takes inquiry beyond dialectic in the *Symposium* (and it is worth noting that Lacan finds this function in the *Phaedo*, too; cf. Lacan, *Transference*, 9), it serves an ameliorating purpose in the *Phaedo*, namely, to pacify the fear of death (114d–e).

18 Ibid., 40.

of divine revelation not merely as instances of a shift in signification, but rather as the advent of the transcendent God entering into the signifying chain itself. Thus, God is *iterated* in the speaking of creation into existence, is *sworn* to the covenant that God freely offers, is *invoked* by the name God freely reveals to Moses, is *explicitated* in the giving of the law at Sinai, and so on, a movement of divine condescension that, in the Christian dispensation, culminates in the incarnation of the *Word*. By entering the signifying chain, God not only presents Godself as lacking what God desires (in this precise Lacanian sense), but the very "domain of not having" is transformed into a domain of radical, self-emptying gift, that is, as the site of revelation in which God comes to occupy the position of lover.

Love Pure and Impure: Ambiguous Identities

In order to present Cyril's diagnostics of love through the lens of the preservation of the possibility of the beloved-lover transformation, we turn to the textual evidence. With respect to love, Cyril's catalogue can be roughly organized along two axes: first, there is the Hegelian-Heideggerian axis, which charts the course from *The Heterodox Hegel* to the forthcoming second volume of *The Anatomy of Misremembering*; second, there is the Gnostic-Behemistic axis along which Valentinian Gnosticism and Jacob Boehme, and their echoes in modernity, are treated in *Gnostic Return in Modernity* and *Gnostic Apocalypse*. Of course, much of Cyril's work has been dedicated to demonstrating that Valentinians, Boehme, and Hegel are of the same genealogical whole, but the focus on love allows some procedural distinctions to be made, even if a bit artificially. In anticipation of the second volume of *The Anatomy of Misremembering*, Heidegger unfortunately must be neglected for the time being.

In a seemingly offhand remark in *Gnostic Return in Modernity*, Cyril sets Marcionism apart from what he calls "full-blown Gnosticism" precisely on the point that Marcion does not collapse into "total myth, total narration."[19] "What prevents Marcionism from becoming total myth," he continues, "is its emphasis on love (*charis*)."[20] That is, Marcion's identification

---

19 Cyril O'Regan, *Gnostic Return in Modernity* (Albany: State University of New York Press, 2001), 64.

20 Ibid. Cyril's parenthetical inclusion of "*charis*" (grace) does not offer it as a gloss for "love" but rather both alludes to Marcion's preoccupation with redemp-

of the hidden God of Jesus Christ with love (in contradistinction to the wrathful demiurgical God of the Hebrews), effectively foregrounds redemption narratively and, at the same time, narratively de-prioritizes the evilness of both the demiurge and creation. Thus, it is the real, historical prospect of salvation (of Christians) at the heart of Marcion's rendition of the gospel that constitutes a significant point of discontinuity with the mythic substructure of his interpretation of the Hebrew Scriptures. What is important for present purposes, however, is the way in which love functions as a sort of grounding principle, shoring up God's relationship to history and prioritizing God's loving intention to save human beings through Jesus Christ.[21]

Though love does not figure prominently as a topic in *Gnostic Return in Modernity*, once love is identified as this sort of grounding principle, what is at stake in Gnostic narrative and its mode of biblical interpretation becomes clear. That is, in order to maintain its hyperbolic emphasis on anthropology, which is narrated exclusively in mythological terms, both divine and human love must undergo a radical degree of contraction and derangement. This level of metalepsis[22] is perhaps most clear in the Gnostic reconfiguration of the Fall, particularly in the shift from the canonical characterization of the Fall in terms of human fallenness to a notion of the fallenness of both the divine and creation as such, which in turn "involves a commitment to divine

---

tion, which foregrounds the Marcionite liturgical impartation of Marcion's own salutary *Charis* (grace) to his faithful, as Irenaeus (and Harnack later) records, as well as marks an internal distance from the use of *Charis* in Valentinian myth.

21   This point should not be overstated; Marcion's notions of history and narrative are not those of canonical Christianity, as evident in his redactions of the biblical narrative (of particular importance is his dismissal of the gospel infancy narratives), but even so, Marcion retains a comparatively thick historical register, especially with respect to the totalizing mythologizing in Gnosticism.

22   As best as I can tell, *metalepsis* first emerges as a grammatical-narratological term for Cyril in *Gnostic Return* as a central means of describing Valentinian narrative's "usurpative hermeneutic practice vis-à-vis the biblical text, and the narrative that it renders or at least shapes its reading" (57). Drawing both from Hans Blumenberg's retrieval of "metalepsis" (originally, "participation") in Aristotle and the literary theory of Harold Bloom, Cyril explains that "one thinks of metalepsis as a revisionary ratio, the way in which a later discourse both neutralizes an earlier discourse and siphons off its authority. Metalepsis indicates retrieval (but only across the gap of difference), and what is retrieved is both disfigured and reconfigured" (57).

pathos" while mitigating "the capability of supporting a truly affirmative view of the world and history."[23]

Thus, in Gnosticism, as well as those discursive traditions in its genealogical wake, the correlation between divine pathos and the developmental logic of divine actualization eliminates the contingency of the Fall (in addition to its shift away from human fallenness) in the mainline tradition. This correlation, moreover, utterly transforms the symbolic value of the Fall from "an opportunity for the just and good God to make visible the gratuity of divine love,"[24] which is accomplished by redemption, to the precise terms by which God must overcome the lack in Godself. Moreover, on this necessitarian rendering of the Fall, love itself becomes a problem *for* God, and for God *in se* within a process of divine actualization, as well as for human knowledge of God.

Love out of Bounds: Hoist on the Tolmatic Petard

To illustrate this deracinating feature of the Gnostic account of the Fall, Cyril points to Plotinus's comparative treatment of "audaciousness" (*tolma*) or "eros for knowledge [of the transcendent]" in his own Neoplatonic system and how it would function in the Valentinian Sophia myth, were Gnostic aeons replaced by philosophical principles. In Plotinus, *tolma* is "nothing more nor less than the legitimate responsiveness of Nous to the diffuse love of the One."[25] Though Cyril focuses here on *Enneads* 6.9, we could also look to 2.9, which Cyril treats elsewhere, where Plotinus charges the Gnostics not only with introducing "an abrupt, cataclysmic break in the hierarchy of being,"[26] but also with seeing in that break the creation of the world. Thus, insofar as Gnostic ontology pivots on an absolute disruption of the hierarchy of being, the diffusive love of the One collapses into an agonism in which diffusion becomes a frustrated dis-integration, uncoupling the natural hierarchical relationship that legitimates the erotic, "tolmatic" response of Nous to the One in Neoplatonism and renders it in a manifestly transgressive register.

---

23 O'Regan, *Gnostic Return*, 20.

24 Ibid., 64.

25 Ibid., 170.

26 N. Joseph Torchia, *Plotinus, Tolma, and the Descent of Being: An Exposition and Analysis* (New York: Peter Lang, 1993), 111.

As Cyril notes, this decoupling does not foreclose the communication of divine perfection, but unlike Neoplatonism, Gnosticism recasts it "*across* discontinuity, *despite* tear and gap that signify a refusal of divine communication [and renders it] a kind of expressive excommunication."[27] Thus, within the Gnostic myth, lack is located at the level of perfection itself, which constitutes a thoroughly erotic construal of divine perfection that, in Cyril's words, "is developmental and pedagogic in a way that Plotinus refuses."[28] Whatever we make of God's (or the One's) capacity for love in Gnosticism, it is radically different from Irenaeus's God of pure love, Plotinus's diffuse love of the One, or even Marcion's alien God of redemptive love. In other words, love in Gnosticism in no way resists mythologization, but is rather eagerly subsumed entirely by the mythic drama of agonistic divine self-becoming.

In Boehme's speculative system, this developmental and pedagogic trait is hyperbolized, despite the apparently Neoplatonic re-substitution of Principles for aeons, which for Boehme, and unlike Plotinus, refer to "domain[s] of essence (*Wesen*), thus a dimension of existence radically distinct from the Unground [the mystical being of the divine or the groundless ground of God] and the Quaternity [the union of God's threefoldness and divine wisdom]." Yet, most importantly, "[a] Principle refers to a domain of life (*Leben*)."[29] The triadic structure of the Principles includes a fire or dark Principle (First Principle) associated with wrath, a light Principle (Second Principle) associated with love and mercy, and the dialectical coincidence of the dark and light (Third Principle), in which both are overcome in the realization of form according to which the world is created, human beings are created to bear the *imago dei*, and the Christ figure emerges.[30]

Furthermore, though these Principles are themselves antagonistic to one

---

27 O'Regan, *Gnostic Return*, 171.

28 Ibid.

29 O'Regan, *Gnostic Apocalypse*, 40.

30 It is certainly worth noting, as Cyril does, that this structuration of the three Principles shows the clear influence of Paracelsus. For Boehme's full account of the Three Principles, see Jacob Boehme, *De tribus principiis, oder Beschreibung der drey Principien* Göttliches Wesens, Bund II, *Jacob Bohmes Sämtliches Schriften*, ed. August Faust and Will-Erich Peuckert (Stuttgart: Fr. Frommanns Verlag Günther Holzboog, 1960).

another, particularly the First and Second, that antagonism is relationally and developmentally parsed, such that what occurs in antecedent Principles is the condition for subsequent ones. At the same time, however, the Principles correspond to the persons of the Trinity, assigning the Father to the First Principle, the Son to the Second, and the Holy Spirit to the Third. It should be immediately noted that not only is the Son non-identical to the Christ that appears in the Third Principle, but by dint of Boehme's developmental and agonistic logic, the relationship between Son and Christ is itself antagonistic and dialectically separated insofar as the Third Principle is the sublation of its antecedents, though Christ appropriates all the properties of the Second Principle.[31]

Furthermore, love is conceived of as a quality of the Second Principle, though it is particularly associated with Christ. Yet given the relational and dialectical transition from First to Second Principle, love is both the overcoming of wrath in freedom, as well as the freedom to choose love over wrath. Moreover, "if sometimes identified unequivocally with Christ," Cyril writes,

> the Second Principle is more nearly a christic principle, which includes in addition to an agonically marked divine love, a pneumatologically marked expressiveness, expressibility and power of naming, and a sophiologically marked paradise.[32]

It is in the Second Principle that the divine is truly actualized, divine goodness gains its effectiveness, and—most important for my purposes—the divine pathos of the First Principle is raised into joy. Cyril is clear, however, that, unlike Valentinian myth, Boehme's erotic model does not exclude *agape* insofar as "[a]gapaic expression is possible for a fully real or perfect divine."[33] Yet at the same time the possibility of agapaic expression is contingent only upon the realization of perfect divinity; it is not the simple self-expression and communication of God as God, as we find in the canonical tradition and perhaps most notably in Irenaeus. If *agape* is realized

---

31   O'Regan, *Gnostic Apocalypse*, 42.

32   Ibid., 77.

33   Ibid., 78.

in Boehme's system, its realization is always-already the realization of *eros*, "for it is only in such a totality of expression or self-objectification that the divine fully appropriates itself and becomes capable of agapaic love."[34]

Thus, a critical element of Cyril's Irenaean profile begins to become clear, namely, his agapaism. In addition to the Irenaean form of his genealogical and narratological analysis, Cyril claims a more personal Irenaeanism, suggesting that the whole of his genealogical project constitutes an answer to the open question posed by John Milbank's *Theology and Social Theory* "as to who or what kind of discourse will play Irenaeus to modern Gnosticism."[35] It is perhaps typical of Cyril not to identify *himself* but rather the genealogy he constructs as the Irenaeus *redivivus*. It is all the more striking in light of the fact that throughout Cyril will speak of Irenaeus the man, in addition to his utilization of a whole network of "Irenaean" modifiers. Yet if there is anything with which to take issue, it is this metonymic move to have his genealogy stand in on his own behalf.

My contention is that what is obscured here is the Lacanian question of desire. What does Cyril desire in the construction of his discourse? The same question, of course, could be posed to Irenaeus. Interestingly, however, Cyril himself gives us clues as to how the question might be answered for Irenaeus precisely by highlighting the ways in which Irenaeus's anti-Gnostic polemic is so thoroughly Johannine. "For Irenaeus," Cyril writes,

> John's Gospel fundamentally interprets the relation between God and world, just as John's Gospel also provides the lens in and through which to read Genesis. God is a God of pure love, of *agape*, of God who gives existence and life, who communicates his presence to human beings before and after the fall ..., [and] reestablishes our right relation with God our Father.[36]

The pressing question, then, is not *why* Irenaeus marshals John's gospel in the frontlines against *gnosis* (as that is patently clear), but is rather what Irenaeus is seeking to preserve by inveighing against Gnosticism to begin with.

---

34 Ibid.

35 Ibid., 18.

36 O'Regan, *Gnostic Return*, 156.

The insistence that God is a God of pure love and the perfection that entails counters the divine agonism of Valentinianism, on the one hand, while his insistence on the gratuity of creation and created life counters both the evil status accorded to creation in Gnosticism as well as the ontological necessity of the fall. *Mutatis mutandis*, the Irenaean argument can be easily adapted, as Cyril does in *Gnostic Apocalypse*, to assess Boehme. Yet this leaves the question of preservation unanswered, as surely neither Irenaeus nor Cyril intends to defend canonical Christian doctrine merely for its own sake. That God is pure love, that God created the world freely and gratuitously, and that such beliefs are identified as doctrines by the Church, as doctrines revealed in Scripture and by the incarnation of Jesus Christ, is precisely what introduces the register of signification. That the revelation of these doctrines is a loving and gratuitous act of divine self-communication is exactly what Irenaeus and Cyril both seek to preserve.

Doctrine as Signified Revelation: The Logic of Theological Articulation

Doctrines, of course, have strange significatory properties, precisely at the point at which they purport to express revelation. What is introduced is a strange sort of split, a split that doubles rather than divides. In Eric Santner's words, it is a split between the "'*that* it signifies' over the '*what* it signifies'"[37] that sees in the identification and articulation of doctrine the implicit question of address. That is, *that* God reveals to us is logically prior to *what* God reveals to us.

To put it a bit differently, the content of revealed doctrine is always-already preceded by the gratuity of God's revealing *to*, which is experienced as a surplus, as something in excess of the content of revelation, as Paul put it, as being caught up to the third heaven, hearing "things that are not to be told, that no mortal is permitted to repeat" (2 Corinthians 12:2-4). The often traumatic experience of this revelatory surplus characterizes many of the biblical encounters with God (or the angel of the Lord) such that the recipient of divine address responds with fear and must be told, "Fear not." It is the locus of this fear of being divinely addressed that is particularly interesting from a psychoanalytical viewpoint. Furthermore, in the biblical context at least, that fear must be abated before revelation is given.

---

37 Eric Santner, *On the Psychopathology of Everyday Life: Reflections on Freud and Rosenzweig* (Chicago: University of Chicago Press, 2001), 38.

What this implies more generally is that the trauma of being revealed *to*, the subjective confusion that arises when being addressed by God, is both the impediment to and the condition of receiving revelation, and, further, it is only by the initiative of the addressor that the addressee resolves this confusion and configures herself as a subject of revelation. As a point of comparison, we should consider the fascinating notion of "the nothingness of revelation" that is discussed in a letter from Gershom Scholem to Walter Benjamin. He writes:

> You ask what I understand by the "nothingness of revelation"? I understand by it a state in which revelation appears to be without meaning, in which it still asserts itself, in which it has *validity* but *no significance*. A state in which the wealth of meaning is lost and what is in the process of appearing (for revelation is such a process) still does not disappear, even though it is reduced to the zero point of its own content, so to speak.[38]

Scholem is describing a mode of signifying address in which the *that* of revelation persists in the absence of the *what*, such that the addressee is able only to discern that she is being addressed without knowing by whom or to what end.

Slavoj Žižek finds the same phenomenon in the novels of Kafka in which the protagonist "is interpellated by a mysterious bureaucratic entity … [but] this interpellation has a somewhat strange look: it is, so to say, an *interpellation without identification/subjectivation*."[39] Kafka's subject, in the absence of the proper identificatory cues, is unable to identify with the one who addresses and is left to flounder under the empty sign of a contentless call. Thus, the fundamental question that the possibility of this mode of address raises is in what these identificatory cues would consist, if they were present. In other words, what is the critical distinction between biblical divine inter-

---

38 Gershom Scholem, Letter to Benjamin, 20 September 1934, *The Correspondence of Walter Benjamin and Gershom Scholem 1932–1940*, trans. Gary Smith and Andre Lefevre (New York: Schocken, 1989), 142, quoted in Eric Santner, *On the Psychopathology of Everyday Life: Reflections on Freud and Rosenzweig* (Chicago: University of Chicago Press, 2001), 38.

39 Slavoj Žižek, *The Sublime Object of Ideology* (London: Verso, 1989), 44.

pellation and the Kafkaesque? Both modes of interpellation are subjectivizing, bringing about a certain transformative awareness of being identified as a certain kind of subject under a certain kind of demand, though they admit different ends. For Santner, following Rosenzweig, divine interpellation is itself a demand for love, a demand to be loved by the addressee. Moreover, Santner identifies two modes of divine interpellation, one in which the addressee is identified as a part or member of a larger whole, and the other in which the addressee is singled out as having no larger whole.[40] It is the latter mode that "transpires in and through a call of love"[41] and at the same time short-circuits the totalizing logic of the former.

Thus, we see here the traces of the beloved-lover transformation that undergirds the significatory dynamics of John's epistle. The implications of this dynamic are staggering: not only have we located in the act of revelation itself a glimpse into the way in which God's own desire is inscribed into the structure of divine revelation as such, such that God addresses us in love precisely as the demand to be loved in return. Revelation, insofar as it transformatively addresses its subject, makes it possible for the addressee to surpass the deadlock of a self-enclosed subjectivity, hitherto unillumined by God's call. Thus, as Santner writes, it is in this way that revelation can be understood to be "the language game of divine love."[42]

More important is that God, who should occupy the position of beloved *ad infinitum*, takes on the indignity of being lover to those who should love God and love God naturally, but often do not and certainly do not naturally. On Santner's account, it should be clear just how any notion of genuine divine revelation depends on Irenaean-Johannine principles as the very condition of its possibility; for if God is not pure love, there can be no legitimate demand to be loved in return that is not also erotically over-determined, which is to say, self-interested. If God is not pure love, divine revelation itself must ultimately be understood as transgressive, as an instance of divine *tolma* in which God desires and demands from human beings what is lacking in Godself.[43] Finally, if God is not pure love, the creation of the

---

40 Santner, *Psychopathology of Everyday Life*, 65.

41 Ibid.

42 Ibid.

43 One of the most sophisticated presentations of a Christian understanding of a

world and life in it cannot be conceived as existing in any key other than aboriginal and constitutive alienation.

Yet the Irenaean-Johannine frame in which Cyril's discourse articulates itself extends far beyond the level of speculation of divine things. In John's language, as we have seen, it is by loving that we know God, for God is love. It is to respond to the call of love by loving, or more precisely, by accepting the interpellative prompt in divine address to accept the subjective position as beloved and to complete the circuit by loving God back. If the beloved-lover transformation is inscribed in the act of divine interpellation itself, it is ex-scribed, written out, in the actualization of human response. In the language of Irenaeus, this ex-scription is given a clear soteriological valence:

> And Paul in like manner declares, "Love is the fulfilling of the law:" (Rom. 13:10) and [he declares] that when all other things have been destroyed, there shall remain "faith, hope, and love; but the greatest of all is love"; (1 Cor. 13:13) and that apart from the love of God, neither knowledge avails anything (1 Cor. 13:2), nor the understanding of mysteries, nor faith, nor prophecy, but that without love all are hollow and vain; moreover, that love makes man perfect; and that he who loves God is perfect, both in this world and in that which is to come. For we do never cease from loving God; but in proportion as we continue to contemplate Him, so much the more do we love Him. (*Against Heresies*, IV.12.2–3)

That this passage is taken from the *Adversus Haereses* is not insignificant, as it is precisely on the possibility of this transformation of beloved to lover that heresy gambles. For Irenaeus, moreover, God's demand to be loved is not agonistically construed, as God gains nothing in being loved; rather, in the human response to return that love, to become beloved lovers of God and neighbor, we are perfected, even unto salvation: as love, the giver is perfect.

---

non-competitive, complementary relationship between divine *agape* and *eros* can be found in Pope Benedict XVI's encyclical *Deus Caritas Est*; see Pope Benedict XVI, *Deus Caritas Est*, especially pp. 13–33.

In both Irenaeus and in Cyril, insofar as he operates within Irenaean-Johannine parameters, we see the twofold structure of revelation, the *that* and the *what*, in play. *That* God loves and does so efficaciously by inviting us to re-constitute ourselves as beloved who are called and even demanded to love, structures and motivates the anti-Gnostic discourse of each. The fact that Cyril takes direct aim at the modern iterations of Gnosticism represents more than an updating of the Irenaean problematic to the modern field; it is more so the identification of the persistence of the same age-old risk of making impossible the transformation of beloved to lover, which is likewise both the very possibility of the reception of revelation as well as salvation.

Thus, if we can discern the desire behind Cyril's anti-Gnostic discourse, it is the desire not only for the putative openness of an abstract possibility for the beloved of God to become lovers of God; it must also be the transitive desire for its actualization in the lives of actual human beings, a desire itself made possible by the individual reality of this very transformation, or at worst an approximation of it. Or, to put it in more recognizably theological language, it is the desire for the salvation of others, in which the biblical injunction to love your neighbor finds its highest expression.

CHAPTER TWELVE

The Unity of Cyril O'Regan's Work

Narrative Grammar and the Space for a Post-Modern Theology

Anthony C. Sciglitano, Jr.

Perhaps Cyril O'Regan's finest attribute as a scholar and thinker is knowing the cost of an argument, especially an argument with a worthy opponent. The "perhaps" is to be taken seriously, as one might easily argue for his intellectual range across the three disciplines of literature, philosophy, and theology, including the massive secondary literature on major figures in each; his generosity to alternative or even inadequately articulated views; his combination of fidelity to tradition and hospitality to contrasting voices; his ascetic refusal to pad essays with details unrelated to the argument at hand; or his philosophical rigor. Affinity for modest undertakings can be ruled out as virtue or vice attributable to Cyril. Indeed, I choose the "cost of an argument" because for his overall project, all of the above is required and in evidence. His expenditure is unreserved but not exhausted. Indeed, Cyril seems to be publishing at a more furious pace than ever. More importantly, his project as a whole, perhaps clear to him from the beginning, has begun to come into focus for others. To give a persuasive account of the unity of this project, even if only in its broad contours, is the challenge of this essay. I will argue in three parts that Cyril's work exhibits a unified if highly ramified effort to show the possibility and even desirability for a post-modern Catholic theology, and, more importantly, for the intellectual viability of Catholic ecclesial existence in the post-modern age.[1] That Cyril is able to see where the most definitive challenges to Catholic ecclesial existence lie, and that he engages them wholeheartedly, distinguishes him from those who begin a constructive or systematic theological effort from "post-modernism" assuming both that this is intellectually viable and that it can provide a kind of "sign of the times" that orients theology. While many of these efforts thus make overtures to the cultural moment, it is never clear why the cultural moment would or should care.

To specify this claim, we can say that Cyril's approach has two major prongs: the first supports or recommends thinkers and theoretical formulations supportive of a post-modern theology;[2] the second refutes thinkers who would (a) render theological pluralism impossible, (b) render theology impossible, or (c) eliminate or derange Christian doctrine and forms of life under pressure from modern intellectual assumptions and regulations that frequently act as stipulations rather than arguments. These two prongs are sometimes joined, as in two essays on John Henry Newman and in Cyril's first volume on Balthasar and philosophical modernity.[3] Often, however, Cyril employs what we might call an "ascetic generosity": that is, he restricts himself austerely to one task, but engages that particular task with an overwhelming capaciousness and intensity. This is the case with the text I will discuss in Part I, *The Heterodox Hegel*,[4] in which Cyril strives to uncouple mainline Christian traditions from Hegelian revisionist interpretation.

---

1   This is especially clear in his recent text on Hans Urs von Balthasar and in an essay on the pluriformity of tradition. Both of these will be discussed below.

2   This is most clear in *Anatomy of Misremembering: Von Balthasar's Response to Philosophical Modernity,* Vol. I: *Hegel* (New York: Crossroad, 2014), where Balthasar is read as a post-modern theologian who welcomes and maintains plural theological vision. We can easily include here William Desmond, who is not a theologian, but a philosopher (thus, my choice of the term "thinker" above). I will refer to this volume as *AM* throughout.

3   See Cyril O'Regan, "Newman and the Argument of Holiness," *Newman Studies* 9, no. 1 (Spring 2012): 52–74, and "Newman and Anti-Liberalism," *Sacred Heart Review* (Fall 1992): 63–88.

4   Cyril O'Regan, *The Heterodox Hegel* (Albany: State University of New York Press, 1994). I will refer to this volume as *HH* throughout.

A somewhat hidden target of this uncoupling, however, is the post-modern critique of Christianity.

If, however, Cyril's argument in *HH* stands, it is nevertheless the case that a post-modern theology would have trouble grounding itself in Derridean disdain for the semantic. The sense that post-modernism is code for relativism and is thus hostile to any kind of Christian—but especially Catholic—metanarrative (or metanarrative itself)[5] would create a seemingly unbridgeable chasm that no Catholic theology could cross. Yet Cyril clearly believes that both plural theological formulation and the attention to particularity of concern to any self-respecting post-modern thinker do, in fact, matter. The question then becomes one of sponsorship. What sponsors this pluralism and attention to particularity? A Catholic post-modernity must derive its sponsorship of plural theological formulation from some place other than semantic refusal or semiotic absolutism. Legitimation of Derrida will not be Cyril's priority. Here, opposition to Hegel finds accompaniment in critiques of Kant[6] and Derrida,[7] and an essay on H.S. Harris[8] on the one hand, and support or promotion of theological voices supportive of pluralism on Christocentric grounds (i.e., Newman, Balthasar, Möhler) on the other. Part II of this essay will show Cyril's support for theological visions that promote theological pluralism by way of Christocentric excess. Finally, Part III of this essay will show that he also offers a theory of doctrine that endorses such pluralism. Here I will investigate the positive importance of the idea and possible uses of Cyril's Christian Narrative Grammar (CNG).

---

5 Cyril observes that the proscription on "metanarrative" in Lyotard is due not "simply to its comprehensive range, but rather in addition it has built into it the metalinguistic function of the justification of its discourse and its rights to preside over all other narratives" (AM, 285).

6 Cyril O'Regan, "Kant: Blind-Spots, Boundaries, and Supplement," in *Christianity and Secular Reason*, ed. Jeffrey Bloechl (Notre Dame, IN: University of Notre Dame Press, 2012), 87–126.

7 Cyril O'Regan, "Hegel, Sade, and Gnostic Infinities," *Radical Orthodoxy: Journal of Theology, Philosophy, and Politics* (September 2013): 383–425.

8 Cyril O'Regan, "The Impossibility of a Christian Reading of the *Phenomenology of Spirit*: H.S. Harris on Hegel's Liquidation of Christianity," *The Owl of Minerva: Journal of the Hegel Society of America* 33, no. 1 (Fall/Winter 2001–2002): 45–95.

I. Heterodox Hegel: The Great Uncoupling

One has only to look at the two volumes recently published by Slavoj Žižek to recognize the contemporary relevance of the Hegelian corpus.[9] Žižek observes that for two centuries philosophy can be "defined by taking distance from Hegel."[10] Georges Bataille, however, perhaps sets the stage for the approach taken in Cyril's magisterial *Heterodox Hegel* when he writes, "Hegel's thoughts are interdependent to the point of it being impossible to grasp their meaning, if not in the necessity of the movement which constitutes their coherence."[11] "Bataille knew," according to Derrida, that to take Hegel's system seriously "was to prohibit oneself from extracting concepts from it, or from manipulating isolated propositions, drawing effects from them by transportation into a discourse foreign to them...."[12] Cyril strives to take

---

9 Slavoj Žižek, *The Most Sublime Hysteric: Hegel with Lacan*, trans. Thomas Scott-Railton (Cambridge: Polity Press, 2014); Žižek, *Less than Nothing: Hegel and the Shadow of Dialectical Materialism* (London: Verso, 2012). It is arguable that Hegel provides the locational and substantive center for Francis Fukuyama's influential argument in *The End of History and the Last Man* (New York: Free Press, 2006 [1992]). See, especially, chapters 13 and 18. Given Žižek's estimate of Hegel's importance and cultural authority, it would not be outlandish to think of Cyril's *HH* as analogous to a commentary on the *Sentences*, especially as it was his doctoral dissertation. In *HH*, Cyril takes each theological episode as treated in Hegelian texts and weighs Hegel's interpretations against those of the mainline tradition. Of course, the style and form are nothing like a scholastic treatment, but the fine distinctions, the calling to mind the tradition, and the wrestling with an authority all look similar.

10 Žižek, *The Most Sublime Hysteric*, 1. Cyril quotes Derrida to a similar effect from Derrida's *Positions*: "We have never finished with a reading or rereading of Hegel, and, in a certain way, I do nothing other than attempt to explain myself on this point." Quoted in *HH*, 12. The original is in Jacques Derrida, *Positions*, trans. Alan Bass (Chicago: University of Chicago Press, 1978), 77.

11 Qtd. in Jacques Derrida, "From Restricted to General Economy: A Hegelianism without Reserve," *Writing and Difference* (Chicago: University of Chicago Press, 1978), 253.

12 Ibid. Cyril would also seem to agree with Bataille and Derrida that "Misconstrued, treated lightly, Hegelianism only extends its historical domination, finally unfolding its immense enveloping resources without obstacle" (Derrida, *Writing and Difference*, 251). Agreement with this view is most clearly found in his essay "Marion: Crossing of Hegel," in *Counter Experiences: Reading Jean-Luc Marion* (South Bend, IN: University of Notre Dame Press, 2007), 95–150. See also his statement on H.S. Harris's *Hegel's Ladder*: "... Harris's text succeeds in showing

Hegel whole. Yet the overriding question of *HH* is a seemingly simple one: is Hegel's claim that formal sublations from representation (*Vorstellung*) to concept (*Begriff*) do not alter Christian content true with respect, especially, to the Christian theological tradition? Otherwise put, once a consensus that Hegel's philosophy is best served at least penultimately with a religious interpretation,[13] is Hegel's claim to Christian fidelity sustainable, or does some other religious formation or no religious formation better represent his ultimate position? The "simple" turns out to be immensely complex (a) because the movement from representation to conceptual articulation is, arguably, how Hegel conceives the primary task of philosophy,[14] and (b) because adjudicating the "fidelity" issue involves massive knowledge of the philosophical and theological traditions, knowledge of the highly contested field of Hegel interpretation all coupled to a method of analysis that helps reveal the depth grammar of Hegel's system.

The Hegelian promise, for Christian thought, is extremely seductive. Hegel promises not only to preserve Christian content, but to show that Christian revelation is "true reason" and thus to legitimate Christianity across a modern breach that would vitiate central doctrines such as Trinity and Christology, among others. Along with Christianity, Hegel simultaneously authorizes the modern age. Thus, to be Hegelian is doubly attractive: Hegel allows Christianity to retain and even secure its content while cele-

---

that the *Phenomenology* outdoes and completes all previous philosophy by sorting through, in the light of ancient skepticism as much as the modern challenges posed by Hume and Kant, how an adequate philosophical discourse is possible" (Cyril O'Regan, "The Impossibility of a Christian Reading of the *Phenomenology of Spirit*: H.S. Harris on Hegel's Liquidation of Christianity, *The Owl of Minerva* 33, no. 1 (Fall/Winter 2001–2002): 82).

13   *HH*, 4.

14   See, for instance, Hegel, *Encyclopedia of the Philosophical Sciences in Basic Outline, Part I: Science of Logic*, ed. and trans. Klaus Brinkman and Daniel O. Dahlstrom (Cambridge: Cambridge University Press, 2010), §3 and §5; see also the introduction, p. xiv. Citations will be written as *Encyclopedia* followed by the section numbers and page numbers. "Zu" stands for "*Zustand*" or additions that were put into the text later by students as reflective of Hegel's oral presentation of the materials. Cyril discusses again, in one of his most intensive pieces, the relation of *Vorstellung* and *Begriff* in "Hegel and the Folds of Discourse," *International Philosophical Quarterly* 39, no. 2 (June 1999): 173–93.

brating modern culture with its attendant lures of autonomy and equality.

This all makes Hegel intriguing, but for Cyril also serpent-like: the promise is a lie, the double a counterfeit.[15] Uncoupling or undoubling Hegel from Christian tradition is crucial, especially as Hegel's system not only "deranges" Christianity itself, but also renders confessional forms of Christianity (and Judaism) logically passé. Cyril agrees with Harris's conclusion on the *Phenomenology* that Hegel does not maintain Christian content through formal shifts.[16] With deliberate and near-forensic care, Cyril argues in *HH* that Hegel's thought is best read as a complete rewriting of Christian tradition, its thoroughgoing hermeneutic warping with respect to all Christian doctrines both individually and as a system, and its valorization of knowledge and divine transparency over against apophatic mysticism in its pre-modern and modern (i.e., post-Kantian) forms.[17] Hegelian "speculative rewriting"[18] or "derangement"[19] of traditional Christian narrative grammar serves his end of systematic, transparent, and total knowledge. Such knowl-

---

15   This is to invoke William Desmond's view of Hegel's system as a "counterfeit double." See William Desmond, *Hegel's God: A Counterfeit Double?* (New York and London: Routledge, 2017).

16   Harris thinks that any view holding that change in form can leave content unaltered is naïve in general, but especially so with respect to Hegel. Cyril is non-committal as to what Hegel claims. Admittedly, there is textual evidence for Hegel stating that the role of the movement is to sustain content not to overturn it (*Encyclopedia* §5, 32); however, a conclusion that this means "content as traditionally given" would in fact be naïve. It is more nearly the case that Hegel gives a non-traditional interpretation of different biblical and traditional theological representations such that they become more easily conceptualized later. Thus, he can say that he is preserving content, but the content has already been thoroughly re-interpreted. See, for example, his reading of the story of the Fall in *Encyclopedia* §24zu.1, 58–66.

17   See *HH*, 31–44, for Hegelian elimination of divine mystery in principle. It is important to note, however, that Hegel does so on the basis of defending Christianity and doctrine against what he sees as the substitution of feeling (and thus doctrine as either secondary or beside the point) for knowledge of a self-revealing divine inherent to the Christian message. On this point, see especially *HH*, 31–32.

18   *HH*, 339; see the entire seventh chapter of *HH* entitled "Representation and Concept: Speculative Rewriting," 331–70.

19   For his use of this term, see Cyril O'Regan, *Gnostic Return in Modernity* (Albany: State University of New York Press, 2001), especially 12, 59.

edge must be integral and proceed through logical necessity. To be total, O'Regan explains, it must be both self-reflexive and find closure.[20] Narrative, in this case, is not merely a type of discourse, but rather indicates the unfolding of the divine in and through time as it moves from an abstract and non-serious form of being toward its end of self-realization/determination and full self-comprehension. The term "ontotheology" or "ontotheological narrative" means here that Hegel forges a connection between theology and philosophy, the divine and being, such that being comes to full self-transparency. In broad, hermeneutical terms, the movement from representation (*Vorstellung*) to concept (*Begriff*) substitutes for the eventfulness of revelation a kind of "manifestation," eliminates succession and happening, marginalizes at best any focus on the empirical Jesus of Nazareth and seeks to remove all traces of divine transcendence. To take one example, Hegel makes creation an iteration of the fall, thus negatively revaluing creation itself; in addition, the fall becomes a logically necessary rather than contingent event of human will and disobedience.[21]

If Hegel represents a temptation for Christians, he also sets the bait for post-moderns who take him at his word to have represented Christianity faithfully. Thus, post-modern thinkers such as Derrida can take a victory over the former as a defeat of the latter.[22] The post-modern critique gains energy from Hegel's pretensions to total explanation, from the justification of violence that this explanatory system appears to countenance, from a

---

20   *HH*, 57–59.

21   On creation and fall in Hegel, see *HH*, 151–88; also all of chap. 3, "The Second Narrative Epoch: Creation and the Epoch of the Son," 141–88.

22   See O'Regan, *Anatomy of Misremembering* (*AM*), 252. For a more focused discussion of Derrida's *Glas* regarding this taking the counterfeit for the real, see O'Regan's essay "Hegel, Sade, and Gnostic Infinities," *Radical Orthodoxy: Journal of Theology, Philosophy, and Politics* (September 2013): 383–425: "... he [Derrida] never raises the critical question as to whether the discontinuities between Christianity and Hegelian thought are as superficial as Hegel suggests. In contradistinction to both Hegel and Derrida I argue here that they are more significant than either allows, and that the gap is such that Christianity can defend itself not only against the charge of logocentrism (and the implied charge of theodicy), but also against the charge of violence and repression," 387–388. Cyril argues here that Derrida misses the inherent violence in the way he frames his deconstruction in *Glas* by obscuring the history of Sadean effects in the French literary tradition of Jean Genet.

desire to protect the irreducibility of the particular, and from a rejection of the dominance of philosophical discourse vis-à-vis other discourses such as literature, religion, and art. Cyril shows that Balthasar shares many of these concerns.[23] To uncouple Hegel from the mainline Christian tradition, then, is to shield Christian tradition from post-modern critiques that take the former for the latter.

That Cyril has in mind post-modern interpretations of Hegel is evident both in the early and later stages of *HH*. At an earlier stage he sides with Derrida against interpreters who hermeneutically foreground history and temporality in Hegel, thus underestimating narrative closure,[24] and also, it would seem, against those such as Peter Hodgson who would find a lack of narrative closure in Hegel's system.[25] Arguments between Hegel and post-moderns in general (and Lyotard, Ricoeur, Bataille, Heidegger, Mark Taylor, and Derrida in particular) return to the foreground in the final chapter. The central issue here seems to be Hegel's desire to maintain narrative apart from the contingency or contingent events common to narrative as a form of discourse, but also to close the narrative in such a way as to render meaning transparent. Apart from narrative closure or ending, meaning forfeits the teleological ground of its possibility. Markers of contingency include a "discourse of happening,"[26] "successiveness," "sequentiality," and "punctiliarity" typically related to biblical events such as creation, incarnation, crucifixion, and resurrection, among others.[27] O'Regan observes, however, that for Hegel, these features inherent to narrative discourse are problematic:

> [These elements of representation introduce] "happening" and "accident" into the depiction of the divine that affects the kind of coherence required to constitute the divine as truth (also science) (*Enc* #1, 9; *LPR* 1 1821 MS E 247–248, G 156; 1824 E 334, G 236). This coherence is guaranteed if and only if what Hegel refers to as

---

23 See *AM*, 68–69; cf. 56–57.

24 *HH*, 13.

25 *HH*, 57–61. For Hodgson and O'Regan's exchange on the issues, see *Owl of Minerva* 37, no. 1 (Fall/Winter 2005/2006).

26 *HH*, 338.

27 *HH*, 340–41.

"the connectional matrix" (*LPR* 1821 MS E248–249, G 156–158) is structured by necessity rather than by contingent event (*LPR* 1 1821 MS E 255–256, G 163; 1827 E 401–402, G 296).[28]

In addition to deconstructing any "language of happening and accident," Hegel wishes to rid his "speculative rewriting" of all remnants of divine will or action—that is, theological voluntarism broadly defined.[29] Cyril reveals in his analysis of Hegel's denarratizing operation not merely that *Vorstellungen* or representational discourse is to be sublated into conceptual discourse, but rather that Hegel hierarchically orders *Vorstellungen* such that higher grades can critique lower ones, all of which receive their grades on the basis of the degree to and ease with which they are conceptually redeemable. Cyril then details the precise mechanisms, or "denarratizing operators," by which narrative receives its sublation in the Hegelian system at nearly every turn.[30]

Yet Hegel's de-narratization of Christian discourse does not, in O'Regan's view, mean the utter deletion of narrative, at least as defined by ordered progression, within Hegelian conceptual space.[31] He gives several rea-

---

28 Ibid., 338.

29 *HH*, 347. Indeed, very broadly. We are not talking about nominalism here so much as the general Christian idea that God acts on creation at all, that is, divine agency.

30 There is something interesting and perhaps telling in Cyril's language of "denarratizing operators." Surely Hegel wants one to feel the organic movement of his entire system of Spirit. A logic, yes, but a beautiful, epical logic of Being that arrives at modernity and freedom. Cyril's use of the term "denarratizing operators," however, suggests that force external to the system is at play, that not all is a providential march to modernity. Indeed, the term "denarratizing operator" whispers of the Industrial Revolution, its mechanization and destruction of human life that must be justified by the movement of Hegelian *Geist*. And in this whisper, perhaps, we hear an echo of Marx and his critique.

31 This is a crucial point because the rest of *HH* is given to arguing for a reading of Hegelian philosophy as a rewriting of Christian narrative grammar in such a way that it ends up as a nineteenth-century revisioning of Valentinian Gnostic grammar. O'Regan argues that Hegelian dialectic is not merely a panentheistic dialectic, but also, in its depth structures, a narrative dialectic. Indeed, the dialectic gains its meaning from its ontotheological narrative context. See *HH*, 298, for this point. If narrative is entirely deleted by Hegel, even in the final stages, this argument would suffer.

sons for this interpretation. First, whatever "logic" means to Hegel, it is not of the "Kantian analytic"[32] type, and it is not merely formal logic;[33] rather, it incorporates being itself and strives to know the infinite. Second, he contends that it is at least plausible, and perhaps probable both textually and analytically, to understand Hegelian philosophy as a second-order discourse designed to save "metaphoric-narrative discourse by assimilating it, while at the same time supplying reflective argumentative warrants that metaphoric-narrative is incapable of supplying."[34] This is an important point for two reasons: (1) should logic be first-order, then narrative would ultimately be eliminated for pure conceptual articulation; (2) that narrative is underwritten rather than eliminated allows Cyril to argue that some forms of narrative or metanarrative discourse will prove more conceptually salvageable than others for the Hegelian system. Perhaps also for a third reason. As second-order discourse, philosophy is involved in the total legitimation of the entire metanarrative at a level that faith discourse is not. This is the logocentrism that Derrida and Lyotard decry but also conflate with Christian theological/ontotheological discourse.

Cyril, at this point (1994), is still working out his Gnostic return thesis, but suggests at various points in *HH* that the narrative of the heterodox Lutheran, Jacob Boehme, and the second-century narratives of Valentinian Gnosticism are significant possibilities as taxa for Hegel's system.[35] The "denarratizing

---

32 *HH*, 340.

33 Hegel makes this clear in the *Encyclopedia* both in his opening discussion of logic, §10, §19, and also throughout his discussion of the Critical Philosophy in §40–45.

34 *HH*, 363; cf. 357.

35 "Suggest" is too weak a word here, but useful to note that Cyril does not want to make the full-fledged argument in *HH*. He has already begun significant work on his Gnostic return thesis within *HH* through penetrating critiques of other candidates for Hegelian revision such as neo-Platonism, Eckhartian mysticism, and Spinozism, to name three. In addition, he notes throughout various points at which Boehme or Valentinian Gnosticism make better sense than any of these others. The full methodological discussion for ascription of Gnostic return, however, can be found in *Gnostic Return in Modernity* (Albany: State University of New York Press, 2001). Boehme will be the major modern conduit of Valentinianism to modernity. See *Gnostic Apocalypse: Jacob Boehme's Haunted Narrative* (Albany: State University of New York Press, 2002), 2. A volume is planned and mostly written on Hegel in the series.

operators" that he adduces function to remove contingency and the lack of integration inherent to lower levels of *Vorstellung* especially, but also to give necessity to Hegel's heterodox narrative configuration and the content he wants to underwrite. So narrative discourse remains, but as underwritten and under-writeable by Hegelian logic. What remains of narrative is limited, but essential. Although necessity replaces contingent event and divine willful action—and to some extent and in some places human agency—there remains a kind of master syllogistic *narrative* order of Universality moving through Particularity to Individuality[36] (U-P-I) within Hegelian logical space. These points are crucial for Cyril's reading of Hegel's system as an instance of Gnostic return, for he will interpret Gnosticism as an ontotheological *narrative* reconfiguration of Christian narrative grammar that structures the divine itself. Should Hegel excise narrative, Cyril's argument that he presents a narrative rewriting of Christian tradition would fail.[37]

In *HH*, then, Cyril has shown that Hegel's ontotheological rendition of Christianity is not consonant with any traditional (i.e., Augustinian, Patristic, Lutheran) Christian form.[38] In addition, he persuades here and else-

---

36 Also called the "theological syllogism" (*HH*, 355) in that it structures divine becoming in Hegel's ontotheological narrative. That this is Hegel's master syllogism finds some evidence early in the *Encyclopedia* §24zu.1, p. 61. Speaking of the syllogism, Hegel writes: "It is that determination in virtue of which the particular is supposed to be the middle that joins the extremes of the universal and the individual together. This form of syllogistic inference is a universal form of all things." Of course, he says this in the first part, which is the logic. Cyril adduces more significant evidence still. See *HH*, 354–56.

37 I again want to flag O'Regan's discussion in "Hegel and the Folds of Discourse." He argues there for a hermeneutical "reflexive" view of philosophy's autonomy vis-à-vis other discourses from which it gains content to "think-over" as Hegel says in the *Encyclopedia*. Philosophy gains its autonomy through its critical hermeneutical work on other discourses and its ability to legitimate them (which they cannot do for themselves). This essay marks a development of chapter seven of *HH* both in relation to the complexity of the "between" in Hegel's interpretation (between theological reduction and absolute philosophical autonomy) and in relation to the discourses of modernity—in particular, Kant and the French Encyclopedists.

38 H.S. Harris agrees with this view, at least with respect to the *Phenomenology* (1807). In *HH*, Cyril works predominantly from the *Encyclopedia* and *Lectures on the Philosophy of Religion*. Of course, nearly all of Hegel's texts play some role in addition to a massive number of commentators. Cyril is amply aware that this does not

where that Hegel is a key site if not the key site of anxiety for post-modern critics. While he gives some credence to the post-modern critique of a lack of metaphoric or semantic excess in the Hegelian system,[39] post-modern traction ultimately seems weaker than Hegel's ability to respond. Or, perhaps more accurately, they fight to a draw.[40] If a post-modern critique points out the existence of metaphor and narrative within the Hegelian system, Cyril shows that, in fact, not only is it present, it is protected and legitimated by Hegel's philosophical second-order discourse. Cyril addresses all of this to post-modern detractors of Hegel. There will be no easy post-modern victories over Hegel. Nevertheless, *HH* shows that a victory over Hegel, should it occur, is not a victory over Christianity.

II. Christian Excess

The prospect of a post-modern Catholic theology faces significant opposition and, perhaps rightly, causes some anxiety. To the extent that post-modernism absolutizes perspectivalism or undercuts the privileging of meaning and truth, it fails as a candidate for Catholic theological appropriation. Nevertheless, for a Catholic theologian less than enamored with modern strictures on Christian content, practices, and forms of life, desirous of plural theological formulation and wanting to keep theology open to a variety of discourses (i.e., philosophy, literature, art), post-modernism appears as a breath of fresh air. This middle section of the essay observes Cyril's promotion of theological visions that offer resources for contesting modern and Hegelian restrictions to theological formulation and phenomenological description of Christianity and Christian practice.[41] I will highlight several lo-

---

rule out someone saying that it should be the Christian form. Peter Hodgson comes to mind here. See Hodgson, *Hegel and Christian Theology: A Reading of the Lectures on the Philosophy of Religion* (New York: Oxford University Press, 2005), 16–17.

39 See O'Regan's comment on Ricoeur and Bataille in *HH*, 362.

40 "The agon would continue, the battle simply played out on a different level. This itself, however, would be eloquent. Hegel would continue to be the hallowed enemy worth fighting, post-modernism's named other, perhaps the angel with which it wrestles to be blessed at daybreak" (*HH*, 370); cf. 368–70.

41 It is worth mentioning here that Cyril, in a number of places, has challenged Martin Heidegger's genealogy of modernity and his collapsing of pre-modern and modern in a critique of both. Cyril observes in *HH* that post-moderns frequently

cations where Cyril promotes the work of Balthasar and Newman to make the point that the option for plural theological formulation and Christian forms of life are to the fore in Cyril's work, often in opposition to a Hegelian undermining of such plurality.

That Balthasar stresses the generative excess of Christ for theological formulation, genre, metaphysical description, doxology, and Christian forms of life is no secret. Balthasar refuses both Catholic reduction to Thomas Aquinas and Hegelian discursive closure, which would involve the philosophical sublation of art, religion generally, and Christianity in particular.[42] These various "sublations," on Balthasar's reading, often presuppose a too-thin rendition of Christian doctrines and Christian traditional reflections, but also of the traditions of poetry and art.[43] On Cyril's reading, Balthasar seeks to undermine Hegel's renditions at nearly every point, while offering a massively capacious theology—or gallery of theologies—attractively presented for contemporary edification. Cyril eloquently encapsulates the generative excess for Balthasar of Christianity's Christological center:

> ... tradition consists of the articulate memories provoked by the glory of God disclosed in the cross and resurrection of Christ. These memories will be various as they reflect the unique perspectives and performances of individuals, communities, and historical periods. Moreover, they will be various as a matter of theological principle and not simply as a matter of fact. As the phenomenon of phenomena, Christ is exhausted neither by any single perspective nor their

---

follow Heidegger's genealogy of ontological forgetfulness uncritically. See *HH*, 366, and also his "Von Balthasar's Valorization and Critique of Heidegger's Concept of Modernity," in *Christian Spirituality and the Culture of Modernity* (Minneapolis, MN: Eerdmans, 1998), 123–58. More perspicacious from his point of view, then, would seem to be the connection of pre-modern and post-modern. Ann Astell interestingly made this point with reference to Cyril's poetry and the city of Alexandria in her essay "O'Regan as Origen in Alexandria," earlier in this book.

42   The anti-Hegelian stream of Balthasar's thought is foregrounded in the five volumes of *Theo-Drama*. The first volume, *Prolegomena*, also contests Hegel's death of art thesis. Cyril shows that *Glory of the Lord*, volumes 4 and 5 on metaphysics ancient and modern, contests Heidegger's genealogy.

43   *AM*, 20.

sum. Still, it is the case that the multiplicity and variety of perspectives provide a more adequate response to a reality than individual perspectives however singular.[44]

Balthasar seeks to upend modernity's forgetfulness and/or mis-remembering of Christian tradition to "impress and express the energy that comes only from excess."[45] Articulate faith response to the triune God, whose self-gift makes the tradition possible, "is both plural and highly differentiated; the tradition is genuinely multi-voiced and polyphonic."[46] The center of a plurivocal Catholic theology, then, is the semantically excessive divine self-revelation in Christ rather than a language that falls short of meaning or an overly dogmatic language that pretends to exhaust it.[47]

At a more structural level, Cyril makes a compelling argument that Balthasar is at times more interested in laying down protocols for particular doctrinal issues than giving a once-for-all position. This is especially the case, he argues, with respect to divine impassibility-passability disputes. The essential point for us here has not to do with issues of impassability, but rather with what Cyril sees as Balthasar's recommendation for a plurality of voices, each of which strives toward articulation of the mystery of God and each succeeding in important ways, but none of which are better alone than with the others. At some point, while explanation ought to be tried, in the end "the theologian must forsake explanatory for protocol discourse."[48] So, for example, he writes:

---

44   Ibid., 8. Further, Cyril writes of human being as the image of God: "whose vocation is a kind of transparence to the mysterious depth of a triune reality best characterized as infinitely deep and inexhaustible giving" (30–31).

45   Ibid., 31.

46   Ibid. Cyril shows that response to excess and mystery is key to both Balthasar's own view of tradition and acts as a measure of forms of thought generally, including those that would take "clear and distinct" as the final arbiter of truth. On the latter, see 31. Excess is present throughout the text. Neo-platonism receives plaudits from Balthasar for being "responsive to excess, mystery and giftedness" (67).

47   Nor is one left, as seemingly with Bataille, with excrement/waste, death, or transgressive sex as the only exits from the total consumption—because non-assimilable or digestible—for divine self-development of the Hegelian system.

48   *AM*, 244.

Thomas is strengthened when he is paired with Bonaventure, who more emphatically defines the entire Trinity as love, and whose cruciform credentials shout at us more loudly. But even together they are not sufficient. We can best know where explanation breaks off when we have truly attempted it. But explanations from both sides will, Balthasar insists, surely need to break off at some point. All explanations are referred to a height and a depth that is beyond them and into which they disappear. The trinitarian God is epistemically an asymptote.[49]

A final Balthasar example will further make the point that plural theological formulation is central to what Cyril seeks to promote. Cyril's essay "Balthasar: Between Tübingen and Postmodernity"[50] directly addresses the issue of a plural tradition that nevertheless has meaningfulness or semantic richness as its core and font. The argument of this essay is fascinating, especially as it has, once again, a post-modern terminus without being reductively apologetic. Here, however, we can only point to an earlier version, less obviously advocatory, of Balthasar's post-modern position supported in AM.[51] Cyril makes the essential point early in the essay:

With some reservation, then, it can be said that not only are each of the perspectives presented in *GL2–GL3* equally worthy of retrieval, but that they are also equally *capable* of retrieval. As the Prolegom-

---

49 Ibid., 244.

50 "Balthasar: Between Tübingen and Postmodernity," in *Modern Theology*, 14.3 (Summer 1998): 325–53.

51 *AM* is interesting in Cyril's work for any number of reasons. For one, his discussion of Balthasar seems more demonstratively or tonally anti-Hegelian than the remarkably irenic and deliberate *Heterodox Hegel*. In part, I suspect, this is due to his writing more nearly in a Balthasarian rhetorical register in *AM*. The other development is that while in the Balthasar-Tübingen essay he does not explicitly support Balthasar's pluriform rendition of tradition, it seems in *AM* he clearly becomes something of a promoter. This is evidenced in his using his own theory of narrative grammar to help with genealogy and his forceful justification of symbolic discourse. It would be odd to bring this in if he did not, in fact, see Balthasar's anti-Hegelianism and pro-plurality position as one to support.

enon of *GL1* makes clear, the plurality and variety of the tradition, which is inductively demonstrated in *GL2–GL7*, can be provided with explanatory warrant. As one might expect, Balthasar makes no appeal to the discourses of sociology or anthropology that might support a plurality claim. Plurality has, in his view, a theological ground. This ground is the *mysterium Christi*. The mystery of Christ exerts such fascination that it demands a vision which, since it is finite, is always only a point of view, and thus limited. Moreover, the excess of Christ with respect to any point of view encourages multiple and different perspectives in order partially to correspond to its literally infinite number of aspects. Needless to say, a tradition, which is the sum of perspectives on the *mysterium Christi*, does not exhaust this mystery. Correspondence in this context does not imply adequation. In what perhaps is best construed as a compliment to a perspectivalism, most clearly articulated by Cusanus, the coincidence of perspectives and their differences are found only in Christ, who is their provocateur.[52]

Clear from this paragraph are the two points we have heretofore been pursuing: Balthasar's support for plurality of theological tradition and formulation generated, evoked, and provoked not by a Kantian cognitive shortfall, but rather through Christian faith response to Christ precisely as inexhaustible revelation. The engagement with the Russian literary theorist Mikhail Bakhtin helps highlight Balthasar's inclusion of theologically informed discourses in poetry and theater that become included as theological resources (not to say, "sources") crucial for a time that frequently abandons beauty for argument and ethical rules.[53] If he is not quite as expansive as Bakhtin, nevertheless, Balthasar reaches for more plurality than either his Tübingen forerunner (Johann Adam Möhler), neo-Scholastics, or Hegel could countenance.[54]

---

52 Cyril O'Regan, "Balthasar: Between Tübingen and Postmodernity," 328.

53 This is a central point at the outset of *Glory of the Lord: Theological Aesthetics*, Vol. I: *Seeing the Form*, esp. 18–19.

54 When Cyril is critical of Balthasar, it is essentially regarding two points: first, a paucity in some of his argumentation, and second, in his aesthetic tastes where, at times, he seems to recur too strongly back to the sixteenth-century masters and thus exclude more art than is necessary.

Some justification is needed for a transition to discussing Cyril's work on Newman when the latter obviously cannot be a post-modern thinker in anything like a chronological sense. It is important to notice the dual role Newman plays in Cyril's work. On the one hand, Newman serves to cut through modern rational religion's pretensions to have made arguments against more traditional religious forms. Modern opposition to traditional Christianity's emphasis on prayer, its creedal fealty, hope for and official marking of sanctity joined to a doctrine of grace, and its view of the ubiquity of sin that must and can be overcome is deep and broad. Cyril beautifully excavates Newman's arguments against these standard complaints against doctrine, sacrament, prayer, and sin in two essays, but also discusses Newman's relation to Balthasar's theology of glory in an earlier piece.[55] Newman argues for a liturgically, doxologically, ascetically, and prayerfully rich Christianity. The explicit target of these essays is the Lockean atmosphere that permeates nineteenth-century England,[56] but also informs many of our contemporary assumptions with frequent reduction of religion to feeling, on the one hand (the Evangelical wing for Newman), and ethical or doctrinal formulas on the other (rational religion). Like Balthasar, Newman contends for a Christ whose glory outstrips any individual doctrinal formulation with a non-dogmatic, gloriously excessive center. Perhaps implicitly, however, Newman also plays the role of nineteenth-century antithesis to Hegel and a pointer to a reading of Hegel that, if he is ultimately cast in the garb of a neo-Gnostic thinker, he also comes to seem like the apotheosis of modern rational religion by other (apocalyptic) means. If, for Cyril, Newman shares ahead of time Balthasar's recognition of the gracious excess of divine revelation in Christ that calls forth awe, gratitude, and praise, Hegel is the philosopher who begins with worship but systematically overcomes these more "limiting" features of Christian thought and practice that have their condition of possibility in divine transcendence and mystery. Promissory notes of this reading of Hegel are to be found in *HH* and in an article on H.S. Harris's reading of the *Phenomenology of Spirit*.[57] *Anatomy of Misremembering*, however,

---

55 "Von Balthasar and Newman: The Christological Contexting of the Numinous," Eglise et Théologie 26, no. 2 (1995): 165–202.

56 On the atmospherics of the Enlightenment, see O'Regan, "Newman's Anti-Liberalism," 86–87. On the importance of Locke (and the Lockean assumptions of his own age) as a Newmanian target, see "Newman's Anti-Liberalism," 94, 101, 102, 107.

57 On Cyril's reading of Harris's position, Hegelian holiness is "marked by the

reads Balthasar in the most forceful of ways, exposing Hegelian rewriting of worship as philosophy without remainder, rendering prayer monological, and eliminating the gratitude that lies at the center of Eucharistic practice.[58] All of this is to suggest that the essays on Newman help support Cyril's case not only against modern rational critiques of Christian practice, but also as a bulwark against a Hegelian "liquidation" of particular Christian practices and forms of life. Much more could be said about the Newman articles, but I will close with just one more observation. Hegel, in the fourth chapter of the *Phenomenology of Spirit* and again toward the end of his *Lectures on the Philosophy of Religion*, makes clear that for him Catholicism is an alienating and joyless affair: alienating because beholden to an institutional mediating body that mediates not that which is present, nor what is intellectually grasped, but an impossible, immutable beyond that requires sacrifice of intellect and will; joyless because of required renunciations of worldly enjoyments through "fastings and mortifications."[59] Cyril's discussion in the Balthasar-Newman piece, then, not only serves to bring these two thinkers together, but also shows that for these two Catholic thinkers the ever-greater glory of God encountered in Christ, which gives rise to awe and even a sense of one's iniquity, focally and decidedly brings joy.[60]

III. Narrative Grammar and Theological Plurality

---

terrors of otherness, mystery and heteronomy" (74). Holiness here is "communitarian" and involves "liberation from dependence on Christ" as its condition (74, 75). For Harris, Hegel's *Phenomenology* is the "liquidation" of Christianity insofar as "transcendence, mystery, and contingency" are factors "basic to the definition and self-definition of Christian discourse as such" (ibid., 70). On worship and its overcoming, see 78–79. The suggestion here is that whatever worship might still mean for Hegel, it would seem to be "non-doxological." See also *HH*, 246.

58 For a fuller discussion of these issues in *AM*, see my "Death in Cyril O'Regan's *Anatomy of Misremembering*," *Nova et Vetera* 14, no. 3 (2016): 1003–14.

59 G.W.F. Hegel, *Phenomenology of Spirit*, trans. A.V. Miller (Oxford: Oxford University Press, 1977), pp. 136–37, §226–29.

60 Of course, any such discussion also has a rebound effect. To the extent that institutional or theological practice occludes or enervates the excessive glory encountered in Christ, and registered in the New Testament in the experience of joy and rejoicing, then correction becomes necessary.

Since *HH*, Cyril has expressed his preference for the systematic over *aperçu*.[61] Thus, his approach to Hegel, if not his conclusions, differ entirely from that of Kierkegaard.[62] This preference for systematicity and theory gets amplified in *GR*.[63] Indeed, his particular form of theory serves a clear anti-Hegelian agenda and a rich and plural conception of Christian tradition and doctrine.

The anti-Hegelian front comes not only from his development of a Gnostic narrative grammar and association of Hegel with it, but also in his methodological preference for narrative coherence over and above logical coherence. Narrative grammar would overturn the Hegelian impetus toward total knowledge and self-legitimation and thus give apophatic space its due. *Apophasis* is code for neither "anything-goes" pluralism nor for a content-less Christianity, the latter of which might actually serve the former. Rather, for Cyril as for Balthasar, *apophasis* inscribes an excess that resists closure and total transparency. Cyril's appropriation of narrative theory for doctrine has the effect of elevating multivalent *Vorstellung* and demoting a would-be transparent and total conceptual articulation. Instead, conceptual formulation, while remaining significant, is always subject to narrative-grammatical purification, contextualization, and supplementation by other formulations. Of course, this has the correlative effect of a re-narratization of Christian revelation and thus the admission of finitude, both epistemically and ontologically, not as something to overcome through logic, but as part of the gift of being, the very space for plurality. Indeed, the post-modern critique of meta-narrative *per se* as self-legitimating and fully transparent remains a target for Cyril in *GR*: "Related to the interest in promoting a generous orthodoxy implicated in a grammatical reading of the biblical narrative is the interest in defending the metanarrative of Christianity, whether trinitarianly rendered or not, from charges that its discourse is totalitarian and self-legitimating."[64] Thus narrative grammar serves ge-

---

61 *HH*, 6.

62 In his essay on H.S. Harris, Cyril notes that while Harris may be right to bemoan Kierkegaard's lack of philosophical sophistication vis-à-vis Hegel, Kierkegaard's conclusions with respect to Hegel and Christianity are borne out by Harris's own discussion.

63 Yet Cyril shows himself fully aware of the deficits of systematicity and theory, namely, the tendency of each to exclude data and experiential richness for clarity.

64 *GR*, 14.

nealogically to uncouple Hegelian meta-narrative from Christian, to allow for the rightful place of apophasis within theology, and, more positively, to generate an alternative theory of doctrine that formally allows for plurality, or what he calls in *GR* a "generous orthodoxy."[65]

Generosity, for Cyril, is a function of both style and theory. His rejection in *GR* of a demonological or hysterical orthodoxy for a "middle-voiced"[66] and irenic style supports his overall aim for a generous orthodoxy. Demonology chills discourse and prematurely squelches self-criticism and insight.[67] A second key move toward generosity is the shift from a prioritization of content or propositional conception of doctrine to a grammatical conception. Narrative grammar is an attempt to construe the unity of doctrine within a vast array of christianly desirable plurality due to both alethic excess and cultural, historical, and even individual differences (i.e., individual talent, emphasis, or insight). It is crucial, however, that Cyril's particular grammatical rendition works in a thoroughly *a posteriori* manner rather than seeking to control data through *a priori* restriction.[68] This option means that Christian Narrative Grammar (CNG) does not exist independently of

---

65 See *GR*, 13 and 14 for uses of this phrase.

66 See *GR*, 11, 15, and 16, for his discussion of low-, high- and middle-voiced rhetoric. Essentially, low is history of ideas/disinterested genealogy; high is reduction to interests and has a kind of polemical thematic; middle is irenic, analytical, and dispassionate, but not disinterested. See, in this book, Corey Barnes's wonderful essay, "Theology in the Middle Voice: Thomas Aquinas and Immanuel Kant on Natural Ends," for a more complete discussion of the importance of Cyril's rhetorical style. Cyril rejects polemics later in the text (144).

67 This refers to his emendation of Irenaeus, who, he observes, brilliantly describes Gnosticism's relation to Christian truth and practice, but both descends into hysterics on occasion (143–44) and would seem to restrict unnecessarily the diversity of Christian theological option through his strict adherence to the rule of faith (145). On his own narrative grammar formulation, Cyril writes: "Here I am especially interested in opening up the rule of faith to a grammatical interpretation that underpins the diversity in the reading of the biblical narrative" (145). It is perhaps worth pointing out that Cyril believes Irenaeus, at his best, to be a more sophisticated interpreter of Gnosticism than many a modern critic prone to throw Valentinianism in the general file of dualistic Hellenism. Cyril thinks this entirely misses the hermeneutical relation of Gnosticism and the biblical text.

68 Cyril suggests the difference between Sartre's *a posteriori* method and Descartes' *a priori*. He is choosing for Sartre (11) in this matter.

a reading of the Christian tradition in its mainline authors. That is, CNG is an abstraction from the works of theologians such as Irenaeus, Augustine, Aquinas, Maximus, Luther, and so on.[69]

Aspects of narrative and of grammar each provide for the unity of doctrine or truth over time. The first aspect is precisely that CNG works *a posteriori* from mainline Christian authors. In addition, CNG operates prescriptively with respect to narrative order. The Christian narrative from creation through fall, covenant with Israel, salvation in Christ, and consummation in the life of the triune God provides the grand story into which Christians traditionally locate their lives and from which Christian communities find meaning, identity, and mission. To rearrange major plot points, whether in a play or novel or in the biblical narrative itself, is to change significantly the meaning of the whole. The second-century Gnostic text, *Hypostasis of the Archons*, provides an example of this type of alteration or "rewriting," where a fall in the divine realm precedes, reinterprets, and negatively revalues creation.[70] Moreover, in this Gnostic revision, the God of the Jews receives nothing less than mockery rather than worship. It reads as a direct attack on the Shema. Narrative rearrangement leads to semantic revision, which leads to the elimination or relocation of Christian praise. Narrative also has the advantage of exhibiting relationships among particular Christian doctrines such as creation and salvation. Narrative has its rules of coherence unlike those of logic, but coherently meaningful nonetheless.[71] Formally speaking, narrative issues in singular events that connect through succession, agency, consequence, character, and so forth. More specifically, the Christian narrative makes evident the unity of creator and redeemer, the semantically rich and internally differentiated relation of creation and redemption, and the unity of both with consummation in the life of God.

---

69 Nowhere as of yet does Cyril discuss Christian Narrative Grammar as a theory of doctrine outside of his employment of it for genealogical purposes. Thus what is discussed here is a kind of abstraction of an abstraction. Nevertheless, he does make clear that CNG is meant to support a generous orthodoxy.

70 See "Hypostasis of the Archons," in *The Nag Hamadi Library* (New York: HarperCollins, 1990), 161–89.

71 This is broadly an anti-Hegelian point and relates to the difference between a transcendent divine subject rendered by narrative and the divine as made purely immanent through conceptual sublation.

The conceptualization of doctrine as grammar also serves the unity of doctrine. Grammar is a system of rules for making sense and for distinguishing nonsense from sense. Christian grammar tells the community if doctrinal statements or claims make Christian sense in relation to other rules considered important by the community. *Creatio ex nihilo*, for instance, is an important grammatical rule for Christian speech. It is not clear that we know what a creation from nothing actually is or looks like. As a propositional claim, creation *ex nihilo* might suggest that we can match and judge its level of correspondence to an intended object. Such a formulation pulls creation *ex nihilo* out of its reference to other Christian beliefs and practices. It also suggests that we know what a creation from nothing is or looks like and, therefore, probably claim too much for it, thus threatening to erase apophatic humility. A grammatical treatment, by contrast, grasps that creation *ex nihilo* transcends human understanding. Nevertheless, it is a rule for Christian speech because it relates to and protects key Christian beliefs and practices—namely, the giftedness and goodness of creation, the freedom and agency of human beings, the creator-creature difference, the relative autonomy of the created order, and so on. These other claims, all of which can and have been abrogated by a variety of creation *ex deo* doctrines, relate not only to doctrinal statements, but also to the underlying reasons for Christian praise.

To summarize: "grammar" has at least two virtues related to the integrity of Christian truth: first, unlike doctrines viewed as propositional statements, a grammatical conception of doctrine more clearly acknowledges the transcendent, mysterious nature of the divine object; second, grammatical rules for Christian discourse point to the interrelationships among doctrines for Christian belief, practice and forms of life. Like narrative context, these grammatical rules also support and deepen appreciation of the relations between and among different sites of doctrine. Taken together, doctrine conceived as narrative grammar promises to exhibit the narrative coherence of Christian teaching, but also grounds that teaching in the Bible, in Christian practices, forms of life, and, in particular, worship.

Our main contention, however, is that CNG serves plurivocal theological formulation. How might this be the case? First, grammar is not the same as vocabulary, and narrative order does not imply semantic identity. To take the latter first, we can see that Irenaeus, Augustine, Luther, Calvin, Thomas, and Bonaventure (among many others) hold to the same pre- and post-lapsarian order. That is to say, none of these theologians move the fall into the divine realm, or conflate it with creation itself. From a Catholic perspective, Luther may seem to underwrite the marginalization of creation theology or philosophy's role within theology, but he nevertheless remains within the flow of Christian narrative grammar. Certainly, Augustine and Irenaeus have different emphases, but again both views, whether a more "optimistic" Irenaen view of the fall or a more "catastrophic" Augustinian view, fit the grammar and narrative plotting of Christian teaching.[72]

It may be that "grammar" is more nearly the key to plural formulation. Grammar is not vocabulary. Grammar tells us how to make sense, but not precisely what to say. If narrative allows for different tellings with different nuances and emphases, a common grammar allows for different intellectual and linguistic vocabularies. Different "vocabularies" can include philosophical aids to theological articulation (i.e., Platonic, Aristotelian, Marxist, analytic, etc.) and different cultural-linguistic realizations (i.e., Syriac, Indian, Chinese, etc.). As an example, we might take our earlier observation that creation *ex nihilo* supports the Christian teaching that creation is fundamentally good. Nevertheless, how one speaks to the goodness of creation will differ. One might see vestiges of divine power and wisdom (Bonaventure), a basic luminosity or intelligibility for the human mind (K. Rahner) or even analogies to the paschal mystery (Balthasar), the livingness of God (Aquinas, E. Johnson). Very different formulations are possible and plausible that remain within the same grammar, follow the same narrative vector, and serve to express the excessive glory of God that impresses itself upon all who encounter it.

Conclusion

I began with the suggestion that knowing the cost of an argument is the distinguishing feature of Cyril's work to date. Certainly, the texts he writes and the path he follows suggest as much. Cyril's books and essays evince considerable wonder at the breadth of authors he not only considers, but treats with care and deep knowledge. The path he follows is challenging,

---

72 It is interesting to note that while Cyril has clear favorites among different forms of apocalyptic theology and thought, he nonetheless seeks to articulate the finer points of all relevant thinkers in his Père Marquette lectures, *Theology and the Spaces of Apocalyptic* (Milwaukee, WI: Marquette University Press, 2009), and in *AM*. Criticisms of Metz and Moltmann are real, but their equally real insights should not be lost.

to say the least. He seeks a post-modern theology fully responsive to the thinkers and obstacles that stand in its way. He seeks a generous orthodoxy not as a quaint nod to the past, but as a genuine option for Christian and ecclesial living in the present and future. Žižek is right to recognize that philosophy seeks to distance itself from Hegel; Derrida and Bataille are right to say that to do so one must be vigilant, one must not take Hegel lightly. Yet their "solutions" bring one to traditions of inarticulacy and, indeed, the inarticulable. Cyril shows in *The Heterodox Hegel* (and elsewhere) that "Hegelian" is not isomorphic with "Christian," that total ontotheological transparency and the self-legitimating circle of reason does not and cannot translate the excess of Christian truth.

Cyril rarely works in the first person. Thus, our second section sought evidence of his views in treatments of other thinkers—namely, Newman and Balthasar. Here he finds friends to elevate against the ecclesially and theologically enervating effects of modernity. Newman undermines modern liberal or rational religion both by showing that it stipulates rather than argues, ignores massive amounts of evidence, and thus constitutes a reduction of Christianity to a kind of moralistic or emotional core. Newman thus justifies post-modern fears that modernity frequently offers only a reduction to the same. Unlike post-moderns, however, Newman, like Balthasar, is an apostle of the more, the greater glory of God that evokes and provokes praise and joy. It is this "more" that can sponsor a Catholic post-modern theology.

In *Anatomy of Misremembering* and throughout various essays, Balthasar receives a capacious and generous treatment from Cyril. Balthasar even more than Newman supports plural theological styles, Christian forms of life and practices from a gloriously excessive center in the *mysterium Christi*. The revelation of God in Jesus Christ cannot be exhausted by any system, regardless of how profound. Indeed, there is a generosity born of divine self-giving that must lie at the foundation of any theology, coupled to a liberating trust that what one does inadequately will be completed, better said, or filled-in by another.

Cyril offers a style and a theory to support such plurality-in-unity in the future. The Gnostic return thesis continues an irenic style that can be heard by its detractors. It also refuses the modern reduction of religious and intellectual currents to slogans and *a priori* categories of what "religion" must be. It might even be considered an exercise in love of enemy. Clarity of expression is certainly a virtue, but not if paid for by those one seeks to express. Instead, Cyril determines to give full voice and nuance to the Gnostic other even if it is precisely that other who threatens Christian identity at every turn. Christian narrative grammar promises to support speculative theology within the range of a generous orthodoxy.

Hegel knew perhaps as well or better than anyone that where one ends is more profound than where one begins. We began naming the "cost of an argument" as perhaps Cyril's most prominent feature as a scholar. He certainly bears this cost with a lightness that makes it more than bearable, even edifying. Our suggestion, however, cannot be redeemed. Argument is significant, and Cyril thinks that philosophy should not eschew it for phenomenological presentation alone. Yet argument in the last analysis is a distant second to generosity. In truth, this is Cyril's most prominent quality as a scholar, thinker, and teacher. He seeks to be generous to those whose views he considers, both friends and intellectual and cultural adversaries alike. He works to put this generosity into a theory that supports it ecclesially and doctrinally. This is a generosity to the future, to those scholars of different times and places who enter the mystery of Christ from an unforeseeable angle of vision, with unforeseeable experience to seek and express the ever-greater glory of God. Of course, no one who knows him will be surprised. For it is that same generosity that defines his person.

POETIC EPILOGUE

Cyril O'Regan

On the Nile

If the world is a stretch
In the possible, it might
Be I was never there, nor here,
Only rehearsing instruction
To the soiled and the broken.

But dreams are not continent
And if my mind starts with
The image of the teacher ferried
On the river's uncatchable center,
It ends with sympathies, blurring
Already vagrant identities

And I am the river plodding
Before the rainy season, wind
Blowing over sly brown silk
Catechizing the cabbage plant
And the dirty sunt.

Wise old thing I make the cabal
Of kites wheeling above plotless.
But I find my calling when
I enter the pores of the girl-
Woman who will always find

Her way to the edge
At the time of flush
Turning bruise till
Night's gauze heals
Her eyes' unasked questions
And we both forget.

If the world is a sketch
In the possible, it may
Be I am never here, was not
There, fated only to remember
Another's notes and words
In the fog of the never happened.

Still dreams give on dreams
And in my sleep I am awake
On some mountain where
My wet comfortable breath clasps
Damp skins shuddering
At the dog's midnight bark.

So hard to make one's way
In the labyrinth. Perhaps
It does not matter as long
As the silence is arable
And I can throw my seed.

Waiting for the Barbarians I

The citizens have grown impatient and can
No longer wait. We have taken
To writing letters some claim
They know where to send. Words

Sing the praises of our fathers
In such general terms no one
Can accuse us of error.

We have begun to seek out strangers,
Emptied our jails. Smiles are knowing
The talk still vague.

Cranks come forward saying they met
Our deliverers such and such a year at sea
In the desert, on the mountain.

After a drink some claim they see
Them coming out from a rock
in which they swim and from the air
which to them is solid ground.

A visage monstrous to one is child-
Like to another. Yet we know
Their existence is more than rumor.

For a on-agreeable city like this
Could not dream one thing without
That thing existing. Else how

Explain the reel, young men and women
Like the world turning visioning
Their coming smelling like bread.

We feel like the morning after
Too much eating. They feel the morning
They put into their mouth and eat

As if it were a live animal trying
To die of fear. We choke
On a bone here.

We wish them our lungs,
To thin our thickening blood
To feel the chill running down

The mountain into the dead
Valleys or linger as night eddies
In the desert's whirlpool of silence.

We choke on a bone here. Brain-
Gorged on impossibilities. Looking
To lessen, to draw the fluid.

We choke on a bone here.
Listlessness prays for its night,
Hopes that they will teach us again

That the old thing is the new
The world does not grow old.

If they come they will find us
Dead-eyed with empty smiles

Like chevrons at the gate
Imploring them to enter.

Requiem for Marguerite (d. 1310)

1
Marguerite, explicable this blur
of faces on the next to the last day,
this lick of heat on the feet,
even as a scream expires
the coils of a body that purrs
and springs in desire.

But inexplicable this finalizing of flesh
to paper curling at the edges, first brash
yellow, then sullen brown, dull black
to end in no color at all, ready
to fly to the blue beyond the steady
chattering of windless morning,

this folding in which bones see
and the tempest of ash sniffs
the apocalypse of beauty.

Jaw-clenched serene you are arriving
at the place beyond places insinuating
an empty bowl, a piece of cloth tucked
near the skin, a picture of the Madonna,
a gap at the center, Jesus plucked
from her lap.

Earth in flame the sky bends to chance,
a last look as a finch rests on a sill,
song tilting the world toward another dance.

Perhaps also just enough time to recall
a girl who bears a likeness lying
on her back pressed to the gall
of the earth, waiting

for the black sun
to cut out her heart.

Biblical Rachels we grieve at a distance,
risk errancy in which we lose our names.

Walk and your words drug our pain.

Gather in rooms cold as stained glass,
your words whirl and skirl.

I am the desert without memory,
a crust breaking like lips, silence
gushing toward the everywhere of light.

2
Love is wet; seed and sweat,
steam rising from the pot
creating a circle. Insinuating rot
in beds, underclothes, in fretted
windows, in days that do not rain
and cannot be dry,

in the thunder of salt breaking
on steeples of low-lying towns,
without hint of sail or rigging,
without the shove of water down
beyond a feasible dark.

Our food chides and charges us.
Porridge weighs us down, green
lentils make us swell, hard to preen,

not to heave sour breath, the skin

not to break open, to envy
the angel's translucent wing.

Then there is the wet of our failings,
our small worlds of not love, sodden
pleasures of one-up, damp imaginings
of tit for tat, sudden

moist heat of our breath
as everything takes a toll,

as we lessen before the priest,
as our mind's scuffle with promises
and threats over the beggar bowl.

How otherwise to address you?
Ointment to our wringing of vice,

hot cloth to our kneading of virtue,
finger pointing to an amazed world?

Words return to silence.
No memory of leaving.

3
Marguerite, you floated like a cork
down a green river. We inhale the wine.

Had we looked we might have seen
narrow grey eyes, sparse hair
of no particular color, startled
flesh flushed from its lair,
beginning to keel and keen.

Nothing here but cipher

a space for our hope, a way
to thread the litany of hours.

Our eyes suck your sinewy lines,
our ears trace the curve of voice.
Our toes shape its weave
Of undulating and firm strokes.

Map the mind, and it reveals
a million suns in love with a billion moons.

4
Even in the shivered mirror
light refracts. The shards
of a brown jug give glimmers

of the blue shout of the mind
putting a dent in circumstance.

She is the remains of humor
in the rustling of leaves,
what there is of wit in the quarrel
of squirrels in the trees.

Her sky feels me unsheltered.

Waiting on the threshold, sphincter
of pure fear, a rope weaving spirals
of could to circles of would.

Seeing cups the hot core of not.
The wind insists there are no eyes
to spy, heart to elope
with the perfect stranger.

5
After examination, exhortation, the knot
of repentance, recantation, and renege,

the voice of the pleader with no
stomach for it, the silence of the torturer who
cannot live in a disheveled world,

mechanics are all. Faggots piled high,
concern is whether the wood is dry.

Anticlimactic. Fire catches quickly.
Too soon she is the holocaust
of her book,

exposition of impossible peace,
childless, motherless, fatherless,

alone at the dawn of creation
before and after all things are.

I am the house sucked into the dark.
Roofs, walls and windows without eyes,
floors, the patted earth, and finally
the standing water from which we came
amphibian.

6
We suppliants are the scattering, birds.
of all seasons flying north or south.

She is the ladder into the mansion,

the world of essence of perfume, hind
of the far of his near, the near of his far

holder of the key of scansion
in the tiniest nook of the mind,
the deepest cranny of the heart.

Peace could not be more blatant.
Its hot breath eats us to the bone,

Morning's apothecary of light
nonchalantly makes inroads
on the fever of the dark.

Soundlessly the light accepts
Effortlessly lets go.

CONTRIBUTOR BIOGRAPHIES

Ann W. Astell (Ph.D. 1987, University of Wisconsin-Madison) is Professor of Theology (2007–) at the University of Notre Dame. Prior to that appointment she was Professor of English at Purdue University (1988–2007), where she also chaired the program in Medieval and Renaissance Studies. The recipient of a National Endowment for the Humanities fellowship and a John Simon Guggenheim Memorial Fellowship, she is the author of six books on medieval religion and literature, including *Eating Beauty: The Eucharist and the Spiritual Arts of the Middle Ages* (2006), and the editor or co-editor of seven volumes of collected essays. She is the past President of the Colloquium on Violence and Religion and past President of the Society for the Study of Christian Spirituality.

Corey L. Barnes is an Associate Professor of Religion in the Medieval Mediterranean World at Oberlin College. His research focuses on medieval scholastic thought, with a concentration on discussions of causality, providence, analogical predication, and Christology. He is the author of *Christ's Two Wills in Scholastic Thought* (2012) and has published articles in *The Thomist*, *New Blackfriars*, *Nova et Vetera*, and *Modern Theology*.

John C. Cavadini is Professor of Theology in the Department of Theology at the University of Notre Dame. He served as Department Chair from 1997 to 2010. Since Fall 2000, he has also served as the McGrath-Cavadini Director of the McGrath Institute for Church Life. His main areas of research and teaching are patristics, that is, the theology of the early church, with a special focus on the theology of St. Augustine and on the biblical spirituality of the Fathers of the Church. He has also published in the theology of miracles, the life and work of Gregory the Great, catechetical theology, the theology of marriage, and so on. In November 2009 he was appointed by Pope Benedict XVI to a five-year term on the International Theological Commission and was also made a member of the Equestrian Order of St. Gregory the Great, *classis civilis*, by Pope Benedict. He has served as a consultant to the USCCB Committee on Doctrine since 2003.

Lawrence S. Cunningham is John A. O'Brien Professor of Theology (Emeritus) at the University of Notre Dame. The author or editor of nearly thirty books, he is interested in the intersection of systematic theology and spirituality. In retirement he still contributes essays and reviews to both popular and scholarly journals and is working on a book on the theology of prayer.

William Desmond, born in Cork, Ireland, is currently David Cook Chair in Philosophy at Villanova University and Professor of Philosophy Emeritus at the Institute of Philosophy, Katholieke Universiteit Leuven. He taught at Loyola University in Maryland before going to Leuven, where he was Director of the International Program in Philosophy for thirteen years. He is the author of many books, including the trilogy *Being and the Between* (winner of the Prix Cardinal Mercier and the J.N. Findlay Award for best book in metaphysics, 1995–1997), *Ethics and the Between* (2001), and *God and the Between* (2008). Other books include *Is There a Sabbath for Thought?: Between Religion and Philosophy* (2005) and *Art, Origins, Otherness: Between Art and Philosophy* (2003). He has also edited five books and published more than 100 articles. He is past President of the Hegel Society of America, the Metaphysical Society of America, and the American Catholic Philosophical Association. His most recent book is *The Intimate Universal: The Hidden Porosity among Religion, Art, Politics and Philosophy* (2016). *The Intimate Strangeness of Being: Metaphysics after Dialectic* and *The William Desmond Reader* appeared in 2012, and the second edition of *Desire, Dialectic and Otherness* was published in 2014.

Jean-Luc Marion is Professor Emeritus of Philosophy at the University of Paris-Sorbonne Paris IV, Dominique Dubarle Professor of Philosophy at the Institut Catholique de Paris, Andrew T. Greeley and Grace McNichols Greeley Professor of Catholic Studies at the University of Chicago Divinity School, and a member of the Académie Française. Notable among his many publications are *God Without Being* (1991), *The Idol and Distance* (2001), *Being Given: Toward a Phenomenology of Givenness* (2002). His most recent book is *The Rigor of Things: Conversations with Dan Arbib* (2017).

CONTRIBUTOR BIOGRAPHIES

James Martin is a doctoral candidate in Systematic Theology at the University of Notre Dame, specializing in Catholic systematics, political theology, post-structuralist thought, and comparative religion. He is also the Co-Director of the Science & Religion Initiative at the McGrath Institute for Church Life. His dissertation is a critical assessment of the intersection of Christian trinitarian theology, Marxism, German idealism, and psychoanalytic theory in the death of God theology of Slavoj Žižek.

Jennifer Newsome Martin (Ph.D., 2012, University of Notre Dame) is an assistant professor in the Program of Liberal Studies with a concurrent appointment in the Department of Theology at the University of Notre Dame. Martin is a systematic and historical theologian with areas of specialization in twentieth-century Roman Catholic systematic theology, particularly trinitarian and eschatological discourses, theological aesthetics, religion and literature, Catholic retrieval, and the nature of tradition. Her recent research engages the religious character of modern philosophical thought, particularly in the German Idealist and Romantic traditions, as well as pre- and early Soviet-era Russian religious philosophy. Her first book, *Hans Urs von Balthasar and the Critical Appropriation of Russian Religious Thought* (2015), one of ten international winners of the 2017 Manfred Lautenschlaeger Award for Theological Promise, analyzes the submerged presence of modern speculative Russian religious thinkers on the aesthetic, historical, and eschatological dimensions of the theology of Swiss Catholic theologian Hans Urs von Balthasar. Other work has appeared in *Modern Theology*, *Spiritus*, *Communio: International Catholic Review*, and *Christianity and Literature*, and in several collected volumes of essays.

Danielle Nussberger, Ph.D., is an Associate Professor of Systematic Theology at Marquette University. She has published in the areas of trinitarian theology, feminist theology, and the relationship between theology and spirituality in Hans Urs von Balthasar and in John Henry Newman. For the past three years she has been a member of the administrative teams for the Hans Urs von Balthasar Consultation and for the John Henry Newman Interest Group for the Catholic Theological Society of America. Along with Brian W. Hughes, she is currently co-editing a volume of essays produced from the three-year Newman Interest Group on Newman and the Crisis of Modernity.

Andrew Prevot is Assistant Professor of Theology at Boston College. He completed his Ph.D. at the University of Notre Dame under the direction of Cyril O'Regan in 2012. He is the author of *Thinking Prayer: Theology and Spirituality amid the Crises of Modernity*. His published articles in the area of philosophical theology include "Dialectic and Analogy in Balthasar's 'Metaphysics of the Saints,'" *Pro Ecclesia* 26, no. 3 (Summer 2017): 261–77; "Responsorial Thought: Jean-Louis Chrétien's Distinctive Approach to Theology and Phenomenology," *The Heythrop Journal* 56, no. 6 (Nov. 2015): 975–87; and "The Gift of Prayer: Toward a Theological Reading of Jean-Luc Marion," *Horizons* 41, no. 2 (Dec. 2014): 250–74.

Rev. Brendan Purcell was born in 1941 in Dublin, Ireland, and studied at University College Dublin and the Pontifical Lateran University, Rome. After ordination for Dublin diocese, he did a research M.A. at UCD on "Aspects of Method in Human Psychology," drawing on Jean Piaget's and Bernard Lonergan's methodology. He then began "Wewards: Theoretical Foundations for a Psychology of Friendship" as a Ph.D. in psychology at Catholic University of Leuven, completing it at UCD. From 1972 to his retirement in 2008, he lectured at UCD in logic, psychology, political philosophy, and philosophical anthropology. He is currently an adjunct professor in the School of Philosophy at Notre Dame University Australia (Sydney Campus) and assistant priest at St. Mary's Cathedral, Sydney. Publications include *The Drama of Humanity: Towards a Philosophy of Humanity in History* (1996); an edition and translation, with Detlev Clemens, of Eric Voegelin's *Hitler and the Germans* (1999); *From Big Bang to Big Mystery: Human Origins in the Light of Creation and Evolution* (2012); and *Where Is God in Suffering?* (2016).

Anthony C. Sciglitano, Jr., is an Associate Professor in the Department of Religion at Seton Hall University in South Orange, New Jersey. He formerly chaired the Department of Religion and directed the University Core Curriculum housed in the Institute for Interdisciplinary Studies. His essays on Gianni Vattimo, Kant, Pope Benedict XVI, and Hans Urs von Balthasar have appeared in *Modern Theology*, *Pro Ecclesia*, and in several books. His first book is *Marcion and Prometheus: Balthasar against the Expulsion of Jewish Origins from Modern Religious Dialogue* (2014).

CONTRIBUTOR BIOGRAPHIES 243

Todd Walatka serves as the Assistant Chair for Graduate Studies in the Department of Theology at the University of Notre Dame and specializes in contemporary Catholic systematic theology. His research includes work on Hans Urs von Balthasar, Latin American liberation theology, Archbishop Oscar Romero, and the interpretation and reception of Vatican II. His book *Von Balthasar and the Option for the Poor: Theodramatics in the Light of Liberation Theology* was published by Catholic University of America Press in 2017. He also works in the field of pedagogy and pedagogical formation, both in his role as Assistant Chair for Graduate Studies and in his research.

David Walsh is Professor of Politics at The Catholic University of America in Washington, D.C., where his teaching and research is in the field of political theory broadly conceived. His focus has been on the question that the modern world poses for itself at its deepest level. Does our civilization possess the moral and spiritual resources to survive? In response to that question, Walsh has traced the modern retrieval order in a trilogy of works. First, there was the catharsis evoked by the totalitarian crisis that called forth an affirmation of truth beyond the abyss. This is explored in *After Ideology: Recovering the Spiritual Foundations of Freedom* (1990). Second, there was the emergence of a minimal order within the abbreviations that became the liberal democratic form. *The Growth of the Liberal Soul* (1997) tracks both the contemporary debates and the historical unfolding of the principles that maximize individual liberty while also sustaining civic virtue. Finally, *The Modern Philosophical Revolution: The Luminosity of Existence* (2008) reflects on the overarching philosophical horizon of modernity. It finds that the narrative is best characterized as a re-founding of the classical and Christian project rather than a radical departure from it. One of the results of these studies has been a renewed interest in the centrality of the person from whom order radiates into social and political existence. The first phase of this new direction has appeared in *Politics of the Person as the Politics of Being* (2016), to be followed shortly by a companion volume, *The Priority of the Person*.

OTHER TITLES OF INTEREST

Gerhard Ludwig Muller
CATHOLIC DOGMATICS
For the Study and Practice of Theology

Dogmatic theology addresses the tension between God's self-communication and modern attempts to translate them into our own worldview and milieu.
Hardcover, 175 pages, 978-0-8245-2232-2
Paperback, 175 pages, 978-0-8245-2233-9

Robert P. Imbelli, Ed.
HANDING ON THE FAITH
The Church's Mission and Challenge

Renowned theologian and teacher, Robert P. Imbelli, introduces the work of leading Catholic theologians, writers, and scholars to discuss the challenges of handing on the faith and to rethink the essential core of Catholic identity.
Paperback, 264 pages, 978-0-8245-2409-8

Eugene J. Fisher, Ph.D, Ed.
Rabbi Leon Klenicki, Ed.
THE SAINT FOR SHALOM
How Pope John Paul II Transformed Catholic-Jewish Relations
His Complete Texts of Jews, Judaism and the State of Israel 1979–2005

Pope John Paul II's efforts can serve as a model for reconciliation, inspiring both believers and non-believers to pursue deeper understanding and work together in harmony to help improve the world and achieve Shalom, the Hebrew word for Peace, wholeness and right-relationship, for all humankind.
Paperback, 398 pages, 978-0-8245-2682-5

Support your local bookstore or order directly
from the publisher at www.crossroadpublishing.com

To request a catalog or to inquire about
quantity orders, please e-mail
sales@CrossroadPublishing.com

www.ingramcontent.com/pod-product-compliance
Lightning Source LLC
Chambersburg PA
CBHW030109010526
44116CB00005B/173